Modern
Saltwater
Fishing

MODERN SALTWATER FISHING

Vic Dunaway

Winchester Press

Library of Congress Catalog Card Number: 74-16874
ISBN: 0-87691-168-8

Published by Winchester Press
205 East 42nd Street, New York 10017

Designed by Robert Bull

Printed in the United States of America

DEDICATION

In 1959, Dr. Webster (Doc) Robinson of Key West, Fla., was stricken with the urge to fish big game, an ambition readily endorsed by his wife, Helen. Similar inclinations, of course, have smitten countless sportsmen—but seldom in such tardy fashion. Doc was sixty-three years old, Helen fifty-nine. Neither had ever taken a big-game fish, although Doc had for many years been a top-flight light-tackle angler.

Four years later, Doc sat down in the den of his oceanfront home in Key West and began adding up figures out of his personal log. During those four years he had spent 259 days fishing for big game in Panama, Peru, and Chile, and had caught, among many other prizes, 115 black marlin—more than double the total ever before taken by another individual.

Helen, in the same period, had landed 37 black marlin, including a women's world record in the 80-pound-line class (796 pounds), and a record for both men and women in the 50-pound class (584½ pounds).

While the statistics correctly indicate great perseverance, they give no hint that such overwhelming success was due almost equally to Doc Robinson's amazing facility for researching and absorbing known angling techniques, down to the tiniest detail, and then expanding and improving them whenever he found it necessary—and in certain instances to work out an entirely new approach.

Doc really did not intend to become the world's highest-scoring black-marlin fisherman, but merely to reap the full extent of physical and mental satisfaction from setting his own challenges in angling and then meeting them.

"To me, fishing always is a project," he once told me. "It's something to be researched, studied, investigated, improved. My aim never is simply to catch a fish, but to catch the fish I want, the way I want to. The catch doesn't seem very important unless it represents a goal I've set up, or a target for experimenting with new ideas on tackle and methods."

Doc's career had been that of security analyst and financial consultant.

"Every decision I made in business," he recalled, "seriously affected both my client and myself. But in fishing I found something I could experiment with to my heart's content, and with success or failure affecting nobody.

There was no pressure to be right; only annoyance when wrong, and pleasure when results were good."

The most famous result of Doc's experimental approach to angling was the development of a system for *consistently* hooking sailfish and marlin on a cast fly. He was the first angler to capture a sailfish by "pure" fly-casting, and he went on to land a number of others, plus several striped marlin. But his greatest satisfaction came later when he observed that other anglers were able to employ his tactics and do the same.

Another major Robinson development was a revolutionary system for battling heavyweight marlin, which not only reduced the physical punishment involved but also vastly increased the odds on landing a marlin once it was hooked.

Both those developments are covered extensively in this book, thanks to past interviews with both Doc and Helen, plus voluminous personal notes Doc turned over to me before his death.

Those same notes contained many more of his innovative ideas and practices. While none are so spectacular as his two major "systems," they are nevertheless important contributions to fishing success in numerous heavy-and light-tackle areas. They deal mostly with riggings and baits, and have spread into wide usage, generally without acknowledgment of their developer.

But Doc never sought, nor expected, any applause.

"Almost everyone who fishes attentively," he said, "is bound to contribute something to the sport sooner or later, perhaps without even realizing it himself. Sportfishing is not the invention of one man, or a dozen, but is the cumulation of the knowledge, experience, and ingenuity of thousands of anglers over many years.

"If I've been able to add anything to this great store of fishing know-how, it's little enough payment for all I've gotten out of it."

Webster Robinson, of course, added far more than a one-man share. In my opinion he was the most innovative ocean angler since Zane Grey.

This book is dedicated to him.

—Vic Dunaway

CONTENTS

INTRODUCTION

Saltwater fishing is a sport encompassing many different opportunities and styles: among them, offshore trolling for big game fish; bottom fishing from bridge or pier; angling in the surf; trolling or drifting in bays and inland waterways.

At one time, fishermen were pretty well limited to one or two of those approaches, but the modern angler is reaching out, crossing the old boundary lines, and trying many things. Today he may cast in the surf; tomorrow go after sailfish or marlin. And next week he may get the chance to try his hand at one of the ambitious modern specialties that range from casting flies to billfish, to kite-fishing, to stalking fish on clear shallow flats, to deep jigging in offshore waters with tackle that, only a few years back, was considered suitable only for bay fishing.

All those horizons, and more, have been opened up by modern air transportation and convenient scheduling. A Florida bonefish flat is within quick— if expensive—reach of anglers living in New York or Cleveland. Closer to home, the angling menu has been expanded by modern developments in boats, motors, and related marine equipment. Yesterday the little boats stayed inshore and the big boats went offshore. Nowadays, thousands of private skippers command vessels that can safely and efficiently put them into all kinds of fishing water, from a tidal creek to the deep blue sea. Moreover, those same boats may be trailered several hundred miles, over good highways, to new waters for long weekends or vacations.

While it's true that most of us are always happy just to "go fishing" and catch whatever might be available to us, it's also true that the avid saltwater sportfisherman is constantly seeking new goals, new species, new tackle accomplishments, new techniques. But whether the aim is simply to catch a few fish, or to accomplish some ambitious undertaking, a considerable portion of the satisfaction comes from mapping the practical approach, doing things right—and doing them for yourself.

That's what this book is all about. It's designed as a textbook—a complete manual of instruction for the coastal angler. It's a book dealing exclusively with the techniques, systems, and procedures for most of the different salt-water fishing specialities. Regardless of species or geography, basic game-fishing techniques remain much the same. Therefore, you won't find anything here about the biology of the striped bass or the range of a white marlin.

This is a book calculated to give newcomers to the sport—and anglers who switch from one specialty to another—the detailed instruction that's usually lacking in more generalized books: step-by-step guidance in selecting tackle, putting it together, rigging baits and leaders, and then going after fish in a proficient manner all the way.

Insofar as important angling skills go, no detail is overlooked, nothing left dangling. The reader will learn not only how to get fish on his line, but how to play them most effectively with all kinds of tackle, and how to handle them and land them once they are at boatside or shoreside.

One thing you won't get out of this book, or any other, is that all-important helping of fisherman's luck. But it's an obvious fact that the angler who is well prepared—and keeps his bait in the water—can thrive with only a modicum of assistance from Dame Fortune.

Part I
Tackle and
Equipment

1

RODS AND REELS

While it's obvious that just about any kind of rod and reel can be used *some-where* in the wide world of saltwater fishing, the serious angler should make a careful evaluation of the types that figure to be best suited to his own opportunities and interests. There is plenty of room for compromise, of course, and in many instances the choice of gear is not at all critical. Nevertheless, familiarization with the different rods and reels and their general applications is necessary in order to make a reasonable choice.

BIG-GAME AND TROLLING TACKLE

This is the elite category of saltwater fishing tackle, featuring rods and reels carefully matched for best performance with a particular size of line, and with price tags ranging from moderately expensive to "ouch!" It is often referred to among offshore anglers as "trolling" tackle, although its usefulness is not strictly limited to trolling, nor is it the only type of tackle suitable for trolling. Other terms used to describe such gear are "class" tackle or "IGFA" tackle—both terms referring to the line classes in which the International Game Fish Association keeps world records. These classes range from 6-pound test to 130-pound test. In each case, the rod action is matched to that line, and the reel is chosen according to the best balance of size, weight, and line capacity for the line test involved.

Big-Game Rods

Since sophisticated trolling rods are invariably labeled according to class, a lot of shopping bother is eliminated to start with. That means any stick labeled, say, 20-pound, will do an adequate job with 20-pound-test line, and so on through all the classes. Note, however, that there *are* minor variations in action, and still room for personal selection based on action alone. Faced with a choice between two different actions, the general rule is to take the stiffer of the two if you plan to use monofilament line, and the more limber if you use Dacron line.

There also is room for a choice based on components, decoration, and trim—all of which influence the price of the rod.

Virtually every "class" rod features a full set of roller guides and a roller tip-top. An exception is the 6-pound class, for which the rod is so light that many anglers choose ring guides, the best of which are the Speed Guides. These have rings of aluminum oxide—smoother than traditional guides and capable of dissipating heat much faster.

Butts must be of hard material to resist wear in the rod holders, but again there is a choice—hardwood, solid fiberglass, or aluminum, in ascending order of cost. The butts are, of course, gimbal-slotted.

Big fish call for strong rods and large-capacity reels. Traditional star-drag reels are favored by most offshore anglers.

In the two heaviest classes—80 and 130—more expensive curved butts are available, and are chosen by virtually all giant-tuna anglers, and many marlin fishermen.

Big-Game Reels

Traditional star-drag reels of appropriate size are entirely adequate for putting together "class" outfits. Despite being relatively inexpensive, their ability to hold up well while taking all the major gamefish is well established, and they are available in all required sizes up to giant 14/0 and 16/0 models (more about comparative reel sizes later).

But even better are those ocean reels in which the familiar star-drag wheel has been replaced by a dual-drag mechanism. One phase of this drag arrange-

A Fin-Nor machined trolling reel with single-lever drag system.

ment is preset to provide a *range* of drag pressure. The other, a lever, can be used to adjust the drag instantly, anywhere within the preset range. The operation of both the star- and dual-drag systems is explained in detail in Chapter 7.

Dual-drag reels are expensive. Some brands cost more than others, but none will be found on the bargain counter. The hefty price is not due entirely to the more elaborate drag setup. Spools are machined from solid bar stock, and so are most of the other major parts.

Being fairly new in design and manufacture, the majority of dual-drag reels are labeled, like trolling rods, according to the line class for which they are best suited. Star-drag reels have a much older system of nomenclature, referred to as the "0" system. The smallest of reels under this system is 1/0, and the largest is 16/0.

Here is a table which should help in selecting the proper 0-size reel for particular line-test classes:

Line class	Reel sizes
12-lb.	1/0, 2/0
20-lb.	2/0, 2½/0, 3/0
30-lb.	3/0, 4/0
50-lb.	6/0 to 9/0
80-lb.	9/0 to 12/0
130-lb.	12/0 to 16/0

The ultrasophisticated matched outfits under discussion are obviously of most interest to dedicated offshore fishermen, who either own their own sport-fishing cruisers or charter regularly. Many own one or more outfits in every line class, representing thousands of dollars in cost.

But the part-time offshore fisherman must look at things a little differently. If he decides to buy "class" tackle at all, he seldom needs consider more than one or two line categories, and can get by at a cost ranging, on the average, from $100 to $300 per outfit. Or he could manage very well with multi-purpose boat tackle instead of refined trolling tackle, paying far less. The choice must be based on personal offshore ambitions, and on budget.

For newcomers to offshore fishing, the first choice of line class probably should be 30-pound, which is as near as you can come to "all-round." A 30-pound outfit will handle anything you're at all *likely* to hook in bluewater trolling, and is light enough to provide excellent sport on fish as large as white marlin, or as small as school tuna. You'd be in trouble if the rare blue marlin, swordfish, or jumbo tuna happened to slug your bait, but that's the kind of trouble you don't mind, and you'd at least have a fighting chance with 30-pound.

BOAT AND MULTIPURPOSE TACKLE

Literally, the term "boat tackle" could be taken to mean any equipment used from a boat. In common usage, however, the name signifies a rather broad array of multipurpose saltwater tackle designed more for trolling, still-fishing, and live-baiting than for casting.

Boat Rods

The majority of boat rods are built of solid glass, although some tubulars are used. Solid glass can withstand much more abuse than tubular, and so is never a bad choice so long as casting action is not a factor. Even some quite expensive "class" rods are built on solid blanks.

Choosing a suitable boat outfit from among the seemingly endless selection of rods and reels available might at first seem like a hopeless task. But by following a few simple guidelines you can put together a rig without much trouble.

The heaviest boat rods, with tips as big around as your thumb, are designed mainly for heavy-duty deep fishing in offshore waters. They are most often used with 50- or 60-pound-test line, but some can easily handle as much as 80- or 100-pound line. For inshore fishing, they are pretty much restricted to shark or jewfish. Though rods in this category generally feature detachable butts, a lot of fishermen who go after bottom-hugging lunkers insist on models in which the blank extends all the way through the butt.

Dropping down to the next heaviest category, we find the most popular boat-rod range of all—sticks that are designed to handle 30- to 50-pound line, with 30 and 40 being fairly standard.

Incidentally, even-numbered line sizes refer principally to monofilament lines. Nylon line, which often is used on boat tackle, is not marked in multiples of ten but in multiples of three, and therefore wears such size designations as 27-pound, 36-pound, 45-pound. Lines are discussed in Chapter 2.

Within this lineup of boat outfits you find the truly all-purpose saltwater fishing tackle, as far as revolving-spool outfits go. They can be used for bottom fishing, light and heavy, and for trolling with small lures for mackerel and big baits for snook, striped bass, or salmon. And they'll do a good job on occasional bluewater trolling trips (if your reel has sufficient line capacity). A boat rod isn't the sportiest outfit you could choose for many of those things, but it is an efficient one.

You'll find very thin boat rods on the market, too, which can take lines as light as 12- or 15-pound test. However, those line sizes are much more often used with spinning or plug tackle. For economy's sake, some bay fishermen may buy the little boat rods for nondemanding types of work, such as fishing for fluke, spot, croaker, or grunt.

Unlike "class" rods, boat rods are seldom marked as to specific line size. One reason for this is that a solid-glass blank can handle an amazing spread of different lines without creating too much of a problem. Many manufacturers do, however, provide some sort of line suggestion on the label.

Several options are available with medium and heavy-class boat rods. For instance, you can get a roller top, or a roller top in combination with a rolling first guide. Another popular option is the gimbal butt.

Boat Reels

Two types of saltwater reels already have been mentioned—the refined dual-drag instruments, and the star-drag gamefishing reels that are designated by the O-size numbers. Several other types, and numerous other models, can be found for reasons of economy or specialization. They all share the basic salt-water-reel features of adjustable star drag and manual free-spool operation, but slight differences in design might make some of them more attractive for your own purposes than others. Here is a rundown.

NARROW-SPOOL REELS are popular for trolling with wire and lead-core lines, and also for deep trolling, deep drifting, and bottom fishing with monofilament or braided lines in offshore waters. The spool is narrow, but deep enough to provide an adequate line capacity for these specialties. Their use with metallic lines, however, is limited to the smaller diameters and to situations where about 200 yards, or less, of such line serves the purpose. Where heavy wire line and large capacity are called for, a 6/0 or 9/0 game-fishing reel is generally chosen. The narrow-spool design means that more line is picked up for each turn of the crank. In combination with the faster gear ratios found on some of these reels, the narrow design really affords deep-probing fishermen the rapid pickup they need in trying to get fish away from bottom as quickly as possible.

SQUIDDING OR CASTING REELS certainly are not limited in appeal only to surf and pier fishermen. A great many boating anglers select a reel of this type because they are frequently called on to toss a live or dead bait, or sometimes a large lure, well away from the boat. It is possible to get off a cast with other types of saltwater reels, but it takes a practiced hand to do so, and even then the results aren't apt to be spectacular. Large reels designed for casting can often be identified at a glance by wider spools. But all casting reels don't have the wide spools; their casting capability is due entirely to interior design refinements and to spool construction.

Best casting results with these larger surf and saltwater casting reels are obtained when the reels have plastic spools. This means that braided line must be used, since monofilament can destroy a plastic spool (see Chapter 2).

Best and most expensive of the reels in this particular category are certain ocean casting reels that amount to enlarged versions of quality bait-casting reels, and wear the same familiar names.

LEVEL-WIND REELS offer an obvious convenience. Like bait-casting reels, they wrap line evenly on the spool during retrieve, meaning that you need not worry about performing this important function with your thumb—as you must do with all other kinds of conventional saltwater reels, in order to keep line from piling up in one spot and binding against end plate or pillar. But the limitations of a level-wind mechanism pretty well limit the usefulness of these reels to fairly light saltwater duties. The largest model holds approximately 300 yards of 30-pound line and does a good job of handling larger coastal gamefish such as snook, king mackerel, channel bass, striped bass, and bluefish—even big tarpon. Many charter boats use them for such work because inexperienced fishermen need not concern themselves with thumb-leveling. But the reels have neither the capacity nor the ruggedness needed for long-running offshore fish.

In smaller models, level-wind reels serve a great many purposes and have a raft of staunch supporters. Though less expensive than star-drag bait-casting reels, they can be used for many of the same applications, while serving extra duty for bay bottom fishing, light trolling, and live-baiting. They are mostly used with 12- to 20-pound line.

BAY AND BOAT REELS. These labels are commonly given to light and medium saltwater reels which do not have any of the specialized features outlined previously. They range from very small and cheap all-plastic models up to some that are strong and dependable enough to handle 40- and 50-pound line in types of fishing which do not require great line capacity. All reels in this very wide category are modest in price—the best of them cost less than any of the offshore gamefishing reels marked with 0- sizes. As you can guess, most reels that are matched with low- and medium-priced boat rods come out of this family.

PLUG-CASTING OR BAIT-CASTING TACKLE

The terms "bait-casting" and "plug-casting" are interchangeable, but neither is very descriptive. Be that as it may, they refer to a style of fishing that employs revolving-spool reels of small size, usually fitted to one-hand casting rods.

Since this is primarily an artificial-lure system, the name "plug-casting" probably was coined by purists who resented the implication of natural bait in the older term "bait-casting." But the newer label doesn't quite hit the target either, since jigs, spoons, and other artificial lures are commonly used, along with plugs.

Modern bait-casting reels are marvelous instruments capable of tossing lures much farther than spinning reels, if lure weight, rod action, and line test are roughly equivalent. They can be free-spooled for casting by pushing a button, but the gears re-engage automatically when the crank is turned. Also, the spool is nonreversing, which means you don't have to keep your thumb on it all the time to prevent line from jumping off unexpectedly.

A plug-casting reel with star drag and level-wind mechanism.

In combination with the anti-reverse is an adjustable drag and the familiar star-wheel of larger saltwater reels.

Two sizes of plug reels have become pretty much standard over the years, and both sizes are offered by most manufacturers. The smaller one holds about 200 yards of 10-pound line, the bigger one about 200 yards of 15-pound. Even larger models are available, but they raise a debate. Are they really bait-casting reels, or do they belong in a class with larger saltwater casting reels? A minor point, maybe, but purists bicker over much less than that.

Saltwater plug-casting enthusiasts seldom use lines heavier than 15-pound-test, which may sound strange at first, considering that freshwater bass fishermen often go as high as 25-pound. But it really isn't strange at all. In salt water, you generally have room to let a fish run, and so the added capacity of 15-pound line is more desirable than a shorter length of 20- or 25-pound test.

The only situation that comes to mind where a salty plugger might consider going to line heavier than 15 is casting for snook in tight quarters—and the problems there are much the same as bass fishing in snags or heavy weeds.

If you happen to think that a freshwater "worm rod" is a heavy stick, consider some of the plug rods used for different saltwater specialties. Deep-jigging rods are almost like broomsticks. You'd swear they didn't have any action at all—until a husky offshore fish puts a bend in one. But casting action is not needed, since heavy deep jigs are simply dropped overside and allowed to sink (see Chapter 18).

Not much lighter are the bait-casting rods used for tarpon fishing, offshore surface casting, and casting inshore with heavy plugs and lures. They do have *some* casting action in the forward section, but remain pretty rigid near the butt, and are still far more powerful than a worm rod.

For inshore work that encompasses lures of average weight (½ to ⅝ ounce) used on snook, smaller tarpon, school channel bass, stripers, bluefish, and, in fact, the everyday demands of just about every coastal area, the rod still must be fairly stout, but at least can be chosen with more of a view to comfortable casting action.

In all examples mentioned so far, 15-pound line is generally the angler's choice, and so the larger-capacity bait-casting reel is better suited.

If you use 12-pound line or less, there's a decision to make. The larger reel will, of course, give you more capacity. Probably you should take that one if most of your fishing is done with easy-to-cast lures. But the smaller one does cast better, particularly if you go down to lures weighing as little as ⅜ or ¼ ounce.

It's no secret that spinning is a much more widely chosen system for light lures, but a lot of bait-casting enthusiasts do use very light outfits with 10-pound-test line and whippy rod, for applications ranging from bonefishing to potluck angling for a variety of small species. Even for bonefish, 200 yards of 10-pound line is generally adequate.

Whatever your rod needs, light or heavy, it's advisable to use one-piece bait-casting rods in the salt—that is, rods in which the butt is neither offset, nor removable. The shaft should extend all the way through the butt. Such rods are frequently called "straight-handle" rods.

SPINNING TACKLE

The family of spinning outfits is a huge one that ranges from ultra-light all the way to heavy rigs capable of handling lines as heavy as 30-pound-test. All spinning reels, however, have a common denominator in the fixed-spool system of operation.

With other reels, the spool revolves when you cast line or let it out. The spinning spool remains stationary at all times. When you cast, lure weight pulls line forward over the end of the stationary spool; when you retrieve, a pickup mechanism revolves around the spool, wrapping line onto it.

There are two principal advantages to the fixed spool. One is that less force is needed to simply peel off line than to turn a spool. Thus, lighter lures can be used with a spinning outfit than with equivalent classes of revolving-spool tackle. Second, since the spool does not turn at all, there is no danger of its overrunning and causing a backlash.

This feature, of course, is the one biggest factor in spinning's great popularity.

Spinning outfits in various sizes are used in so many different kinds of salt-water fishing that the applications can't be counted. But it's important for the angler to realize from the start that there are some salty specialties for which spinning tackle isn't at all suited—and many others for which it can be used, but is less practical than revolving-spool gear.

One obvious limitation is in line size. The heaviest spinning reels are not suited for more than 30-pound line, at best, and most spin-fishermen of experience place the outside limit at 20-pound.

For offshore trolling with lines up to 20-pound-test, spinning can be used, but the revolving reel is much more efficient. In general, revolving reels are often preferable for the simple reason that they do not twist the line as spinning reels eventually do, even if handled with utmost care.

But when any kind of casting is involved, most of the advantages swing to the side of spinning—at least for those fishermen who are not well practiced at conventional casting.

Getting back to the matter of line twist, this is the one big drawback with spinning reels. You can live with it, but you certainly can't ignore it. The main reason it keeps cropping up is that the pickup mechanism imparts a slight amount of twist as it wraps line on the spool. This twist rapidly multiplies when helped along by such factors as baits or lures that spin on the retrieve, or by the common practice of turning the reel crank when a fish is taking out line.

Even the best tackle-handlers will get a lot of twist during an extra-long fight with a fish, or several tough fights over a period of time.

When line twist develops, it can be removed by clipping off your entire terminal rig and trolling the twisted length of line behind the boat.

Selecting the Right Spinning Outfit

Probably the most versatile of all saltwater spinning outfits is one built of a 6½- or 7-foot rod, and a standard-size reel which holds in the neighborhood of 200 yards of 10- or 12-pound line. The same outfit could be used with line as light as 6-pound.

For a lot of anglers, this outfit might be the only one really needed. It serves beautifully for the general run of inshore fishing—all the way from panfish to many brawny types, such as snook or stripers. And it is suitable for casting, trolling, drifting, and still-fishing.

Even offshore, it can find spot use—for school dolphin and other surfacing fish. And, of course, it has the potential to whip some very large trophies, with the right combination of good tackle-handling (see Chapter 7), working room—and luck.

Ultra-light spinning tackle takes on a slightly different meaning in salt water than in fresh. There are many small coastal fish which would not overmatch the little 4- or 4½-foot rods and 2-pound line sometimes used inland. But the ultra-light devotee in salt water generally likes his rods no less than 6 feet long, and will seldom use line lighter than 4-pound-test.

Now let's look at spinning rigs heavier than the "standard" 10-pound-test setup.

Next step is an intermediate outfit, making use of a reel having a capacity of about 300 yards of 15-pound line. This rig is well liked by spin-fishermen in all areas who do a lot of casting with lures up to 1 ounce or so in weight, or who use heavier bottom rigs or live baits. The rod may be either a beefed-up model of the 7-foot, one-handed configuration, or it may be of some alternate design—possibly a two-handed rod with light-action tip for live-baiting, or a two-handed rod up to 8½ feet long for longer casting potential with big lures.

Big ocean spinning reels, as mentioned, are generally spooled with lines testing 20 pounds, although it is possible to use up to 30. Rods, naturally, are hefty ones in all cases, but again variable as to style.

The light spinning gear so popular in fresh water is surprisingly well suited to most inshore fishing, though longer two-handed rods are required for long casts and heavy lures.

Heavy spinning rods in the 9- to 12-foot range are usually thought of as surf rods, as indeed they are. But in certain cases, the boating angler might choose such a stick, if he sometimes faces the challenge of casting a long way. One example is off the North Carolina coast, where boaters search outside the beach for schooling channel bass (red drum). When found, the fish can seldom be approached closely enough to be reachable with one-hand tackle, and so rigs of surfing proportions are chosen.

Another common use for 9- or 10-foot rods in boats is to meet the challenge of tossing out rather small live baits without a sinker—the kind of thing you might have to face in California party-boat fishing as well as many other kinds of chumming situations.

But when touchy casting problems don't enter the picture, heavy spinning rods used in a boat should be no more than 7½ or 8 feet long for the sake of convenience.

SURF-FISHING TACKLE

It is possible to fish from the beach with just about any casting tackle, spinning or conventional. However, proper surfcasting tackle is specially designed for very long casts and heavy terminal tackle, so that the angler can get his lure or bait out to the fish.

Most surfcasters today use spinning gear. Rods are two-handed and from 8 to 12 feet long; the most common length is 8½ to 9 feet. Reels are intermediate or heavy saltwater models spooled with 15- or 20-pound-test monofilament.

Many expert casters still stick with conventional tackle. Though it is much harder to handle than spinning tackle, casts are longer, and conventional reels are better suited to very heavy lures. Rods are generally longer than spinning rods—usually 10 or 11 feet, and they have been made up to 16 feet. The best are made from one-piece blanks, and are not too portable. Reels, already discussed above for boat use, are called squidding reels and have wide light spools of either plastic or metal. (Heavy spools such as used in trolling reels would increase the danger of backlash.) The best line is braided nylon up to 36-pound-test.

Surf-fishing tackle is discussed in more detail in Chapter 16.

FLY-FISHING TACKLE

People sometimes wonder if they "need" fly tackle for saltwater fishing. The quick and easy answer to that one is "no."

Far more than any other fishing specialty, saltwater fly-fishing is practiced for love of the sport itself—not because it's the most productive way to fish. In fact, the basic approach is at odds with the usual. Most anglers decide what fish they want to go after, and then try to figure out the easiest way to catch them. The fly-fisherman realizes that nearly all his targets could be captured more efficiently and in greater number with other kinds of tackle—and that's why he likes it!

Of course, you don't have to go so far overboard that you flail away with fly rod through thick and thin. Many a saltwater angler uses fly tackle for added zest in spot situations, even though he might put in far more time with other gear.

The information in this book can't get you started in fly-casting nor is it intended to. But for those who already cast, or who are planning to learn, should prove helpful in tackle selection, rigging, lures, and techniques.

Fly Rods and Lines

The important factor in balancing fly tackle is matching the rod to the weight of the line. This is no great trick any more, because all fly lines are marked according to a weight system designated by the American Fishing Tackle Manufacturer's Association. And rod manufacturers label their sticks with the line size (or sizes) they consider best suited. No system is perfect. Minor variations can still be expected, but fortunately, modern rod blanks are capable of handling such variations.

Because of the often large and bulky fly-fishing lures used in salt water, a No. 10 line is the standard. You need a heavy line to carry out a big and wind-resistant fly. Floating fly lines are preferred wherever their use is practical, and so the exact designation of the line under discussion is WF 10 F— the "WF" for "weight-forward," and the final "F" for "floating." "Weight-forward" simply means that the line is tapered, with all the casting weight concentrated in a short length of the line near the tip, another aid to long casting with big flies.

Having selected the line size, it's easy to find a rod marked to match—in fact, a lot of rods. You'll still have some shopping to do for looks, price, and component features. But any rod so marked is supposed to work well with a No. 10 line. Rod length for this line size is invariably around 9 feet or 9 feet, 3 inches.

Two other rod-line matchups have a prominent place in saltwater fly-fishing—one heavier than the preceding, and one lighter.

The heavier one will be needed if you have a yen to tackle giant tarpon, shark, or big offshore fish like amberjack and sailfish. Again, the rod will be 9 to 9½ feet long, but of stiffer action—perhaps with a reinforced butt section— and will be used with a No. 11 or No. 12 line.

If you don't go big-game fishing with a fly rod often enough to justify the cost of the heavier rig, go ahead and use the standard No. 10 outfit when an extra-heavy challenge arises. Just don't apply too heavy a hand during the fight and you probably won't get into trouble.

For a lighter outfit than standard, try an 8½- or 9-foot rod, matched to a No. 8 or No. 9 line. Being smaller and lighter, this rig is much more pleasant to cast, and therefore more enjoyable to fish with when after lightweights like bonefish, weakfish, or any other target for which small and medium-size saltwater flies can be used.

Sinking lines can be very useful in many situations where fish aren't rising to the surface. Virtually all fly-fishermen prefer to use floaters, but still keep a sinking line on hand—either on another reel, or on a spare spool with its own backing attached.

The only difference in labeling between a sinking line and a floater is the letter "S" after the weight number, replacing the "F."

Fly Reels and Backing Line

Saltwater fly reels must be large enough to accommodate both the chosen size of fly line and a long length of backing line, which usually is of braided Dacron, although monofilament and braided nylon are sometimes used. Actual length of the backing must, of course, be whatever seems safe for your particular fishing, but backing is always necessary, since fly lines are only from 90 to 120 feet long. There's no place in salt water you can throw a fly without risk of hooking something that can strip off that amount of line.

A Fin-Nor saltwater fly reel.

Tarpon fishermen like a minimum of 200 yards of 30-pound-test backing. Offshore fishermen cram on as much of the same test line as they can possibly manage. For most other situations, 200 yards of 20-pound-test is a good arrangement.

A few fly reels, with elaborate drag systems and spools machined from solid metal, are quite costly—ranging upward from $100. They are truly advantageous only for tarpon and offshore fishing, where the elaborate drags do important work, but they carry considerable pride of ownership as well.

For about half the price of a top-quality reel, you can get production-line models which also have minutely adjustable drag systems. Much saltwater fly-fishing, however, doesn't require much of a drag at all. A simple click mechanism provides minimum drag pressure, which can be complemented by careful fingering of the spool. Plenty of pressure is exerted on a fish by the sheer weight of the bulky fly line being dragged through the water, and so the simplest single-action reel may be perfectly adequate to your needs. Just make sure it is large enough and well put together.

Fly-fishermen are aware of this, but it bears mentioning that the actual size of the fly line has nothing to do with breaking test. Fly-fishing categories are rated according to strength of the *leader,* or the lightest portion (tippet) of a tapered leader. Competitive tippet-test categories are 6, 8, 10, 12, and 15 pounds. These may be used freely on any size fly outfit, with any line weight.

Information on fly leaders will be found in Chapter 10.

2

CHOOSING AND INSTALLING LINE

Three different types of fishing line are prominent on the modern saltwater angling scene—monofilament, braided nylon, and braided Dacron.

Monofilament is very nearly an all-purpose line. As long as the reel is capable of handling it, mono can be used for any kind of saltwater fishing with any kind of tackle, and for the majority of applications it is the best choice. Certain specialties, however, favor braided lines. And, as hinted, some reels are not suited for monofilament.

Never install monofilament on a revolving-spool reel with plastic spool. A characteristic of the stuff is that it stretches, then later tends to return toward its original condition. After the line is spooled back on the reel, following bouts with a fish or two, it begins contracting. The pressure can quickly break a plastic spool. True, a few spinning reels have plastic spools, but veteran anglers don't trust them for extra-rugged use, even though they hold up to monofilament pressures under everyday conditions.

Another reason why a particular revolving-spool reel might not be workable with monofilament is spool tolerance. If there is sufficient clearance between spool lip and end plate, springy mono will force itself through the gap and jam your reel. If this should happen to you, you can either try a larger diameter monofilament or go to braided line.

Let's consider the three lines separately, exploring the advantages and disadvantages of each, and with particular attention to their major areas of usefulness.

For both mechanical and practical reasons, monofilament is the only choice for spinning reels. In both light and heavy bottom fishing with any kind of tackle it is better than braids because it sinks faster. Far less visible in the water than braids, mono offers a decided advantage in those relatively few saltwater situations where no leader is used.

Being "stretchy," monofilament is less likely to break under sudden snags and strains. It has an elastic property that helps forgive minor errors in drag and heavy-handedness. This doesn't mean you can ignore proper fighting procedures; only that you may have an extra cushion.

As an offshore trolling line, monofilament is often chosen over braided Dacron for all line classes up to 80-pound.

And even among bait-casting enthusiasts, mono has forged ahead of traditional braided lines in popularity.

Braided nylon remains, however, the caster's choice for surf or squidding or ocean casting reels, and is still preferred by some bait-casters. There's no denying that it "behaves" much better on the spool than mono does.

Also, braided nylon is widely used on general-purpose boat reels, and would be the choice if your own reel can't handle monofilament for the reasons already mentioned.

Dacron is mainly considered a trolling line, particularly for offshore work. Its chief characteristics are a quite small diameter and almost complete absence of stretch. Since stretchy monofilament and non-stretchy Dacron are both in common use among trollers, it's obvious that personal views are the determining factor. In general, here's how the opposing views can be stated: Dacron users like the fact that it's easier to set a hook with their line, and that all applied drag pressure is felt by the fish—none being taken up by an elastic line. Mono users are perfectly willing to work a little harder setting the hook in order to gain the added cushion against line breakage which the stretch provides.

The debate goes on, even among old hands. But it should be apparent that anyone who hasn't had a great deal of experience in fighting fish is much better off with monofilament.

All the foregoing applies to lines in the light and medium classes—up to and including 50-pound. When it comes to 80-pound and 130-pound classes, used for giant tuna and marlin, there is fairly general agreement that Dacron is much more suitable, the reason being that monofilament of those large sizes, and used under such heavy drag, is just *so* stretchy that a great deal of the angler's effort is wasted in fighting the line instead of the fish.

But there will never be complete agreement on anything in the world of offshore fishing. At Cairns, Australia, where many American big-game fishermen go each fall in quest of black marlin weighing 1,000 pounds and up, there has been many a rumble between the visitors, who want to use 130-pound-class Dacron line, and the Australian skippers, who insist on monofilament.

Regardless of whether that particular argument will ever be resolved, there another niche where 80- or 100-pound-test monofilament has a use—not for trolling, but for "monster" fishing down deep (warsaw grouper or jewfish), or for shark fishing.

Getting back to saltwater fishing in general, one important reason for the popularity of monofilament is its low cost. True, there are expensive brands of mono on the market, but many tried-and-true brands cost amazingly little, if purchased in bulk.

That's the key—bulk. Not only would you have to buy a lot of 100-yard spools to fill some saltwater reels, but the price mushrooms because of the more expensive packaging.

Bulk monofilament generally is sold by weight, the common spools being ¼ pound, ½ pound, and 1 pound. Often you'll find that a ¼-pound spool of say, 10-pound-test monofilament costs only around twice as much as two 100-yard spools of the same brand, yet contains four or five times as much line. Savings increase, of course, if you buy ½- or 1-pound spools. For some anglers that might be more line than they'd use in several seasons, but bulk monofilament can be stored indefinitely if kept in a dark closet or some other place where it is not exposed to extreme heat for long periods.

FILLING A SPINNING SPOOL

Without aid of a line-winding machine, the best way to fill a spinning reel is to let the line flow off the end of the line spool while you crank it onto your reel spool. Proceed as follows:

Place the line spool on the floor. String the line through your rod guides, open the bail of the reel, and tie the line to the reel spool.

Now comes one important point. Check your reel to see whether the bail rotates in a clockwise or counterclockwise direction. Most move clockwise but at least one very popular model turns counterclockwise. If your reel does turn clockwise, then make sure that line is coming off the line spool counterclockwise, or severe line twist will result. All you have to do to reverse the flow of line off the line spool is turn the spool over and set it on its other end.

Grasp the rod forward of the handle, extending your thumb and forefinger downward so that you can grip the line between them, ahead of the bail. The rod butt is pressed against your stomach. Exert firm pressure on the line with thumb and forefinger while you turn the reel crank with the other hand.

Continue cranking until line fills the spool to the point where the forward spool lip starts its last outward curve. This is not always an easily definable point, nor is it all that critical. If in doubt, go ahead and crank a few extra turns. Better to have the spool a bit too full than a bit low.

Too little line on the spool not only deprives you of maximum capacity, but makes casting considerably more difficult. On the other hand, if a spool is too full it will cause a line snarl somewhere in the early stages of its use. That not much fun, but at least after you cut away the snarl the line level will be just about right.

Unless a hole or clip is provided by the manufacturer on the reel spool itself, you'll have to use a rubber band to keep the line in place after spooling. Tie a knot near one end of the rubber band first, to provide an easy grip when you remove it.

FILLING A REVOLVING SPOOL

A different approach must be taken with revolving-spool reels. In this case, you cannot simply let line slip from the end of the supply spool, or line twist again will result. The supply spool must revolve. An easy solution is to have someone else hold the spool, using a pencil or something similar as an axle.

If nobody is on hand to help you, try this: Cut a wire coathanger at one end, slip your spool over the long wire, twist the cut ends with pliers so they hold together, hang the coat hanger any place that's convenient, and start cranking.

If filling a bait-casting reel or other reasonably small rig, press the butt of the rod against your stomach and hold both rod and line forward of the reel seat with one hand while you crank with the other—applying pressure to the oncoming line with thumb and one or two fingers.

In order to fill a reel too heavy to permit comfortable holding in the manner described, you'll have to look for an alternate way of supporting the rod. You can rest it on a firm support, or have someone hold it—freeing your entire hand for applying pressure to the line.

The heavier the line, the more pressure you must use to assure that the wrap is snug. Loosely spooled line will "bite into itself" under fishing pressure, and will break.

With really heavy lines, you'll have to wear a glove on the line hand, and bear down hard. Wet the glove first, to cut down on heat buildup caused by friction—and re-wet it as necessary throughout the spooling process. Also check the line occasionally to see that it isn't being frayed by the glove pressure. If it is, find a glove with a smoother surface—perhaps a leather or plastic one.

Level-wind reels can be filled to the very edge of the spool. Spools on revolving reels without level-winds probably shouldn't be filled up completely *unless* they are to be used exclusively by practiced anglers who take care to lay the line on evenly as they bring in a fish. Otherwise it's best to leave some leeway in case the line piles up to one side of the spool and starts binding.

3

HOOKS AND TERMINAL TACKLE

HOOKS

Despite a boundless array of hook patterns, finishes, and sizes, the saltwater fisherman needn't wallow indecisively in a sea of technical choices. Three or four basic styles will cover all needs.

Size of Hooks

Saltwater hooks range generally in size from 1/0 (small) up to 20/0. Among those sizes, some basic divisions can be made:

INSHORE FISHING: 1/0 through 5/0, with occasional need for hooks as large as 9/0 for tarpon, big bass, and the like.

GENERAL OFFSHORE FISHING, BOTTOM OR SURFACE: 6/0 through 12/0, with 7/0, 8/0, and 9/0 being used the most.

BIG GAME, SHARK, AND GIANT GROUPER: 9/0 through 20/0, but few marlin and tuna men choose larger than 16/0.

Within those groups, actual size choice is based more than anything else on the size of the bait to be used, though some consideration must be given to the striking or biting habits of the fish that are primarily being sought. In any event, a variation of one, or even two, sizes will seldom cause any serious problems.

Hooks smaller than 1/0 are labeled by a different system, starting with No. 1, the largest. Then, as the numbers go up, the sizes go down. A No. 2 is smaller than a No. 1, and a No. 20 is almost invisible to the naked eye of a middle-aged angler.

But, aside from their fairly common use on lures and flies, hooks smaller than a 1/0 are not prominent in saltwater fishing. You might use some No. or 2 or 4 hooks for baitfishing or panfishing, and sometimes a No. 10 or 1 for catching baitfish with very tiny mouths, such as balao or pilchard.

Hook Patterns

Here are the four basic designs or patterns, that can cover every need:

O'SHAUGHNESSY. This one is the standard for making rigged baits of all kinds in small-to-medium sizes—mullet, balao, strips, and others. For such work, sizes 6/0 through 9/0 are the most common, and an angler should carry them all, because actual size of the baits is bound to vary, even with a single species. Average-size balao, for instance, call for a 6/0 or 7/0 hook; large ones for an 8/0 or 9/0.

The O'Shaughnessy hook has a fairly long shank, ideal for bait rigging, and is obtainable in both needle-eye and round-eye styles. The needle eye can be helpful in rigging certain baits where a round eye seems a bit bulky or hard to handle. Too, the needle eye assures that the eye will not straighten under heavy pressure. While this happens only rarely with a round eye, the possibility must be considered in cases of great strain with heavier lines.

In smaller sizes the O'Shaughnessy isn't bad as an all-round saltwater hook, entirely satisfactory with most live and dead baits, as well as rigged baits.

BIG-GAME. These are characterized not by size alone, but by strength. They must be able to withstand the drag pressures of heavy tackle, the powerful jaws of huge fish, and the prolonged strain of battles that can last for hours. Such hooks are identifiable by the heavy-gauge wire which is forged into a flattened appearance; by the knife-edge point and barb, and by the eye, which is either needle-style or else a round eye that has been brazed to prevent opening up. Though most commonly seen in offshore sizes, 9/0 up to 16/0, these are sometimes used in sizes down to 4/0 for inshore tarpon and jewfish.

OFFSET. This term means that the shank and point are not in the same plane; the bend of the hook, along with point and barb, are turned at an angle to the shank. This arrangement means that once a fish takes the point in its mouth, it is much less likely that the hook can be pulled from the mouth without digging in. Not that you can't catch plenty of fish on a straight-design hook. It's just that the odds favor an offset.

In my opinion, the offset hooks—of which the Eagle Claw pattern 85 is a good example—should be first choice of those who fish primarily with dead baits, especially inshore. They also can be used very effectively with live baits, such as shrimp or minnows. The offset hook, however, is not favored for making rigged trolling baits.

SHORT-SHANK LIVE-BAIT. Many hook styles can be considered "short-shank," of course, compared to those with extra-long shanks. But what we're talking about here is a specific design in which the shank is very little longer than the bite—the appearance being almost that of a U.

First popularized on Southern California party boats, this style allows small live baits to be presented in the most natural manner possible. Yet the hook is made of relatively thick wire and tempered so that it can be used on heavier lines without fear of straightening. Now well established in Florida and elsewhere on the East Coast, it sometimes is still referred to as a "California hook," though a more common name among offshore anglers is simply "live-bait hook."

Offshore, the short-shank is used in sizes ranging from 5/0 to 8/0, with small to medium baitfish on the order of blue runners, pinfish, goggle-eyes, and balao. A size 2/0 is about right for live shrimp and baits of sardine or pilchard size, whether fishing inshore or offshore.

Bridge and pier fishermen find short-shanks especially useful in helping fool certain wary fish which hang around such structures and which are hard to sucker unless presented with the bait of choice, swimming freely and hooked inconspicuously.

If you haven't seen these hooks before, be prepared for the fact that they will look "too small" at first, no matter what size you're considering. But resist the impulse to go a couple sizes larger. Little hooks take big fish, if they're strong enough—and these certainly are.

OTHER PATTERNS. While it's true that the four hook styles already described can serve every saltwater angling requirement, this certainly doesn't mean you can't make additional choices—based on such considerations as availability, regional specialization, or simply your own views of particular personal needs.

The Sproat and Limerick patterns, for instance, are reasonably similar to the O'Shaughnessy and, except for rigging trolling baits, can be used interchangeably. The Siwash, featuring an extra-long bite, is a Pacific-salmon standard that also has many followers on the Atlantic shore. And you might well prefer to use a hook with an extra-long shank simply for ease of removal from the fish's mouth—in cases, of course, where the added bulk seems no detriment to getting bites.

Whatever the pattern, saltwater hooks should be tinned or nickel-plated to help resist rust and corrosion, and the great majority are. Stainless hooks are available, but many anglers object to them on several grounds: they are expensive, hard to keep sharp, and, if stolen by a fish, will not corrode away so the fish can get rid of them.

Hooks with turned-up and turned-down eyes need not be considered for general saltwater fishing. They are used in making flies and jigs, or for snells. Again, they can be used if at hand, but offer no particular advantage with popular saltwater baits.

TERMINAL TACKLE

By definition, "terminal tackle" refers to anything you might stick to the end of your line—leader, sinker, swivel, snap, float, whatever. Following is a general description of terminal items, along with various recommendations. Instructions on working these different components into actual terminal rigs is given in Chapter 10.

Swivels

A swivel serves in two capacities—as a connector between line and leader, and as a safeguard against line twist. In general, you should choose the smallest swivel that is consistent with strength of tackle and weight of leader and bait. If a swivel is overloaded it will not turn freely and the line will twist. If you encounter this problem, go to a larger swivel. For exceptionally severe twist problems, you have the option of a ball-bearing swivel, which is costly but positive.

Swivels may be purchased in either bright or black finish. Black ones are preferable in any situation where toothy fish are likely to be present—mackerel, bluefish, barracuda—which often hit a flashy swivel and cut the line. Black swivels do not completely eliminate such "accidents," but at least they minimize them.

Three-way swivels, featuring three separate connection rings instead of the usual two, are designed for making special rigs. The line attaches to one ring, the leader to another, and either a sinker rig or a second leader to the third.

Snaps and Snap-Swivels

Snaps resemble a safety pin in design, and are furnished alone or in combination with a swivel. Beginning anglers sometimes get the idea that a snap-swivel is a regular and essential bit of equipment—at least they often tie the devices to the end of their line, and then snap on a hook. But the first rule in terminal tackle is to keep it as trim as possible under given circumstances. Neither a snap nor a snap-swivel should ever be used with a baited hook. And their application with lures must be carefully judged on individual merits.

A simple snap gives the convenience of quick lure change, but be warned that snaps can open up when used at the end of a leader where a fish might get the chance to chew on them. Sheer strain can open up a snap as well, so if you use one, make sure it isn't too flimsy for the job.

In my opinion, snap-swivels belong at the end of a leader only when using a spoon or spinner. They hold down twist and, since these lures are shiny and metallic themselves, the snap-swivel isn't apt to discourage a fish from striking.

In offshore fishing, a special type of heavy-duty snap-swivel serves an entirely different and extremely valuable function. It is tied to the end of line, or double line, so that prepared leaders—rigged with a loop at one end—can be snapped on or changed instantly.

Sinkers

Any chunk of lead that helps take a bait below the surface qualifies as a sinker, whether it weighs a fraction of an ounce or a pound. And somewhere in the vast world of saltwater fishing, there is a place for all the sizes.

The rule of thumb in selecting sinker size is nothing more than using the smallest that will do the job for you—and none at all if a little patience will allow the bait to sink to desirable levels. But at times, sinkers are used for casting weight as much as for "sinkability," and so you may have to bend the foregoing rule.

The surf fisherman, for instance, might need a 5- or 6-ounce sinker to match his tackle and carry a bait for long casting distances. Such a heavy blob of lead would seem to make it difficult, or impossible, to feel a bite. However, that important matter is provided for by rigging in fish-finder fashion: the sinker slides freely on the line and, conversely, the line slides through the sinker-eye when tugged on by a fish. An alternate method is to rig the sinker on its own short length of leader, tied to a three-way swivel, so that the feel of a bite need not be transmitted directly through the sinker's weight.

Let's look now at some basic sinker styles and their applications.

SPLIT-SHOT, CLINCH-ON, AND RUBBERCOR SINKERS vary in appearance but their usefulness is much the same. They attach directly to line or leader. The round split shot and elongated clinch-on both have slits in which the line is placed. The slit is then pressed closed with pliers. The chief advantage of these types is that they can be added to existing leader arrangements without having to cut and retie. The Rubbercor, a patented design, is superior to the others because it can also be taken off easily. It contains a rubber insert with "ears" protruding from either end of the sinker. When the ears are twisted, the line spins to the opposite side from the slit. A reverse twist allows removal.

Though often considered a freshwater sinker, the split shot can come in very handy—perhaps adding just that tiny bit of extra weight you need to cast a light bait. The split shot also is used to stop a larger sliding sinker at a given point on line or leader.

EGG SINKERS, also called sliding sinkers, are one of the types which allow free movement of the line, and perhaps are the most popular style of all for every type of bottom fishing. An assortment of egg sinkers in weights of ¼, ½, ¾, and 1 ounce will serve all light-tackle purposes. They are available in weights up to several ounces for deep work.

PYRAMID SINKERS are designed for extra holding power in sand and mud bottoms, especially where strong current or wave action rolls other styles all over the place. Obviously, they are the surf fisherman's standard, but are also useful off piers and jetties and, at times, from a boat.

BANK SINKERS, vaguely duckpin-shaped and with an eye molded into the small end, are used for bottom-fishing rigs in which the sinker is tied directly to the end of the line, with a hook (or hooks) rigged to dropper lines positioned above the sinker. The *dipsy sinker* is an improvement of this design that features a swiveling eye.

TROLLING SINKERS come in several shapes—cigar and keeled being the most popular. The feature they all have in common is an eye at either end for attachment between line and leader, or sometimes directly into the leader itself, usually well up from the hook.

Floats

Made of hollow plastic, cork, or plastic foam, fishing floats are used to keep baits off the bottom, or at a desired depth, and they also signal a bite. An auxiliary function for a shorebound fisherman is that of carrying the bait out a long way with wind or current.

Some floats snap directly to the line by means of a spring clip. Others must be threaded onto the line.

Choosing the correct size certainly isn't difficult. If the float goes under, or doesn't ride high enough in the water to suit you, it's too small. On the other hand, you don't want it so large that a striking fish can't pull it under without being alarmed by the weight.

One type of specialized float—the popping cork—even helps attract fish to your bait. This one has a hollowed-out head that blurps loudly on the surface when you jerk your rod. Popping corks are routinely used everywhere along the Gulf Coast for trout, redfish, and snook.

One of the most versatile—and portable—of fishing floats is an ordinary toy balloon. It can be inflated to whatever size is necessary for a particular bait. Moreover, when pulled under by a fighting fish it usually breaks, so there is no extra weight on your line. A small package of balloons doesn't take up much room in the tackle box, and therefore some anglers carry them for special situations even though they don't normally fish with floats. The inflated balloon must be tied on, of course, and since it is difficult to tie it firmly to line or leader, it usually is fixed to your swivel.

A breakaway float can also be rigged out of scrap plastic foam. Most fishermen have an ample supply of this in the form of broken foam ice chests, or it can be scavenged all too often from roadside or seashore. Break off a chunk the size you need to support your chosen bait. Unlike the balloon, foam can be affixed anywhere you desire on line or leader, simply by half-hitching the line to it, or wrapping the line a few turns and pulling hard so that it bites into the soft foam. Your float will disintegrate quickly after a fish is hooked.

4
ARTIFICIAL LURES

Most experienced anglers realize that artificial lures will take any predatory species of saltwater fish, and in many situations can be more productive than natural bait. However, newcomers to the sport frequently develop an early mistrust of artificials. They buy a popular model, toss it out a few times with no results, then put it away in favor of a bottom rig that they know will get some kind of bite sooner or later.

Nothing is more important than having confidence in the bait you're using—not because of any mind-power exerted through the bait to the fish, but for the entirely logical reason that you are then more likely to fish the bait properly, patiently, and with the knowledge that it's bound to pay off if you get it to the right place at the right time.

Many beginners have the idea that a certain type of artificial is needed for a certain kind of fish, but the fact is that all predatory species will take many different lures—which must be chosen according to water depth, size, and other specific fishing conditions. Shown here with a Pacific roosterfish are two slender-minnow plugs, one cup-faced popper, an artificial squid, and three skirted trolling lures.

It does take quite a bit of experimenting with difficult artificial lures to develop that kind of confidence. But the way to start is by understanding that there really are only a very few basic *types* of artificials—despite the hundreds of different models and colors offered by various manufacturers. And the situation is rare indeed where it takes a specific size or color or model to get strikes.

It's important, of course, to select a lure that is generally appropriate in size, action, and weight. But the choice is seldom a critical one, and certainly not—as some think—a matter of picking a specific lure for a specific kind of fish. What folks might call a "snook lure" in Florida can be exactly the same one that's called a "bass lure" in New Jersey or a "trout lure" in North Carolina. And in any area it might take a wide variety of predatory species.

A sound basic assortment of lures can be compiled with just a couple of lures from each of the following groups, your final personal selections being based on local preferences, the kind of tackle you use, and the depths you fish.

SPOONS AND SQUIDS

This category contains metallic lures, designed to combine flash with a wobbling or twisting motion. They are among the best of lures for taking open-water predators that commonly feed on schools of silvery baitfish such as menhaden or pilchards, but they are productive in all areas of saltwater fishing, from shoreline out to the deep sea.

Within this category, "spoon" is the name given to obviously spoon-shaped or dished-out models. Similar flashy lures which are flattened, tapered, rounded, or diamond-shaped are generally referred to as "squids" or "jigs," but both those names also refer to entirely different types of lures, as we'll see later. The angler always has to fight the battle of terminology, especially if he moves from area to area on the saltwater scene.

By tradition, not necessity, single-hooked spoons are chosen for trolling and treble-hooked ones for casting. Both basic styles are obtainable in all weights, from less than ¼ ounce to several ounces.

When used for trolling, spoons should be selected on the basis of overall size and hook size—weight being not much of a factor. It's a simple matter of bigger spoons for bigger fish. Unfortunately, size designations of spoons are not constant from brand to brand, but here are some general guidelines, based on hook size: Light trolling (mackerel, trout, etc.), 1/0 to 3/0; medium trolling (snook, school kings, redfish, stripers, etc.), 3/0 to 6/0; heavy and offshore trolling, 6/0 to 9/0.

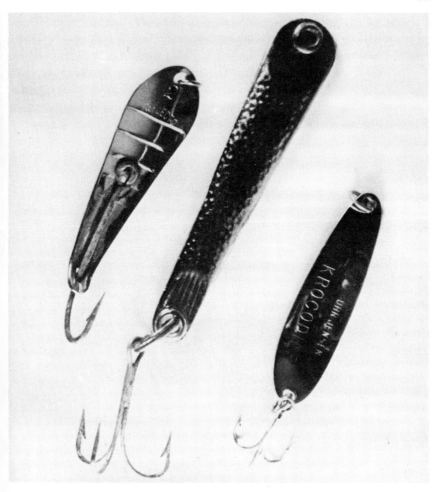

Bright metal lures are among the best saltwater fish-getters. Lure in center is only one of many designs of metallic casting lures called squids or metal jigs. The treble-hook spoon usually is chosen for casting, while single-hook spoons are normally used for trolling. However, they can be interchanged freely.

Treble-hooked casting spoons often are heavier for their overall size than single-hooked models. This is to provide additional weight for longer casting capability. Here, weight *is* the important key to proper selection, since you'll have to match lure weight to your rod and line. These spoons are extremely popular for long-distance heaving from shorebound positions, such as bridge, jetty, or pier, so it pays to use the heaviest your tackle can efficiently handle— whether it be ½ ounce on a light spinning rod, or 3 ounces or more on gear of surfing proportions.

Remarks in the preceding paragraph apply equally to metallic squids, which really are no different in application and action to treble-hook spoons made of heavy-gauge metal. While squids make good trolling lures at times, they are seldom used for this work, being thought of mainly as surfing lures and alternately as "jigging" lures—that is, lures that are sunk in deep water and then worked with an up-and-down motion. In short, wherever a compact but heavy lure seems in order, a shiny squid might well be a great choice.

JIGS

In most fishing circles, the word "jig" refers to a simple lead-headed hook, dressed with bucktail, nylon filaments, shiny Mylar tinsel, or a combination

Popular head styles of bucktail and nylon jigs. The two at top center are "skimmers"—flattened to keep hooks upright for shallow-flats use.

of those materials. In recent years, the "bait-tail" jigs have come along to dominate the field in many saltwater areas. These are jigs in which the hook dressing is nothing more than a bit of plastic worm, molded plastic shrimp, or molded minnow.

Bait-tail jigs are available in many ready-made brands, but the angler can also tailor-make his own, by keeping on hand an assortment of jig heads in various weights and an assortment of worms or replacement bait tails purchased in bulk. Be sure to save all your old bucktail or nylon jigs from which the dressing has been nibbled away or unwrapped. They can ease the strain of buying new heads.

Plastic bait-tail jigs are currently among the most popular and productive of saltwater lures. By keeping a supply of lead-heads and an assortment of plastic tails, the angler can make up his own lures on the spot. Heads at right were purchased for this kind of use; those at left were salvaged from old bucktail and nylon jigs. The screw-tail, shrimp, and worm shown can all be bought inexpensively in bulk, along with several other types of plastic tails.

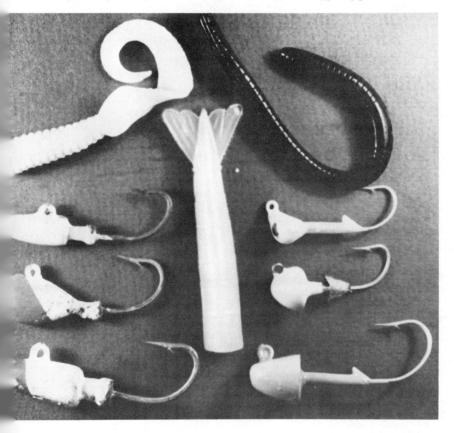

Regardless of whether the jig is dressed with hair or plastic (or a combination), fishing methods remain the same. The single best retrieve for the widest variety of fish is a slow-to-medium bottom-hopping routine. Fast retrieves will produce more fish on occasion, particularly mackerel, blues, and other fast-swimming kinds. Since few jigs have any real action of their own, you must provide it by twitching the rod tip or by pauses in cranking.

In selecting an adequate jig for a particular job, the only thing that might of itself spell success or failure is weight, which must be determined by water depth and, again, by what your tackle can handle. For most inshore work over grass beds, along shorelines, and around bars, the two most useful

This assortment of deep jigs ranges in weight from 1 to 3 ounces. Flattened head styles sink more rapidly than the blunt-nose design shown with plastic shrimp.

weights are ¼ and ½ ounce, with ⅝ ounce being the usual maximum. The same sizes can be used for surfacing fish in deeper water.

You'll need jigs weighing ⅝ to 1 ounce for deep-hole inshore fishing, or outside fishing in water up to perhaps 50 feet deep. Heavier ones are seldom needed except in deep jigging (see Chapter 18), and these require exceptionally stout rods.

Very light jigs, under ¼ ounce, are used mainly for fishing thin flats in quest of bonefish and the like. However, the little jigs should not be overlooked for other work when fish seem reluctant to take the larger ones.

Color cannot be ignored in jig selection, but you have plenty of leeway. From my own experience, I've become convinced that color is mostly a proposition of dark and light, rather than exact hues. I'd probably be content with white as a light tone and yellow as a dark one, but I also use pink, orange, and red as dark colors; or any of the translucent colors in bait tails as light choices. The basic rule is light in conditions of good visibility (from the fish's point of view, that is) and dark when the water is murky or off-color. At any rate, you don't have to load yourself down with all the many colors available. As usual, local preference is always a good clue.

The last remaining factor in jig choice is head style, which, except for certain specialized uses, matters hardly at all.

One such specialty is the "skimmer" jig, which is flattened horizontally. This causes the lure to sink much more slowly than other designs, and tends to keep the hook upright. Its application, obviously, is bonefishing and other thin-water pursuits.

Conversely, when extra-fast sinking is desired, the head should be flattened vertically—knife-edged or arrow-headed or a similar design that lowers water resistance.

Success with any jig depends far more on how well you keep it at the desired level, and work it there, than it does on design or anything else. Pick a weight that's suited to the water you're fishing. The rest is up to you.

PLUGS

By way of description, a plug is roughly fish-shaped and is fitted with one or more sets of treble hooks. Traditionally of wood, many plugs are now made of plastic, and a few of metal.

Like all artificials, plugs must be chosen with regard to size and weight, but they also fall into general groupings based on action. The one broadest division is between surface and underwater models, but there are several action categories in each.

While some larger plugs are designed for specific saltwater applications, most serve double duty as freshwater bass lures. Almost any freshwater plug will draw strikes from saltwater fish, but care must be taken that the components can stand up to salty use. Hooks, for instance, should always be tinned or plated. Bronzed freshwater hooks not only will rust quickly, but many are too flimsy for even "everyday" saltwater species. And for really big saltwater fish, it pays to use extra-strength plated hooks with heavy-duty hook mounts. The most rugged construction of all is to have the hooks fixed to a stout wire running through the plug. With such a wired-through arrangement, the wood or plastic could disintegrate completely under the assault of powerful jaws and teeth, yet the fish could still be landed. That seldom happens, of course, but it's possible with some offshore fish. On the other hand, it isn't at all unheard-of for a lunker to rip a hook-screw from the plug and get away. The wire prevents this.

Surface Plugs

Floaters can be roughly grouped according to the noise and commotion they make on the surface. Splashiest of all are the cup-faced poppers, which make a loud "blurp" and throw spray when the rod is jerked sharply. You can raise quite a ruckus with one of these. And that's what it takes to attract fish offshore, from either a good way down or out. The same noisy action is valuable in the surf or other inshore areas for big, aggressive species, and particularly in a heavy chop where a more modest action might not be noticeable enough. While popping plugs are sometimes useful in still or shallow water, they should be worked in a softer and more restrained manner. But for big stripers or offshore varieties, pop the plug hard and fast.

Most popping plugs float when at rest, but some of the popular surf-casting plugs are sinkers that gurgle at the surface on retrieve. With the proper rod action you can make them about as noisy as you wish, yet the denser, nonfloating material of which they are made gives extra weight for long-distance casts.

Just below the wide-jawed poppers in noisemaking ability is a group of surface plugs characterized by a notched-head design. They are often called darting plugs, since a sweep of the rod tip not only causes them to make a restrained popping noise, but makes them dart under the surface for a few inches. These are used most often in shallower inshore water where some noise is needed to attract fish, but not enough fuss to scare the daylights out of them. Darters have the additional advantage of a nifty swimming motion when pulled under and retrieved fast. A common retrieve for fishing close to shoreline cover is to pop the lure two or three times, then move it back straight and fast. The hope is that any fish which might come to investigate

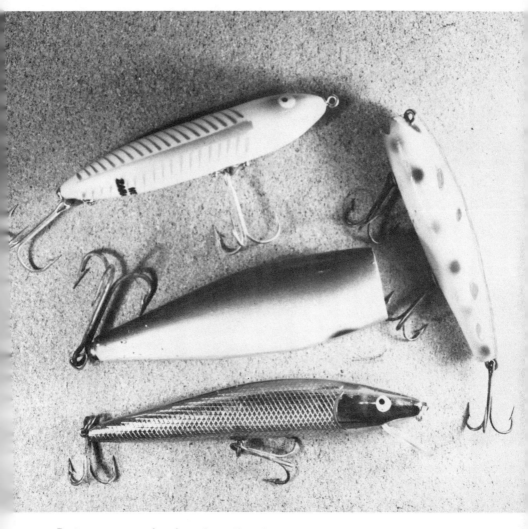

Basic assortment of surface plugs. Top, dancing style; center, cup-faced popper; bottom, slender minnow; right, darting type.

the noise will, if reluctant to hit, change his mind as soon as the lure seems to be making a fast dash for safety. Darters worked in that manner have long been the standard lures for snook fishing near the mangroves.

Another type of surface lure is designed to simulate a fish fleeing and skittering fast across the surface. This is the dancing design, identifiable by a head that is tapered down to the lure eye—no notch or lip to catch the water and make a splash. Also, plugs of this design sit at an angle in the water, head erect. When retrieved with a fast cranking of the reel and constant twitching of the rod tip, they dance across the top, bobbing up and down and sideways. They work on a lot of different fish, but have been especially taken to heart by anglers after snook or spotted seatrout in calm, and often shallow, water.

The least noisy but often the most effective of surface plugs is the slender-minnow design. Balsa-wood models were first popularized by freshwater fishermen, and larger and sturdier models later were made available to saltwater fishermen. They are slender and elongated in shape and have a small plastic lip. Some are made of wood, others of hollow plastic. Very shiny finishes are common. The most popular lengths are 4 to 6 inches.

Though not actually a surface lure, the slender minnow can be treated as such, and it provides the most realistic imitation possible of a near-dead bait-fish barely able to get off an occasional effort to right itself. To achieve this effect, you should give a sharp twitch of the rod, then a long pause. The lure dips, then floats back to the top, wiggling slightly as it does so. The dive makes only a little noise, hence will not attract fish from as far away as other surface lures. But in calm water, the sound travels a reasonable distance, and because of the slow retrieve, fish have time to track it down.

Whenever you have good reason to believe that fish are in close vicinity of the plug—by spotting them in the water, or by seeing surface activity, wakes, birds, or other telltale signs—it often pays to work the minnow in faster spurts, by jerking it again as soon as it rises to the surface.

The slender minnow is a floating-diving plug—meaning that it floats when at rest but dives under and becomes a vibrating subsurface swimmer on a troll or straight retrieve. Yet another of the productive retrieves possible with this lure is to pull it under, then bring it back in a series of erratic yanks, with no pauses that would allow it to surface.

Underwater Plugs

Just as surface lures are roughly classified according to the varying degrees of noise they make, underwater plugs can be typed according to how deep they go with certain retrieves.

Again, it should be noted that all the popular plugs come in an assortment of sizes, and that these general comments hold true regardless of the actual size chosen.

Many diving plugs are activated by a metal lip, which causes them to plane downward in the water and also imparts a vibrating or swimming motion. If the lip is fairly short you can be sure the plug is a shallow runner. The larger the lip (in proportion to overall plug size) the deeper the lure will run. Really deep-diving plugs, then, can easily be spotted by the oversize lip.

There are, however, some plugs in which the planing surface is incorporated into the design, and not obtained by adding a metal lip. These are

deep-bodied plugs with sloping "foreheads" and the lure eye set high or farther back than usual.

Also, there are plugs with no planing arrangement at all. They sink from
sheer lack of buoyancy, being made of solid plastic and perhaps with lead
weights inside. While these are capable of going plenty deep, they must be
fished slowly, and preferably with pauses in the retrieve, if that depth is to be
maintained.

Only the lipped plugs are capable of staying down on a fairly fast straight
retrieve, and so they are generally the ones chosen for deeper trolling.

The lipless underwater plugs are primarily designed for erratic retrieves
and are often called "jerk plugs" or "stick plugs." Those names indicate a

*Some popular underwater plug designs are (top to bottom) the slender min-
now; mirror plug; shad type; lipped swimmer. At lower left is a deep-diving
plug with oversize lip.*

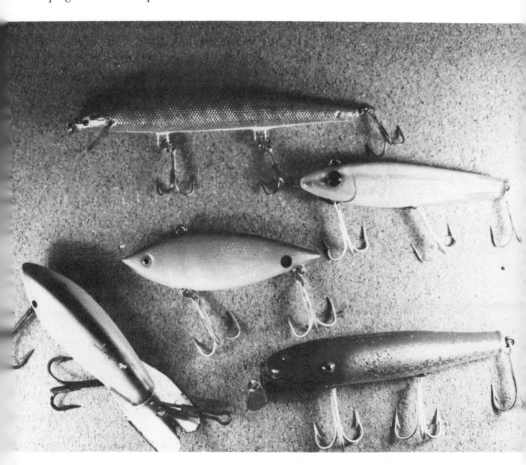

lack of built-in action, but such is not necessarily the case. Many examples, such as the popular mirror-finish plugs, do have a vibrating action which can be brought out by testing for the proper rate of retrieve.

Trolling Feathers and Lures

A few artificials are made primarily for outside trolling and are seldom, if ever, used for casting. Best known of these is the trolling feather—similar in superficial appearance to a jig, but differing in that no hook is incorporated into the lure itself. Leader wire is inserted through a hole in the lure head. The hook is then wrapped to the wire and pulled up so that the feathers dress it.

Similar lures are made of long nylon filaments rather than feathers, or in some cases of other fibers.

Feathers vary in size and in weight, but the weight makes little difference in trolling depth. All stay near the surface, though the heavier ones do go slightly deeper. Actual feather size is chosen to match the hook size desired. Often the feather is rigged in combination with a strip bait or even a whole rigged fish. In that case it is sometimes necessary to use a heavier than usual feather in order to keep the bait completely under the water and swimming.

Another type of "dressing" for rigged trolling baits is a long, multitailed plastic skirt, roughly resembling a squid. This is simply threaded on the leader so it falls back over the balao or other bait. They serve as attractors, and gaudy colors are the most popular—red and bright green.

Fly-Fishing Lures

Saltwater fly-fishing is a relatively new branch of an ancient art, so we don't yet have fly patterns by the endless thousands as the freshwater folks do. But we already have far too many to permit a detailed survey.

Fortunately, there is no real need for such a survey. A few streamers in basic sizes and colors, plus a couple of poppers, can cover the waterfront pretty well. Your kit of flies will then proceed to grow apace with your dedication to the sport.

Simple bucktail streamers are generally as productive as anything. Pulled through the water by short strips of the line, they deliver a most realistic imitation of a minnow. They stay at approximately the same water level all the time, not bouncing up and down as a spinning jig does.

The average saltwater streamer is 2 to 3 inches in overall length, with hook size of 1/0, 2/0, or 3/0.

Flies smaller than that can be used with effect, even for larger fish, if tied on strong hooks. Flies up to 6 inches long, on 4/0 to 6/0 hooks, are used sometimes for big bass, tarpon, and certain offshore fish, though they seldom really need be longer than 4 or 5 inches.

The two basic color patterns are white, with some dark hairs on top to simulate the back of a minnow; and yellow, either with or without a dark back.

An alternate choice to the bucktail is the feather streamer, which can be tied either with a wide-open scissoring action, or a longer, closed, "snaky" action—depending on how the natural curve of the feather is employed. There is

Simple bucktail and streamer flies suffice for most saltwater fishing. Large white flies at upper left are designed for offshore fish and other big species. The small fly at bottom is typical of bonefish flies. The other three are favorite inshore patterns that can be varied in size for anything from tarpon to small mackerel.

no sharply definable guide to choosing between hair and feather streamers. Both may work equally well in the same situation, but at times the fish will show a decided preference for one over the other. Don't be afraid to change. A couple of specialties for which feather streamers are exceptionally strong (though bucktails can work for both) is in tarpon fishing, and casting for surfacing fish offshore.

A few strands of shiny Mylar tinsel add appeal to a great many saltwater flies, regardless of pattern. Some flies are tied entirely with this bright material.

Saltwater poppers are not much different in design from their freshwater counterparts. Saltwater hooks are required, of course, and usually there is a length of hair or feather added to the popping head in an effort to increase the size or bulk of the lure without adding too much weight. A few very large poppers are used at sea—biggest of all being the Robinson billfish fly. The head of this one is made from a foam popping cork, flattened at the bottom, with a dozen long white hackles for a tail.

Anyone who dives hard into saltwater fly-fishing should quickly check with other fly-fishermen in the areas he fishes to determine local views on fly patterns, colors, and sizes.

5

ACCESSORY EQUIPMENT

Every saltwater angler needs a considerable amount of accessory equipment, and the purchase of such gear requires as much careful judgment as the selection of fishing tackle. You'd like to take along everything you might conceivably need, but compromises always must be made in the interest of storage space, portability, or convenience.

Many accessory items are general in nature, being necessary or useful in virtually all kinds of fishing. Others must be picked selectively for certain angling specialties. Still others are not directly for fishing, but simply for the angler's comfort and safety.

Here is a brief survey of the most-used accessories, with the exception of landing nets and gaffs, which are covered in Chapter 11.

TACKLE BOXES

Certainly no other equipment must be more carefully fitted to your own personal needs than a tackle box—or tackle boxes. It may sound nice to have a trunk-size box brimming with goodies in dozens of compartments. But you might have to hire a porter to carry the thing around for you. On the other hand, you don't want a hodgepodge of lures, hooks, swivels, leaders, and tools dumped into a tangled mass inside a box with only two or three divisions. Somewhere in today's seemingly endless lineup of boxes in different sizes and different arrangements, there is the right choice or two for your own requirements—and only you can make the choice.

Modern plastic materials are light but very strong. They also hold up better in saltwater environments and are relatively inexpensive. These days you have to look hard to find a box made of something else, anyway, so there's no decision to make along that line.

Size and interior arrangement—there's the rub. Obviously you need a box

large enough to hold the stuff you carry along, and to keep it in reasonable order. If you're a spin-fisherman, you'll need smaller compartments and more of
them; if a surfcaster, then fewer and larger compartments are the ticket. If
you locate a size and design you like, but with compartments of unfavorable
dimension and layout, be sure to check with the dealer or look at the manufacturer's catalog, since the same box may well be offered with two or more
different interior arrangements.

There are boxes whose whole interior is devoted to smaller, removable
boxes, and some with removable boxes or trays, as well as additional space or
compartments.

There are specialized designs—among them boxes with trays that slide out
like drawers. These are especially convenient in a boat with limited deck
space. Many modern plastic boxes are strong enough to sit or stand on, and
some are actually designed to double as seats for the bank or bridge
fisherman.

Whether or not you choose a box that's equipped with smaller boxes, it's
always a good idea to buy some of those little boxes to tuck away inside. They
separate tiny items like sinkers and swivels, and can be useful as pocket containers when you walk or wade and want to take along only a few lures or terminal rigs.

Of course, there also are boxes made to be carried over the shoulder or on
the belt—again with a variety of designs, with compartments ranging from
surf-plug-size to very small.

Many surf fishermen, however, prefer a heavy canvas shoulder bag to a
rigid box. They tuck their lures inside in small boxes, and also have additional space for bulkier things.

BAIT CONTAINERS

Keeping baitfish and shrimp alive for long periods can be a tricky business indeed, requiring proper equipment and constant attention on the angler's part
to make sure the water stays fresh, aerated, and cool.

Two-piece bait buckets have long been popular. The outer shell is a conventional bucket, with carrying handle. Inside this is fitted a perforated container, with a cover and spring-loaded door. Ashore or in a boat, the outer
bucket is filled with water, and the inner one, containing the bait, is placed
inside. This is for temporary holding until such time as the inner container
can be removed and lowered directly into the water by means of a stout line.
Frequent changes of water must be made if the bait is to be kept alive for any
length of time during transport in the outer bucket.

A fairly recent improvement allows the same functions to be performed by a one-piece bucket of special design—a closed bucket with a watertight lower portion and a perforated upper one with spring-loaded door. In the water, this bucket rests on its side, allowing water to flow through the upper perforations. When the bucket is lifted aboard, water is retained in the lower part so that filling a separate bucket is not necessary. This design is sometimes referred to as a trolling bucket because it needn't be taken from the water when the boat is moved at medium speed—and boat movement keeps new water circulating in the bucket.

A foam ice chest, used with an electric aerator, makes an excellent live-bait arrangement. The foam keeps water temperature stable and also adds a little bit of aerating help.

The trolling bucket is also excellent for the wade-fisherman who keeps the container tied to his waist, since it pulls more easily than a conventional perforated container. Even bridge and dock fishermen find it more useful than the two-piece bucket, if for no other reason than not having an extra component to keep track of.

The limitation of any bucket is that it can accommodate only fairly small supplies of fairly small baits. Larger baitfish and larger quantities need different arrangements, involving aerators, or pumps.

One answer is a large plastic garbage can, fitted with a hinged wooden lid to which a special pump is mounted. Such a setup can be purchased as a unit, or rigged on your own. The garbage can is as easily lugged around as any big container could be.

Perhaps the best containers for long bait life, particularly in hot weather, are foam-insulated ice chests, which, of course, keep water temperatures low for a much longer time than noninsulated cans. One or two pumps (depending on the size of the chest) can be taped or bolted to the chest.

Large and elaborate rigs of this type call for heavy-duty 12-volt pumps which attach by clamps to an automotive or marine battery. In a boat, the setup is simple enough, but for shorebound anglers there are obvious problems. Still, the struggle may be worthwhile for a group of fishermen who need a good supply of frisky bait—especially if they only have to muscle the battery and other stuff to one spot for an all-day or all-night outing. And in cases where you can park close to the fishing spot, the bubbling bait container can be left in the back of a station wagon, or in a car trunk.

Much less difficult to care for are those species of live bait which don't necessarily need to be kept in water—crabs, sand fleas, worms, and shellfish. These need only sand or seaweed to retain moisture, but their container, whether carried by hand or on a belt, should have some perforations to allow circulation of air. This helps keep the bait cool and frisky by evaporation.

ROD BELTS AND HARNESSES

With any kind of rod other than a light one-hand spinning or plug outfit, a rod belt can be considered a necessity, not only to keep your stomach in one piece while fighting a strong fish, but in some cases—surfcasting for instance—to keep the rod butt supported while retrieving or waiting for a strike.

A simple leather cup is the usual design, and nothing more elaborate is needed for surf rods or any other kind of stick with an ordinary butt cap. For rods with metallic gimbal butts, the belt should be fitted with a gimbal socket best mounted to a padded support. In a pinch, the leather cup can handle a gimbal-butt rod, but not so efficiently or comfortably. And the metal gimbal will eventually chew up the leather.

Harnesses are used only with heavy classes of tackle—usually from a boat, but sometimes from shore when fishing for shark, giant sea bass, or huge tarpon. Their use is explained in Chapter 7.

TOOLS

No saltwater angler should be without a good knife and a pair of pliers. Personal preference certainly can enter into knife selection. Even a good pocket knife might serve most purposes. But the almost universal choice is a 6-inch

Possibly an angler's most useful tool is a 6-inch stainless-steel fillet knife. While its main purposes are to cut bait and dress fish, it constantly comes in handy.

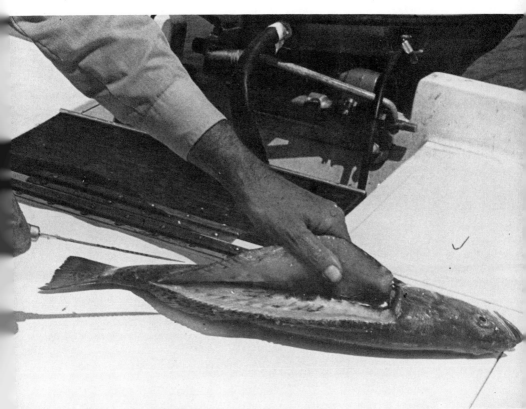

fillet knife with stainless-steel blade. Often carried in a sheath on the belt, this type of knife is ideal for most fish-cleaning work, and for cutting and rigging baits. Many minor variations in blade design exist, but for all-round work the differences can be ignored.

Perhaps the one most useful tool for a saltwater angler is his fisherman's pliers—featuring squared, wrench-grip jaws and a side-cutter. With this one tool you can clip leader wire, trim monofilament, remove hooks, cut off catfish fins, open a bottle of pop, tighten reel nuts, and straighten hooks. It's used so much that you'll probably want to keep it in a belt sheath, close to your knife—or in a hip pocket, anyway.

Long-nose pliers, though not so versatile, can be used for many of the same jobs and they reach farther into a fish's maw for taking out hooks. Or you can get any one of several types of hook removers or disgorgers.

Fingernail-type clippers trim monofilament better than knife or cutting pliers—but don't use them on wire.

A small screwdriver should be at hand to tighten loose screws on fishing reels and the like.

Heavy cotton gloves, or nylon-cotton mixture, are vitally necessary if you fish offshore and have to handle leader wire while gaffing fish.

Since hooks should be kept sharp at all times, you should have a file or sharpening stone. The file does quicker and better work, but you should have a stone anyway to keep your knife sharp.

Surf and shore fishermen can make good use of a sand spike, which is nothing more than a tubular rod holder with a sharpened spike at the end so it can be stabbed firmly into the sand. You certainly don't want to lay your reel down in the sand. And if bottom fishing, you can put your rod in the holder for a rest when bites aren't coming all that fast.

Accessories that are largely restricted to boating applications will be covered in Chapter 6.

ACCESSORIES FOR PERSONAL COMFORT AND PROTECTION

Whether practiced as fast-paced sport or casual relaxation, saltwater fishing is supposed to be enjoyable, but nature seems frequently dedicated against this proposition—beleaguering the poor angler with such ills as seasickness, sun problems, harsh weather, and biting insects.

Seasickness Remedies
Seasickness is not a cut-and-dried proposition. The effects and severity of it vary from individual to individual. A comparatively few lucky folks seem to

be immune to it from the start, while in others it gradually fades away after a number of trips to sea. Some anglers of considerable experience *think* they are immune, then suffer an attack during unusually rough weather or adverse wave direction.

It's pretty safe to say that the majority of boat-riders will have to endure the agony of seasickness at one time or another. And there are those who never miss. They start turning green the second they step on a boat. Surprisingly, a few saltwater fishing experts of acknowledged top rank belong to this unhappy group, but they have managed to log hundreds of days afloat with the aid of medication. But if they forget their pills—well, the most fumble-fisted duffer would be safe in making a bet with them that day.

Maybe you've heard that seasickness is all in the mind. That certainly isn't true. Medical evidence refutes the claim, as does my own experience in witnessing both cats and dogs getting as explosively sick as any human being aboard. Still, mental attitude can obviously control seasickness at times, although it's usually an unconscious attitude. I doubt that you'll be able to "think" seasickness away. For example, I am among many anglers who never get sick while actively engrossed in the business of angling. Whether they're biting or not, if I'm occupied in casting, rigging, searching, or, in short, simply keeping my mind occupied with the business of trying to catch a fish, then I stay healthy. But if I'm on a boring boat ride in rough water—stand clear!

Since the effects of seasickness vary so much, even in the same individual, countermeasures must vary too. Of course, you can routinely take pills for every trip, but unless you just *know* you'll get deathly ill without them, you can save the expense and the possible side-effects. Reserve the pills for occasions when an upcoming trip figures to be particularly rough or uncomfortable.

Should you begin to feel queasy in sea conditions that ordinarily don't bother you, look for contributing reasons. The heat and stuffiness of a closed cabin can be deadly; run for the deck. Exhaust fumes can do in a pretty seasoned sailor; shift your position or change boat direction. Visual focusing on a small jumpy spot can be devastating—much like trying to read in a car. So be careful of the possible onset of dizziness if you look through the finder of a camera too long, or concentrate closely on detail work, such as tying knots and rigging baits. When doing those unavoidable close chores, raise your head and watch the horizon for a moment or two.

In the final analysis, anything that might tend to make you the slightest bit dizzy, nauseated, or even mildly upset on shore will be multiplied several times in a boat, and bring on seasickness. Avoid rich and greasy foods, and try not to go out with a hangover.

Early signs of distress can often be turned off by simple measures before they develop too far. Stay in the fresh air. Take a few deep breaths. Sit down, relax, and close your eyes for a few minutes. If your stomach is rumbling, drink a bit of soda pop or eat a couple of crackers.

When seasickness hits full blast, on the other hand, there's not much you can do about it except try to survive until you reach shore. There's no need to advise evacuating your stomach—just do it overside. After that, the best thing to do is lie down and go to sleep.

Don't waste seasickness pills by popping them into your mouth *after* you're on the boat and start feeling distress. The longer you take them in advance of a trip the better they work. They'll ordinarily do you some good if you take them a couple of hours before going out—at breakfast, say. But for hard cases the most reliable approach is to take one the night before and another in the morning.

Popular over-the-counter brands work well for most people, and your druggist may have good recommendations. The common side effect is drowsiness; children, especially, might snooze all day—not getting seasick, but missing all the fun. Obviously, you should read and heed the label.

If you have a severe and continuing seasickness problem it's a good idea to consult your doctor, especially if over-the-counter drugs do you little or no good. He might prescribe something more effective. At least one drug which seems to do wonders is trade-named Bucladin, and is sold by prescription only. Safe for men, it is not prescribed for pregnant women, or women likely to become pregnant, because of possible birth defects in the child.

Sun Protection

The only good thing about seasickness is that once you get back to shore it will go away. Sun exposure, however, not only deals temporary misery but long-term consequences—possibly serious ones.

A "healthy" tan, it turns out, is not so healthy after all. Dermatologists advise that repeated or consistent tanning over a period of years has the effect, in layman's terms, of "wearing out" the skin—making it rough, dry, wrinkled, and subject to various scaly growths, none of which are attractive and some of which can develop into skin cancer.

The advice generally falls on deaf ears among the young, but doctors recommend careful protection from the sun at all ages. By the time a veteran saltwater fisherman reaches forty or so, and has noted some of the effects, he is only too anxious to comply.

For best protection, shun the ordinary sun-tan preparations and use one that completely screens out all harmful rays. There are several good brands and they can be identified by reading the labels.

Exceptionally tender spots are the face, ears, neck, and backs of the hands. Use sun screen generously, and wear a hat that not only shades your eyes but gives cover to ears and neck. The sun screen should be reapplied a couple of times during the day; more often if you're perspiring heavily or dipping your hands in water.

Long-sleeve shirts and trousers are advisable, but if you wish to wear short-sleeve shirts and/or shorts for comfort in hot weather, then use sun screen on arms and legs.

Lips should get extra-special attention, as they burn easily and, in many people, develop herpes sores—called sun sores or fever blisters—as an after-effect of too much sun. If you've had one of those sores, or clusters of them, you know they are painful and lingering and sloppy. Sun-screen lotions protect lips but don't stay on long. Use a lipstick-type balm that contains screening agents, or try the thick lip and nose salves that come in tubes or small jars. Women who use lipstick generally don't need anything else.

Of course, if you get out fishing only now and then, your main concern is not long-term, but immediate—to protect against painful sunburn and blistering. Again, sun screens and ample clothing make the best safeguard, but if you insist on getting a tan, it must be done gradually. Even with sun-tan lotion, you'll burn if exposed for more than—at most—a half-hour under severe conditions. Exposure time can be gradually increased day by day.

Harmful sun rays are at their worst when the sun is at a high angle, roughly from midmorning to midafternoon. When a day is overcast and breezy it can throw you off your guard, so watch out. You feel cool and comfortable, but don't be lulled into thinking you won't burn.

After a day under the sun, and an evening shower, use skin cream or lotion on areas that have been exposed. If you have a sunburn, they'll make you feel better. Even if you're well tanned, or have been well protected, the lotion is advisable to replace moisture sapped from the skin.

Insect Repellents

Two hungry critters that the saltwater angler is always apt to encounter, in warm and still weather, are mosquitoes and sand flies. Thanks to modern repellents, both can usually be tolerated.

In my experience, almost any commercial repellent is good enough to keep mosquitoes away, though some seem to last longer than others. Sand flies, though, are meaner and hardier. Up until fairly recently, there didn't seem to be anything sold that would keep them at bay. But now rescue is at hand.

The active ingredient in popular repellents has long been a substance called—pay attention because I'm only going to try this once—N, N-Diethyl-metatoluamide. In the trade, this is called "deet." Older brands of repellent contain something like 10 to 15 percent deet, which is enough to put the skids on mosquitoes, as a rule, but not to discourage no-seeum flies.

More recent concoctions have upped the percentage of deet to around 28, with the result that it not only repels flies, but is more effective and longer lasting against mosquitoes. Read the label carefully and look for that 28 percent or so.

Repellent is sold in liquid or cream form, and in aerosol sprays. For exposed skin, the liquid is preferred. Rub a couple of drops in your hands and spread over all exposed skin. Spray costs more, is thinner, and doesn't last as long. However, you sometimes need spray because mosquitoes can bite through light clothing. Use liquid on skin, but spray your clothes.

Though repellents can damage monofilament fishing lines and plastic or varnished surfaces, ordinary application of it, as described, should cause no trouble. Just be careful to avoid spraying or dripping directly on lines.

Protective Clothing and Footwear

Fishermen soon learn the difference between raincoats and foul-weather gear. In a heavy rain, the difference can be measured by the quart, and right down your neck.

Driest gear of all is the full suit—a hooded top overlapping a pair of waterproof long trousers.

In warmer climes, or for use with waders, the top alone will suffice, especially in the longer length called a parka. Wearing a parka without waders means you'll get wet from the thighs or knees down, but if the weather isn't cold you may not mind, and perhaps would prefer the parka over the suit because it is more easily stowed or carried.

The poncho is similar to a parka and gives equal protection, but is not generally as good for fishing purposes because it is loose and floppy. It can interfere with your angling mechanics.

Cheaper versions of both suit and parka are made of vinyl plastic; more expensive ones of rubberized fabric. Vinyl is adequate to the demands, but it tears more easily and has to be replaced often. Also, the hardware is not apt to be so durable.

Even in some of the high-priced fabric raingear, hardware must be considered carefully. Metal snaps and zippers corrode and fail unless given more tender care than most anglers want to devote to the job. Shop for a good pullover top, or models with nylon zippers.

Note also that some parkas and tops have detachable hoods. Sewn-in hoods are to be preferred, since they cannot be mislaid.

Devoted surf and jetty fishermen need good waders. Don't skimp here with light vinyl models. Get sturdy boot-foot waders with chest-high top of rubberized fabric. The boots should be comfortable and of a size to accommodate whatever you might wear under them in the way of heavy socks or trousers.

And the soles should be of a design that affords good traction on slippery rocks. Even then, conditions of extremely treacherous footing dictate felt sandals over the boot soles.

An old belt, or light nylon rope, tied over the waders near the top is a good comfort and safety measure. If you ship water, or take a tumble in the surf, you'll get only a trickle, not a flood. Belted chest-high waders, worn in combination with a foul-weather top, afford about as much protection against water, and wind, as a man can get outside his house.

Shoes with rubber deck soles are standard apparel for any kind of angling on boats. While any soft sole will protect the deck of a boat, the myriad gripping surfaces of true deck shoes are the only decent safeguard against your becoming an unwilling acrobat. If you're style-conscious, boat shoes are obtainable in a variety of styles and colors, and in both canvas and leather construction.

Canvas boat shoes with laces can double as wet-wading shoes. But don't wade in the loafer style; soft bottom will suck them right off your feet.

The best wet-wading shoes are inexpensive sneakers with the tops of the toes cut out. This arrangement helps relieve the buildup of sand and mud inside your shoes.

HEADGEAR AND GLASSES

Mention already has been made of hats as protection from the sun. To an angler they are also useful, in combination with dark glasses, for shading the eyes and thus affording better visibility. Short-brimmed hats and caps, obviously, are not as well suited to this purpose as long-billed ones. The bigger your hat, however, the more likely it is to be blown off your head. Rig a safety cord or remove your hat during a fast boat ride.

Polarizing sunglasses are the only kind that really allow you to see under the water's surface to any appreciable extent—because they sharply reduce reflected glare. Though an absolute necessity for bonefishing and other forms of sight angling, they can be extremely helpful to any fisherman.

Plastic-lens polarizing glasses can be purchased at almost any sundry counter. From among the many styles offered, pick out yours on the basis of lens size and eye coverage, rather than *chic*. If you can find a curved style that affords some shade at the sides, so much the better. All cost only a few dollars.

Anglers who need corrective lenses can order polarizing spectacles of optical glass, ground to their prescription. A far less expensive alternative is to buy plastic clip-ons that fit over regular glasses.

6

BOAT ACCESSORIES

Fishing boats no longer are the neglected stepchildren of the pleasure-craft industry, as they were only a few years back. In every price class and every size you can find boats built with an angler's needs in mind—luxurious sportfishing cabin cruisers; spacious center-console models in 19- to 24-foot lengths that can range anywhere from a quiet cove to far offshore in quest of fish; 15- to 18-foot boats with a raft of built-in conveniences for the fisherman.

Many of the things recommended in this chapter can be found as standard equipment on some boats, and ordered as accessories on many others. Or they can be added to existing boats to improve fishability.

ROD RACKS AND HOLDERS

The deck of a boat is no place for fishing rods. Trip over one and you'll break the rod, or your leg, or maybe both. Ideally, rods should be racked away snugly where no harm can come to them, but remain handy enough for quick access.

Rods can be racked horizontally along the sides of the boat, and this is the most common arrangement. Two supports are needed—one for the butts and another near the tips of the rods. A number of ready-made rod-holder sets are available at marine stores, and for anyone who is even halfway handy with simple woodworking tools, it's no mammoth job to design, cut, and install your own.

One of the simplest designs is also the best—amounting to nothing more than small flat "shelves" supporting butts and tips. The shelves are cut from 2-inch wood and mounted to the boat sides. The advantage of the shelf design, as opposed to a notched or cutout support, is that two rods often can be placed on one shelf, thereby doubling rod capacity. Of course, some provision must be made for keeping the rods in place, and this duty falls to a loop of elastic cord, screwed into the shelf at the back, then stretched over the rod and into a notch on the front edge of the shelf.

Horizontal racks also can be ceiling-mounted, inside a cabin or on the underside of a flying-bridge overhang. These, of course, cannot be of the "shelf" design.

Many anglers with center-console boats are now depending more on upright, console-mounted racks than horizontal racks. The upright system can accommodate more rods in less space, while allowing instant availability. It also can take care of very long rods, which do not fit some horizontal mounts.

Vertical console racking can be achieved in either of two ways. One is simply to mount a row of tubular rod holders at the base of the console. Another is to fashion two console-length brackets out of wood—mounting one near the bottom of the console, the other near the top. Drill holes at measured intervals in the bottom one to accept the rod butts, and corresponding notches in the upper bracket for the rod shafts.

Something will have to be rigged over the notches to keep the rod shafts from slipping out. Swiveling pins are often used, but there's a cheaper and easier way. Place a strip of heavy rubber (such as inner-tube rubber) over the notch, and screw the rubber to the wood on either side of the notch. Then cut the strip in half at the center. When stowing your rod, just push the shaft through the rubber baffle. It can also be pulled out easily, yet the rubber is stiff enough to keep most rods from accidentally falling out.

Single tubular rod holders are used either to hold rods while trolling, in which case they are mounted at an angle toward the stern, or simply as a convenient place to stash a rod, in which case they can be mounted vertically wherever there is a flat surface to hold the brackets.

The best trolling-rod holders are angled ones, flush-mounted through the gunwale decking. This usually is done at the factory, but can be handled by most marine service facilities. Two such holders on each side are the rule, though if your boat is so small that you never troll more than two lines at a time, one holder per side is all you need.

OUTRIGGERS AND PINS

Collapsible outriggers can easily be installed on boats not so equipped at the factory. They should be flush-mounted through the gunwales and, in smaller open boats, located within easy reach of the console or steering station. The mounts are similar to rod holders. A special fitting on the base of the outrigger pole allows it to be turned outboard, in fishing mode, or upright for running. The poles also can be easily removed.

Anglers who use their boats for all sorts of saltwater fishing, including occasional jaunts offshore, will have to decide whether the expense of outriggers

Small-boat outriggers in upright position for running. They can be readied for fishing simply by turning the bases in their mounts.

is worthwhile to them, since they could easily get by in blue water by flat-line trolling alone. But anyone who becomes addicted should certainly equip his boat with 'riggers. See Chapter 13 for descriptions of outriggers in use, and drop-back techniques that go hand-in-hand.

Several types of outrigger pins are available, the most common being the clothespin design, which holds the fishing line firmly between wooden jaws.

The main drawback of this type is the lack of adjustable tension to accommodate baits of different weights: however, the snapout point can be adjusted to some extent by how deeply you position the line in the pin, or by looping the line and clipping two or more thicknesses of it in the jaws. If you don't use a great deal of variety in bait or line sizes, the clothespin should be perfectly satisfactory.

Another type which holds the line in a firm grip is the rotary pin, but this one has adjustable springs that allow tension to be varied.

One design features a snap-open eye rather than gripping jaws. The line runs freely through the eye, and so the distance of the baits can be changed at any time simply by letting line off your reel or cranking some up. Again, the amount of pull necessary to snap the eye open can be variably adjusted.

Clothespin-type outrigger clip is the most common and durable design. If extra tension is needed, a rubber band can be slipped over the jaws.

DROP-BACK FOR FLATLINES

Automatic drop-back devices can be rigged for flatlines so that the rods can be left unattended in holders (but not unguarded). The simplest is nothing more than an outrigger clothespin tied to a stout cord a foot or two long. The other end of the cord is fastened to an eye or cleat on the transom. You let out your line the desired distance, then snap it to the pin. Pressure from the trolling bait keeps the pin and its cord extended out over the transom, so there's nothing for the line to catch on when it snaps from the pin.

If you're using a spinning outfit, you can place the rod in a holder and simply leave the bail open. When line snaps from the pin on a strike, the drop-back line will peel directly off the reel. With a multiplying reel, however, you cannot allow line to be pulled directly off the free-turning spool or a catastrophic backlash will result. Therefore, you have to strip off a quantity of line in advance and coil it in a bucket, leaving the reel in gear. Just be sure the bucket is so positioned that the coiled line will have nothing to snag on after the pin snaps and the line starts moving out.

With spinning tackle, a simple drop-back device can be rigged right on the reel seat. Take a piece of soft wire, copper or Monel, wrap it around the reel seat just forward of the reel, and form the ends of the wire into a hook. Place the line over the hook and open your bail. You can vary the holding tension of the hook by increasing or decreasing the angle of the bend. When a fish takes out line, the soft wire hook opens easily to allow free flow from the spool.

FISHING CHAIRS

The big-game fighting chair with integral foot brace and removable back is normally used only on large sportfishing cruisers, and with 80- or 130-pound line. Occasionally the skipper of a 20- or 25-foot open boat will toy with the idea of installing one and taking a fling at giant tuna or marlin with heavy gear. Usually the price alone is enough to kill the impulse, but if someone really has the ambition and really has the opportunity and really has the money, then it's at least workable.

Swiveling, pedestal-mounted fishing chairs with gimbals are at home on cabin cruisers and open fishing craft alike. Because of the limited cockpit space in smaller boats, they often double as steering chairs at the console, but can be mounted in any location that affords a good fishing position. One great spot that usually isn't even considered is on the sunken forward deck or platform of center-console boats. It isn't difficult to troll from that station, and

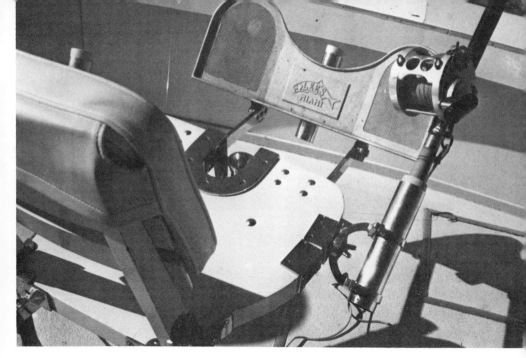

Big-game fighting chair, with foot brace and removable back.

Angler in fighting chair, with seat harness strapped to reel.

when a fish is on, the skipper can do his necessary maneuvering in forward rather than reverse. Of course, if outriggers are used, they might have to be positioned farther forward than normal.

In small open boats, swivel fishing chairs can serve double duty as helmsman's chairs.

Wherever located, the most reliable chairs are those with a pedestal that fastens to a permanent deck mount. Though not instantly removable, the pedestal and chair can be removed from the mount and stored ashore when not needed.

A swiveling gimbal chair with low, wide legs for stability is the best type of portable, or nonmounted, chair. With fairly light tackle and in calm water it will perform nearly as well as a pedestal model, but in rough seas it may bounce around.

There are many lightweight portable chairs that are equipped with gimbals, but they are not likely to satisfy the demands of regular offshore fishing.

DEPTH SOUNDERS

A depth sounder is an invaluable aid to the saltwater fisherman, particularly in deeper waters and offshore. With it you can locate favorable bottom conditions, and possibly even spot bait schools and game fish—depending on the individual instrument. Offshore surface trollers find it just as valuable as deep-bait anglers do, since bottom contours, canyon edges, and rises in the ocean floor generally determine trolling patterns.

Least expensive are the digital and needle-dial types which give only a single direct reading of water depth. They are useful in that they can indicate large holes or dropoffs, but for angling purposes they are, obviously, limited.

Perhaps no more expensive is the flasher type, which gives blips of light on a circular dial. The strongest and steadiest blip is the bottom reading. Additional blips above the bottom can indicate fish. Also, with some experience, you can learn to read variations in the bottom blip and determine the type of bottom and irregularities in its features.

A flasher can indeed be a great tool—but it requires constant monitoring, and even then you can miss many things which flash on the dial and are gone quickly.

By far the best are fathometers which "draw a picture" of the bottom on moving paper—recording fathometers, often nicknamed "recorders" or "scratchers." Even the relatively inexpensive models record irregularities in the bottom with good detail, and will mark some fish, though not any which hug bottom. More sophisticated and sensitive recorders can even do that, as well as give much better definition overall.

Least costly are the combination flasher-recorder models. On these, the revolving blip not only flashes on the dial, but also marks on a piece of revolving chart paper. Or the flasher can be used alone when you merely want to monitor depth. These range in price from about $250 to perhaps $600.

Straight-line, or completely nonflashing, recorders are the costliest of all—and the best. They range in price from somewhat less than $1000 to more than $2000 for sportfishing applications. There's no doubt that they're worth the investment, but one of the flasher-recorders may easily give you what you need at less money.

Whatever your decision, you should study the market carefully at boat shows and marine stores, and also talk to other anglers whose fishing activities are similar to yours.

BAIT WELLS

If live-baiting is your bag and your boat isn't equipped with built-in bait wells that recirculate water, there are several ways to attack the problem.

Easiest and least expensive in the long run would be large removable containers—garbage can or ice chest—with a bait pump that connects to your boat battery. This setup is described in the preceding chapter.

Or possibly your boat has some sort of watertight compartment which can be converted to a live-bait keeper simply by getting an aerating pump.

ANCHOR LINE FLOAT

When fishing with light tackle, you may well hook fish that need chasing—at least, that's what you often hope. And if your boat is anchored, there may not be enough time to haul up the anchor before the fish strips your reel or gets around an obstruction.

The solution: Attach a float to your anchor line just forward of where the line is cleated. When that prize fish hits, slip the line from its cleat and toss it overboard. The float will hold it up so you can return later, lift the line aboard, and either tie up once again in exactly the same spot, or else haul up the anchor and leave.

Any buoyant object can be used as a float, as long as it will support your anchor line. Plastic bleach jugs are excellent, and have a convenient handle to which the line can be looped, even after you're anchored in position. In a pinch, use a floating cushion or life preserver.

MARKER BUOYS

Bleach jugs can also be used to make buoys for marking particular spots. One particular use for such a buoy is detailed in Chapter 18 on deep jigging. But you never know when you might want to mark a particular spot—or simply an orientation point—in any kind of fishing.

Make up one or two buoys and keep them handy in a boat compartment. Here's how to do it:

Use any fairly strong line that's available to you—perhaps old monofilament or braided fishing line. Actual test is not really important, but I like to use at least 30-pound.

Tie one end of the line to the handle of the capped jug. Then wrap the rest of the line around the jug and tie some sort of anchor to it. A sinker or piece of scrap metal can serve as an anchor. For fast sinking in deep water, the anchor should weigh at least a pound.

Now you need only toss the whole shebang overboard. The jug will spin as the anchor sinks, and so unwind the line automatically.

How much line you use must be judged by the depth of water that you're likely to be working. Deep jigging most often is done in water of about 80 to 150 feet, so 200 feet of buoy line would be about right—allowing a little scope to help hold bottom. In shallower water you would use correspondingly shorter lengths of line.

You might wish to leave the marker down, in hopes that it will be there next time you go out. Since it costs next to nothing, the only thing lost would be the time it takes to rig another.

If you pick up the marker, just wrap the line around the jig once more and stow it away for future use.

Part II
Angling Skills

7
FIGHTING SALTWATER FISH

Every angler must suffer through broken lines and lost fish, but why is it that some folks break off relatively few prizes while others snap lines right and left? The answer—no surprise—is experience and the knowledge it brings of proper drag settings, tackle handling, pumping, pressuring, and all the "little" things that are lumped together under the term "fighting a fish."

Regardless of whether you use spinning tackle or big-game gear, the principles of fighting remain the same. The only things that change, according to the strength and power of both tackle and angler, are the methods of implementing these principles.

Understanding drag is the first step. Drag, of course, is the amount of resistance against line slippage from the reel. All modern reels have adjustable drag mechanisms so that this resistance can be set in proportion to the breaking test of the line.

A common misconception in the early career of almost every angler is that a drag can be set just below the test of the line and so afford protection against breakage. But this is not the case. Your drag must be set *far* below the line's breaking strain to provide any real margin of safety, because many different pressures are combining to threaten your thin string. There is the pull of the fish, naturally, but there is also water drag on the line—which continues to mount as more line leaves the spool. And, at the same time, the more line you have out, the more force is required to turn the reel spool, due to the diminishing diameter of line on the spool.

And more. Friction of your line running through the rod guides adds pressure (this can be reduced with roller guides, but never eliminated). And all this time, the fish itself is compounding the problem by jumping out of the water and falling back, or by stopping and starting, or by suddenly changing direction. Since it takes more force to *start* a spool turning than to *keep* it turning, you must allow a lot of leeway for these stop-and-go tactics.

Most experienced hands agree that a reasonable basic drag setting is about one-third the breaking test of the line—and those who disagree tend to set their drags even lighter than that.

But even with the basic one-third setting we have not arrived at an answer to the drag-setting question, only a starting point. In a long fight with a tough ocean gamester, it can be important to use varying amounts of drag during different stages of the battle.

Now this does not necessarily mean you'll be turning your drag-adjustment device back and forth through the fight. With a star-drag reel, or with a spinning reel, normal procedure is to accomplish drag variation by applying manual pressure to the spool with your hand; you preset the adjustable drag to one-third of the line test, and leave it there. Thus you can add more drag manually, as conditions dictate, yet always be able to return instantly to the original low drag setting simply by relaxing your thumb or finger.

Most spinning reels have the drag-adjustment screw located on the front of the spool.

DUAL-DRAG REELS

The most sophisticated drag systems available today are those found on the expensive, dual-drag ocean reels. They are designed so the angler can indeed change his drag settings during the fight by moving the lever backward or forward, yet remain confident that he will not inadvertently apply too much drag.

On these reels there are *two* drag-adjustment devices. One is a finger screw which can be tightened or loosened to provide a particular *range* of drag settings. The other, of course, is the lever, which when pushed fully forward produces the maximum drag obtainable within the preset range. When pulled all the way back, the lever throws the reel into free-spool. Near the forward end of the lever track there is an automatic stop called the "Strike" position. The lever cannot be advanced beyond "Strike" drag (that is, all the way to maximum) unless the angler pushes a button or flips a pin to override the automatic stop.

Usual procedure is to adjust the presetting screw until the lever, in "Strike" position, affords a drag of about one-third the breaking test of the line. When advanced beyond the automatic stop to full forward position, the lever provides a maximum preset drag of perhaps one-half, or even more, of the line's breaking test.

Basically, here are the changes made with a single-lever drag during the course of a battle with the fish:

1. *THE STRIKE.* Lever is in "Strike" position as the angler sets his hook.

2. *THE FIRST RUN.* Immediately after the hook sinks home, the fish usually takes off on its longest, wildest run and, in the case of jumping species, a barrage of acrobatics as well. During the initial outburst, the experienced angler usually will back off with the lever—especially if the fish is an extra big one (in relation to line test) and puts a lot of distance between itself and the boat.

3. *FIGHTING BACK.* When the fish settles down, the angler goes to work—regaining line, pumping, putting on all the pressure he dares. For this work, he returns the lever to "Strike" position.

4. *ADDITIONAL RUNS.* The fish is bound to get off more runs—sometimes one or two, sometimes many. "Strike" drag will be all right for most of these, but in the case of another real sizzler, it is prudent to reduce the drag again. It's largely a matter of judgment, but when in doubt, reduce the drag. Then flip the lever back to "Strike" whenever a surge ends.

5. MAXIMUM DRAG. Often it is not necessary to use the maximum drag setting at any stage of the battle, but occasions for its use do arise, especially with heavy tackle. One such occasion is when the double line reaches the reel. Then, an all-out effort is required to bring the leader within reach, so the angler overrides the automatic stop, shoves the lever to "Maximum" position, and throws all the strength of his back and his tackle into bringing the fish those last few feet. Maximum drag setting may also be used during long periods of tough pumping when the fish is not overly active, but merely resisting stubbornly—or when the problem arises of simply having to raise great weight from the depths.

Despite the instant drag changes available with a lever-drag reel, the angler still may use a great deal of manual drag by means of thumb or hand pressure on the spool. With heavy tackle it is common practice to wear a cotton glove on one or both hands. Since the hands are not needed to support the rod when a harness is used, they are free to squeeze the spool when additional pressure is desired—perhaps for intermittent pumping to avoid flinging the lever back and forth and risk breaking rhythm, or for *really* clamping down to put on even more drag than the lever can provide in "Maximum" position. The latter move is a drastic one, of course, and seldom made except with 80- and 130-pound lines in specific big-game battling situations, primarily giant tuna fishing.

OTHER DRAG SYSTEMS

Though the convenience of a single-lever drag system is apparent, the fact remains that the great majority of reels are without this feature. Most revolving-spool reels used in offshore fishing, from plug reels to big-game models, are equipped with a system called a "star drag." Tension is increased by turning a star-shaped adjustment wheel, located just beneath the crank. Unlike the setup on a single-lever reel, free-spool is controlled by a separate lever.

Drags on most spinning reels are adjusted by turning the spool nut. Many saltwater fly reels feature adjustable drags, again with a nut or finger screw to add or relax tension.

While the actual drag mechanisms vary from reel to reel in the above groups, all are adjusted to one preselected degree of drag and then left at that setting while you fight the fish. True, it is physically possible to change the drag instantly by turning the wheel, but this is highly impractical. You just can't be confident of returning to the precise point of your preset, and so the risk is run of accidentally applying too much tension and breaking off the fish.

So the basic rule is: Set your drag light and do not change the setting. As we've already discussed, a good setting is approximately one-third the breaking test of the line. This should give an ample safety margin against even a long, fast run. Then, in the later stages of the fight, when you need additional spool pressure for pumping or lifting, you get it by snubbing the spool manually. Should the fish make another strong dash, you need only take away the hand pressure to return at once to your original safe setting.

With a spinning reel you can get slight additional pressure by extending the forefinger of your rod hand and pressing it against the lip of the spool.

Extra drag is applied to spinning-reel spool with left hand to prevent slipping on upward pumps of the rod.

But in offshore angling you'll often need more pressure than the single finger can provide, and the best way to get it is by cupping the palm of your cranking hand around the spool, and holding the spool while you lift with the rod.

Since drag pressures and good rod-handling are so dependent on each other, the angler is provided with a simple yet highly efficient system for setting his drag—and no need to use a scale. Here's how:

String your line through the rod guides. Tighten the drag so that line doesn't slip at all. Then tie or hook the line to any stationary object—or have someone else hold the line tightly.

Now, assume the same position you would in fighting a fish with that particular tackle—standing, seated, using a harness, whatever—and haul back on the rod until it is in a good stout bend, as strong a bend as you think you could physically maintain for any length of time.

While holding this bend, back off slowly on your drag adjustment screw until the line begins slipping slowly but smoothly from the spool.

That's it.

All you can do while a fish is running is to keep a strong bend in the rod and let it go. If your drag starts to slip just as the power-bend position of the rod is reached, then you're putting on as much resistance as you dare, while at the same time you're basically protected against line breakage.

Please note, however, that this drag-setting system should be used only with a correctly balanced rod and line. The resultant setting will be quite low—in the ball park with our much-discussed one-third setting—but if you happen to be using a line that is much too light for the rod, then it is likely to break before the rod ever reaches a true power bend.

ROD WORK

Proper and positive rod handling is the key around which all else revolves in battling a rugged offshore game fish. If you employ good rod technique, combined with thoughtful application of drag, you can effectively wage war against gamesters several times heavier than the test of your line.

Again, study and experience are needed to develop the fine points of rod handling, but there is really only one basic objective involved, and that is to keep the power of a well-bent rod against the fish as much of the time as possible. You've probably heard this advice expressed in the common phrase "Keep the tip up."

However, maintaining a staunch bend in the rod can be a demanding chore over long periods—and the heavier the tackle you use, the tougher this job gets. With ocean tackle up through the 30-pound class, and with fly, plug,

Power-bend rod position is what administers punishment to a fish. Maintaining a full bend is often tiring, but always vital.

and spinning tackle, all the strain of keeping the rod in a power bend falls to your arms—and mostly to the one arm that holds the rod, while the other is free to crank the reel.

When your rod arm starts to tire, the natural tendency is to yield, to relax the bend in the rod and remove some of the pressure. Instead, you should do everything you can to *resist* relaxing, and one important step is to get into the habit of using *both* hands for rod work much of the time. Naturally, when there is cranking to be done, the cranking hand must do it. But that hand can be moved freely from reel to rod and back again.

Downward pressure with left hand on rod butt relieves some of the strain from right wrist.

So clamp both hands on the foregrip whenever this will help you keep up the pressure, or swap hands from time to time so the rod arm can rest for a few minutes.

If using a spinning rod or a fly rod, you'll find that by pressing downward on the butt with your cranking hand you can relieve a lot of strain on the hand that's holding the foregrip. A similar effect can be achieved without using the cranking hand at all. Simply let the butt snuggle against the underside of your forearm while you hold the rod by the foregrip. Then, by pressing down with the forearm, you can give your hand and wrist a surprising amount of relief from strain.

Using the left hand to help keep up the pressure with a fly rod.

In order to maintain pressure for prolonged periods, a butt rest for the rod is a necessity when using ocean tackle, and extremely helpful with casting tackle as well. The better ocean rods are all equipped with a slotted butt which fits into either the gimbal of a fishing chair, if seated, or a similar gimbal fixed to a padded belt if standing.

Rod belts fitted with simple leather or rubber cups, rather than the metal gimbal, are used for spinning rods, or for any rod without the slotted butt.

HARNESSES

Considering the strain that can be put on an angler's arms, even with light tackle, it's easy to see why heavier gear calls for a rod harness, so that the angler can put his back, or his entire body, into the job of fighting a big-game fish.

These are the two common types of harnesses:

THE SHOULDER HARNESS, which in effect is a strong vest of canvas or leather. Adjustable straps on the front of the harness are fitted with snaps which connect to the harness rings of the reel. With his rod butt resting in a gimbal (chair or belt) and the shoulder harness in place, the angler can use his *back* to support the rod in power bend, or to pump. And, of course, he can use *both* his arms and his back, or transfer pressure from one to the other.

With a rod belt and shoulder harness, the fisherman can use his entire heft to keep the rod bent while a strong fish is running—and at the same time give his arms a welcome rest.

THE KIDNEY HARNESS, which in effect is a large and heavily padded belt, with adjustable straps and snaps on each end for attaching to the reel. The belt goes around the lower back and is used only when the angler is seated in a fighting chair (not a simple fishing chair). The fighting chair has an integral, adjustable foot brace, and it is really the angler's legs which face the strongest muscular demands. By pressing against the foot brace, against the resistance of the harness around his lower back, the angler is—to a considerable extent—actually using his whole body in mustering the force required

Combination of kidney harness and foot brace enables angler to apply pressure needed to fight fish with heavy tackle.

to work a heavy rod under high drag pressure that averages as much as 30 pounds with 130-pound line.

The kidney harness usually has a padded canvas seat laced to the belt itself. The seat does not contribute to the work, but only prevents the belt from riding up the angler's back during the fight. Also, the back rest on the fighting chair must be removable, or foldable, so that the angler has room to lean far back.

Under what conditions should harnesses be used?

Of course, you'll occasionally run into weightlifter types who try to exceed normal standards, but the usual procedures are to hand-hold tackle up

Snaps on harness connect to rings on the reel. This arrangement is the same with either a shoulder or a kidney harness.

through the 30-pound class, and to use a harness with 50-, 80-, and 130-pound-class gear. However, 50-pound is a borderline class and is often hand-held by experienced anglers in good physical shape.

It should be pointed out, also, that there's no rule against using a harness with 20- or 30-pound tackle, and it is a very good idea to do so in certain situations—such as a prolonged battle by an angler who is a youngster or a lightly built adult.

As to the choice between a shoulder harness and a kidney harness, this is a simple matter. Whenever a harness is used in conjunction with a fighting chair, it should be a kidney harness—although the shoulder harness can be used as an option.

In all other situations—standing or seated in a simple chair without a foot brace—the kidney harness is useless, and so the shoulder harness must be chosen.

PUMPING

Up to now we have discussed rod work in terms of keeping up the pressure, which is primarily the defensive phase of the battle so far as the angler is concerned. When the angler goes on offense, so to speak, the importance of the rod and proper rod handling really takes center stage.

The goal is to bring the fish toward the boat, and this is not accomplished by "winding him in" with the reel, as any angler learns early in his career, but by moving the fish with the rod. Basic procedure is to raise the rod smoothly, but with power, then lower it while cranking the reel on the downward stroke, thus picking up the small amount of line provided by the upward lift. Simple as the description sounds, this procedure, called "pumping," demands a great deal of timing, concentration, and rhythm.

Fairly short pumps, delivered with good rhythm, are far more effective than long ones. Usually on the upward lift the rod tip will travel no more than 2 or 3 feet. And it can be highly punishing to the fish with a lift of only a few inches—provided, of course, that the pumps are rhythmically repetitive.

The exact tempo of pumping is a matter for on-the-spot judgment. At times you are barely able to move the fish, meaning the upward stroke will be rather slow and deliberate, although the downward stroke and cranking remain as fast as usual. Other times the fish will be coming in readily, and in this case you can set up a much faster tempo of pump-and-retrieve.

No matter what tempo you set up, the downward stroke is as important as the upward one—and can cause grief for the inattentive angler. Guard against lowering the rod too abruptly. This causes slack line, relieves pressure on the fish, and can even result in that slack line wrapping around the rod tip and breaking.

Proper execution of the downward stroke requires that you maintain a little pressure, even as the rod is being lowered, and this you do by cranking fast enough to keep the line tight while the tip is going down.

It should be repeated here that you can safely use considerably more drag when pumping than you can when a fish is running. As a matter of fact, your

Despite short butt extension, fly-rod butt can be pressed against stomach while pumping.

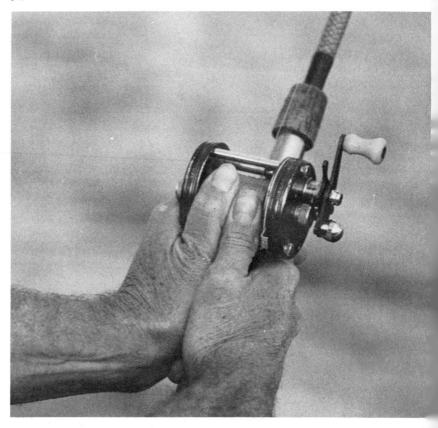

If one thumb isn't strong enough to prevent drag slippage from plug reel while pumping a fish—use both thumbs.

basic drag setting often is not enough to keep line from slipping off the reel as you pump. Therefore, you must hold the spool with your hand to prevent slippage while you raise the rod, as has already been explained.

Pumping techniques are really much the same with light tackle as with heavy, about the only difference being that you have to throw more muscle—or different muscle—into the job with heavier gear and its heavier drag settings.

In summary, successful fighting of husky offshore game fish requires an understanding and a thoughtful application of the following major factors:

1. Drag—basic settings and variations.

2. Rod pressure—applying and maintaining as much pressure as you can throughout the fight without risking line breakage.

3. Pumping—regaining line and moving the fish toward the boat, forcefully and rhythmically, whenever the least opportunity arises to do so.

8

RIGGING
AND HOOKING
NATURAL BAITS

Natural baits fall into three distinct categories—live, dead, and rigged. Live and dead baits need only be stuck on a hook; rigged ones, though dead, must be prepared in some special manner so that they can be trolled or drifted with a lifelike action or attitude.

LIVE BAITS

Many different varieties of live fish are habitually used as bait, and almost any small fish of suitable size *can* be used, including those which are repulsive to fishermen, but not necessarily to gamefish. Stomach examinations of many game species have proved that the most noble types happily gobble "garbage" fish, such as filefish, porcupine fish, searobins, catfish—in fact, just about anything they can get their jaws on when hungry.

This should not dissuade you from selecting the established and popular baits for your area, but when supplies are short, don't be afraid to try alternate species as well.

Regardless of the variety, there are three basic hookups for live baitfish:

1. Through the back or dorsal surface, inserting the hook through one side of the back and coming out the other. Be careful to miss the spine. Most often, the hookup should be made in about the midportion of the back, but if you wish the bait to swim downward, it may help to position the hook closer to the tail. Conversely, a hook positioned toward the head tends to keep the bait up.

2. Through both lips, starting the hook on the underside of the mouth and coming out the top of the head, forward of the eyes. This hookup is preferred

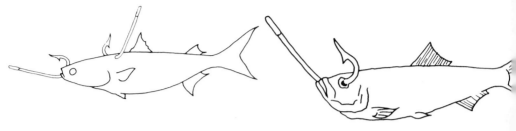

Standard hookups for live baitfish.

when drift or current is so strong that a back-hooked bait would be pulled un-naturally through the water. Mullet and some other bait species have such a small mouth that a hookup through both lips inhibits their breathing. If you're concerned about this, hook through the upper jaw only—inserting the hook point in the mouth and bringing it out on top. This also is the best way to handle live balao.

3. Pilchards, menhaden, sardines, and similar fragile species of bait may not stay on your hook well enough when impaled through back or lips. These can be hooked through the eye socket, over the eyeball and just underneath the bony plate above.

It's always important to use a hook light enough to permit proper bait movement (see Chapter 3).

Live Shrimp and Crabs

Live shrimp should be hooked lightly through the top of the head if they are to swim in near-natural fashion. A horny ridge runs the length of the head. You can insert the hook on one side of the head and out the other, just under this ridge. Avoid puncturing the dark spot inside the head shell or the shrimp will quickly die.

Live shrimp—head hookup.

An alternate and equally acceptable method is to run the hook through the head, bottom to top, forward of that aforementioned dark spot.

A head-hooked shrimp comes off rather easily, but when fish insist on a natural, swimming presentation, there's little else you can do.

However, many fish aren't all that picky. Snapper, weakfish, bonefish, and most bottom feeders—while they may show a decided preference for *live* shrimp—don't particularly care if it's swimming around upright. You can thread the shrimp onto your hook by starting the hook at the tail and working it carefully the length of the body and out under the head. It stays on much better that way. Pinch the fan off the tail before you thread the shrimp. This allows more odor to spread from the shrimp, and it will reduce twisting on the retrieve.

Live shrimp—threaded.

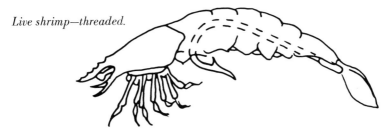

Blue crabs—generally small ones about the size of a silver dollar—are famous producers of permit and tarpon, and will also fool many other gamefish. They should be hooked lightly through the "point" of the shell on either side, starting the hook from the underside. Work the hook in carefully and give necessary support with your fingers to avoid breaking off the tip of shell.

Blue crab hookup.

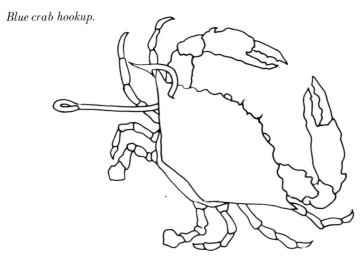

Fiddlers and other small types of crab are usually hooked by working the point inside the shell, through a leg joint, and out the top. Some fishermen break off the fiddler's large claw and start the hook through that hole.

Fiddler crab hookup.

Sand fleas, which are really not fleas but hard-shelled crustaceans, need only be run through once, from the bottom and out the top of the shell. These don't have to be stuck in free-swimming style, because they are almost always used in the surf, or from ocean piers, and wave action keeps them moving around. Also, you don't want them to go digging into the sand.

Sand flea hookup.

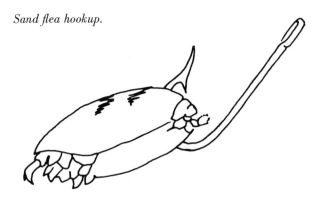

Seaworms pose no special problems. Hook them once or twice through the middle so both ends can wave around. Or hook them several times in bunched-up fashion for small-mouthed biters. Or hook near one end for slow-rolling, drifting, or fishing in a current, so the full length can snake around. For short-strikers, use a double-hook rig with one near the tail.

RIGGED BAITS

First, let's get acquainted with some of the tools needed for rigging various baits:

BAIT NEEDLE—used for sewing. Looks much like an enlarged household needle with a threading eye at the blunt end.

RIGGING NEEDLE—used for pulling swivels and leaders through a bait. Has a hook at the end, rather than an eye.

SEWING LINE OR THREAD—used in conjunction with the bait needle. You can use bait-sewing floss, dental floss, or light braided fishing line.

RIGGING WIRE—used for wrapping balao, and some other baits, firmly to a leader. Sold in precut lengths, in plastic tubes. Still called "copper wire," though mostly it's Monel wire.

DEBONER—used for removing the backbone from mullet and certain other baitfish. It's a length of aluminum or stainless-steel tubing sharpened at one end. The sharp end is worked under the gill flap, then pushed and twisted to cut the spine just behind the head. Then the cutting edge is turned toward the tail and worked slowly by "feel" for the length of the fish—the goal being to contain the backbone inside the tube. The tail is turned at a right angle and a final push with the deboner severs the spine at the tail end. As the deboner is being slowly withdrawn, the bait should be squeezed or bent to help keep the severed backbone from slipping out of the tube. Once the tube is out, a wooden rod is pushed through it to expel the bone. The rod is supplied with the deboner.

See Chapter 3 for sizing baits to hooks.

Rigging Balao

Thaw the balao in a bucket of water, if frozen. Bend it several times to break the spine and make it more flexible. Press firmly on the stomach cavity to expel as much internal matter as possible out the anus. You're now ready to rig.

For balao rigging, a "pin" is left in the leader wire after the hook is wrapped on. The pin should be at right angles to the wire, and on the opposite side of the wire from the hook point. Wrap one end of a length of copper wire around the leader at the base of the pin.

Holding the gill flap open with your thumb, insert the hook point under the gill and into the stomach cavity. Work the point as far back toward the tail as possible, bending the bait to aid you in this, and then bring it out on the underside. Pull on the now exposed hook until the hook eye settles into position under the gill flap.

Rig for balao. Once the hook is inserted, copper wire is wrapped to bill.

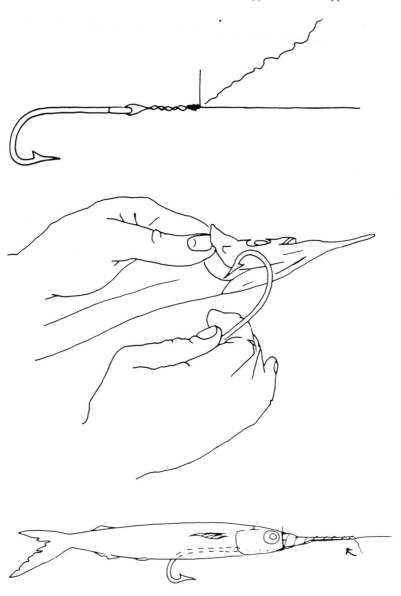

Insert the pin upward, through the head and out the top, between the eyes or barely forward of the eyes. The pin should be centered as nearly as possible. Wrap the copper wire twice around the head behind the pin, then wrap it snugly once or twice forward of the pin to hold the mouth tightly closed. Last, continue wrapping tightly in spirals down the beak for an inch or so. Break off the remaining beak, and if some of the wire is left, wrap it back toward the mouth again until it's all wrapped snug.

With a balao, or any other rigged bait, all the pull should be at the head of the bait. If there is any pulling pressure on the bend of the hook, the bait will spin. Relieve such pressure by using the point of a sharp knife to enlarge the hole forward of the hook.

You'll note that the hook position is well forward in the bait. This is best for all-round trolling, since it provides the most bait action. A second hook would foil short-strikers, such as king mackerel or barracuda, but billfish often feel the extra hook and spit the bait out too quickly.

If you wish to add a second hook specifically for king or 'cuda, it can easily go on *after* the balao is rigged with a single hook. Simply take a ring-eye hook and slip the eye of this over the point of the first hook, then bury the point of the trailing hook upward in the bait.

Balao rig with second hook.

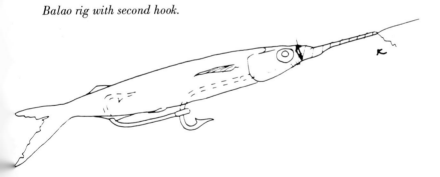

Of course, the eye of the trailer hook must not be so large that it could easily slip off while fighting a fish. Choose a hook of approximately the same size as the rigging hook, or one size smaller. With pliers, carefully press the barb of the first hook down so that the eye of the second can slip over it. Afterward, use a screwdriver and gently pry the barb back into open position.

Mullet or Mackerel Rig, Hook Inside

This rig, though used most often with mullet or mackerel because they are the baits commonly available, can also be used with small bonefish, ladyfish, barracuda, or dolphin.

Larger mullet should be deboned. Small ones may work well if the back is broken once or twice. Deboning is optional with the others, depending on whether or not the action is satisfactory to you. Again, you might get by with just breaking the spine. The extra-supple motion of a deboned fish is more desirable in a swimming bait than a skipping one, so that can guide you as well.

Don't attach the hook to your leader wire in advance.

Place the hook alongside the bait, with the hook eye even with the bait eye. This is a rough measurement to indicate about where the hook point will come out of the fish's belly.

Make a slit at that point, long enough so that you can remove all the entrails.

Trolling bait—hook inside.

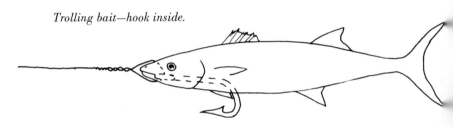

Insert the eye of the hook through the slit and shove it into position inside the mouth of the bait. Now run the leader wire upward through the lower jaw, through the eye of the hook, and out the top of the head. Pull enough wire through to allow easy wrapping, then make a regular haywire twist (Chapter 9).

The gills should be sewn tightly closed, as should the belly slit. Otherwise, water pressure will catch the loose flaps and deteriorate the bait. Another way to close the gills is simply to tie some thread tightly around the head.

A leaded or swimming bait is rigged in almost the same way, with only one obvious difference. First you run a sliding sinker onto the leader, then run the leader through the bait and the hook. Before wrapping, slide the sinker into position tight under the bait's "chin," and hold it there as you make your final wrap.

The lead is not intended to take the bait down very deep—only to keep it completely under the surface, instead of skipping. Thus the size of the sinker isn't overly important. It's usually ¾ ounce or 1 ounce with average baits, 2 ounces with larger ones.

Mackerel or Bonito, Hook Outside

Big marlin baits are often rigged with the hook sewn to the outside of the head.

First, slit the belly, remove the entrails, and sew the slit closed. Sew mouth and gills closed. The belly slit isn't necessary with bonito, since these are going to be fat and rigid no matter what you do. But sew the mouth and gills anyway.

Trolling bait—hook outside.

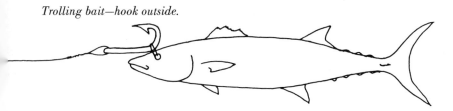

There are two ways of affixing the hook, but both require that the sewing thread first be hitched around the bend of the hook. That accomplished, you can either rig through the eye socket or the mouth of the fish by running the needle through and then tying the thread tight. Needle direction is side to side through the eyes, bottom to top through the mouth.

Trolling Strips

Strip baits, by preference cut from the white belly area of a bonito, are outstanding fish producers, but seldom used by private fishermen because of the time involved in making them.

In fact, they are faster to rig than a balao. It's the cutting of the strips that takes some time and attention.

Bonito often are not available, but strips can be made from any kind of fish you happen to have on hand. Mullet strips work, but are soft.

The strip should be cut in something of an elongated teardrop shape, gently rounded on one end and pointed on the other. Excess flesh should be carefully trimmed away, leaving no more than a quarter-inch thickness. The strip

Trolling strip.

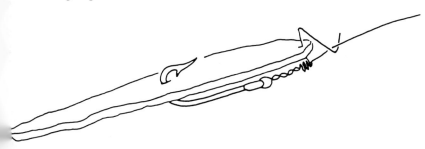

should be about 10 or 12 inches long for offshore fishing. Smaller ones with smaller hooks pay off when trolling for mackerel, blues, and many other small-to-medium fish.

The leader is rigged much as for balao, except the pin should be longer and on the same side as the hook point.

Insert the pin through the head of the strip, then bend it down and around the leader wire to hold it in place. Bunch the strip slightly toward the front as you insert the hook all the way through it. The hook must be positioned just right so that it creates no pull on the strip. All the pull must be at the pin. If you miss the right position slightly, enlarge the hook hole a tiny bit with your knife. But you can't make the hole too large or the hook will fall out. If the hook is grossly misplaced, work it out and try again.

Rigging Eels
Eels are easy to rig, very durable, and make good offshore trolling baits, as well as good inshore trolling or drifting rigs for striped bass, snook, and other gamefish.

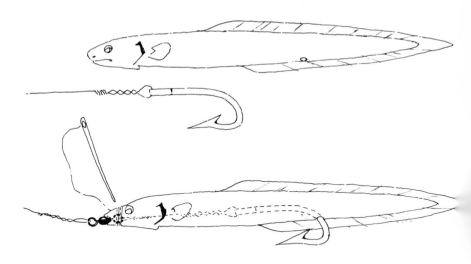

A rigging needle is necessary if you're using monofilament leader. Wire leaders can usually be inserted through the bait without trouble, though if you use very thin wire, or cable, then the needle will help.

A bait needle also is required.

Rig a hook on one end of a piece of leader that is a little longer than the eel. Insert the rigging needle into the eel's anus and work it forward and ou the mouth, pulling the leader with it. Pull until the hook rests lightly at the opening.

Attach a swivel at the other end of the leader, so that only the forward eye of the swivel protrudes from the eel's mouth. Now sew the eel's mouth tightly to the rear eye of the swivel. This, of course, anchors the bait at the head, so that the pull is on the swivel and not on the hook. A regular length of chosen leader is used ahead of the bait, and attached to the swivel.

Rigged with wire, the eel has plenty of action—but a lot more when rigged with monofilament. Of course, you'll have to make this choice based on your type of fishing. For snook or striped bass, 50- or 60-pound mono is ideal. For offshore fish, or critters with teeth, wire should be used.

Rigging Squid

Squid are trolled tail-first. Wrap the hook to the leader wire with a Haywire Twist, then measure the mantle or tail section and secure an egg sinker to the leader wire so that it will lie snug at the tail end when inserted. Insert the end of the leader wire through the head, all the way through the mantle and out the tail. Pull the leader through until the sinker is at the tail extremity. Last, use a needle and thread to sew the wire to the mantle and the mantle to the head at the position of the cross-marks in the drawing.

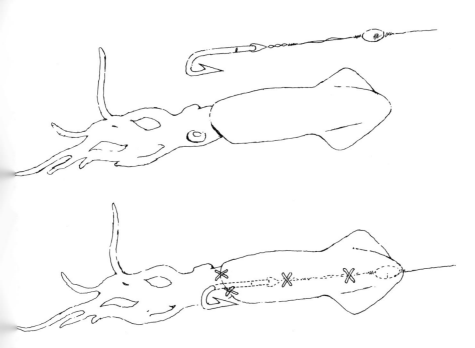

DEAD BAITS

Dead baits attract fish by smell and taste alone, and so there is no need to "action-rig" them. As a rule of thumb, they should go on the hook in as firm a manner as possible. Usually it's best to leave the hook point and barb exposed, though with very soft baits, such as dead shrimp or clams, this is not important.

One type of dead bait that does provide a bit of action is a strip of cut fish or squid, hooked through one end only so that it trails out when drifted or fished in a current. Unlike the trolling strip, however, it can be rough-cut to size and needs no trimming of excess flesh. It is simply stuck on the hook.

Except when fished strip-fashion, cut baits should be hooked two or three times, and the skin of the fish should be left intact for additional holding power.

Rigs for cut baits: chunk, strip for drifting, fish head, small piece of shellfish.

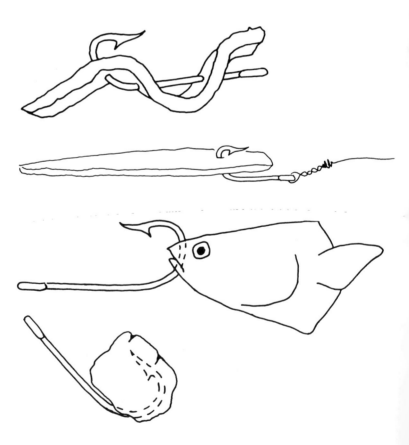

Whole dead shrimp can be threaded to the hook, exactly as described for live shrimp. Never hook a dead shrimp through the head, as the head and body separate easily. For panfish, shrimp can be cut into small pieces. If you leave the shell on, the pieces stay on the hook longer.

Dead crabs, whole or in chunks, should be stuck through the toughest part of the shell, taking care that the hook point is left clear. Though the top shell often is removed on chunks of crab, there is internal shell structure that will help hold the hook.

Clams, mussels, snails, and oysters are another proposition entirely. Run your hook through the toughest piece of stuff you can find in there, as many times as you can, and hope for the best.

9

HOW TO TIE KNOTS AND WRAP WIRE

The hard part of knot tying isn't learning the proper wraps and turns, but training your fingers to take care of the necessary procedures efficiently and—sooner or later—almost automatically.

Whether sooner or later depends on practice. That's the key. All too many folks "learn" a knot from a fishing pal, then never think about it again until they want to use it on another trip—maybe days or weeks later. Perhaps they remember how the knot is formed, but they still struggle to tie it.

To form a short Bimini Twist without an extra pair of hands, start in this position.

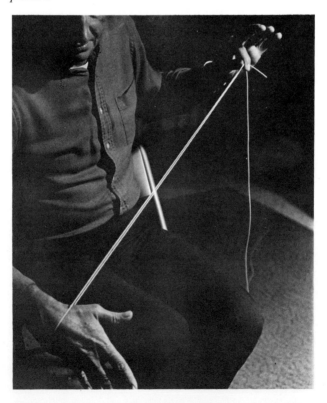

No matter how simple a knot seems, it's best to practice it a number of times—at home or perhaps during lunch while out fishing—in order to train your fingers to the task.

The more steps involved in a particular knot, the more practice you'll need. But even in a seemingly complicated knot—such as the Bimini Twist or Albright Special—the *formation* of the knot isn't complicated at all. The difficulty comes in *handling* things properly from beginning to end. All the printed instruction or oral counsel in the world won't make your hands "act right." Only practice will do that.

I wouldn't venture to guess how many different knots have been developed by and for fishermen. Some of the more avid and versatile anglers get around to using perhaps a dozen different ties, and probably know a dozen more which they can toss around at bull sessions. But when you get to the heart of the matter, you find there are only a few different *applications* of knots for the fisherman. If you learn but one knot for each application that concerns your own angling needs, you're in good shape. Thus, your approach to knot tying boils down to three things: (1) Select a knot suitable to your purpose; (2) Learn its step-by-step formation; (3) *Practice* until you can tie it smoothly.

BIMINI TWIST

Application: To form a double line at the end of your fishing line.

The only known way of *constantly* obtaining 100 percent line strength is to use the Bimini Twist to form a double line, and then rig whatever terminal tackle you're using to the double line.

Use your knees to hold the loop open and taut as you twist the free end of line up the standing end.

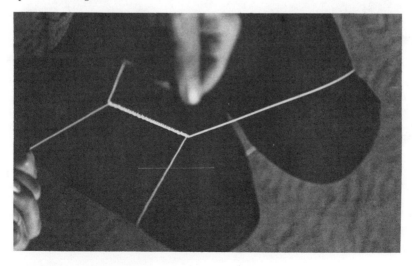

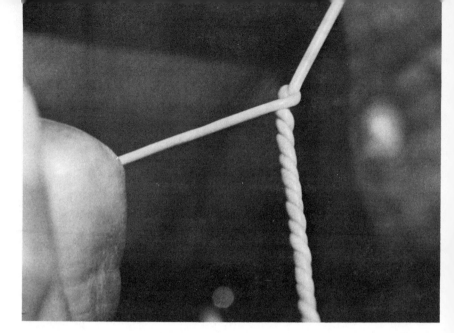

Once you have sufficient twists—20 or so—start back down with the free end of line.

Take the overlaying spiral all the way down, and then make one half-hitch of line around one side of the loop, as shown in the upper diagram on the next page.

Now make another half-hitch around both sides of the loop, and draw up snug.

Traditional use of a double line is in offshore trolling or big-game fishing. The double line can be 15 feet long, in line classes up through 50-pound, and 30 feet long in the 80- and 130-pound classes. Those are the maximum lengths allowed under angling rules of the International Game Fish Association.

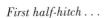

First half-hitch . . .

. . . and second half-hitch complete the Bimini Twist.

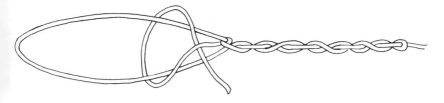

In recent years, spin, plug, and fly fishermen have adopted the Bimini Twist for making a very short double line—only enough to permit tying on a leader. The reason, of course, is to guarantee 100 percent line strength.

The Bimini is king of those "complicated" knots mentioned earlier. It would be easy to tie if you had three or four hands. Indeed, to form a 15- or 30-foot double line you need a helper. For a short double line, the method illustrated here allows you to use your knees as "extra hands."

SPIDER HITCH

Application: To form a double line. It's faster and easier to tie than the Bimini Twist. Tests 100 percent at first, but tugs and yanks reduce strength considerably.

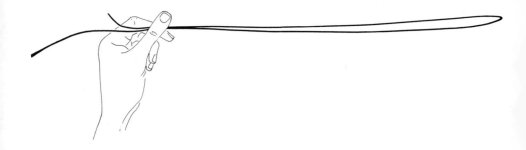

1. Double the line.

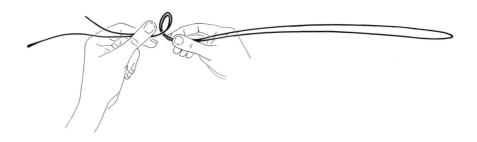

2. Form a small loop.

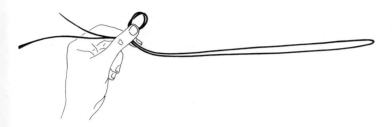

3. Grip loop at base between thumb and forefinger. Be sure to leave thumb extended as far as possible over finger.

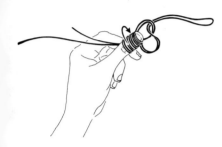

4. Wrap line around thumb eight or ten times, starting back on thumb and wrapping toward tip of thumbnail. Insert end in loop.

5. Pull on end, causing wraps to slip from thumb, one by one, and go through loop. Maintain pressure with thumb and finger after all loops are pulled off, and tighten knot by pulling down slowly and firmly.

6. The finished knot. Excess end can be trimmed very close; no need to leave more than a nub.

IMPROVED CLINCH KNOT

Application: To tie a hook or swivel to the end of line or monofilament leader.

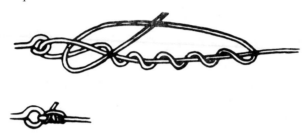

Improved Clinch Knot.

Run the end of line through eye, then wrap end around standing line five or six times.

Turn end downward and run it through opening between eye and first wrap. This creates a large loop.

Turn end upward again and run it through the wide loop.

Hold end until sure it will not slip out, and tighten knot with firm opposing pressure on line and hook.

PALOMAR KNOT

Application: Same as Improved Clinch Knot. You may find it easier to tie.

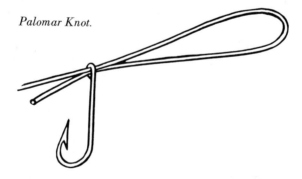

Palomar Knot.

1. Pass line through eye of hook and then return end through eye, leaving a 3- or 4-inch loop.

2. Tie an overhand knot as shown. Pull it down, but do not draw tight.

3. Slip loop over hook.

4. Pull down with opposing pressure on line and hook.

SURGEON'S KNOT

Application: To tie monofilament leader directly to monofilament or braided line. Use when leader is no more than about four times heavier than line—that is, 10-pound to 40-pound, 6-pound to 20-pound, etc.

Surgeon's Knot.

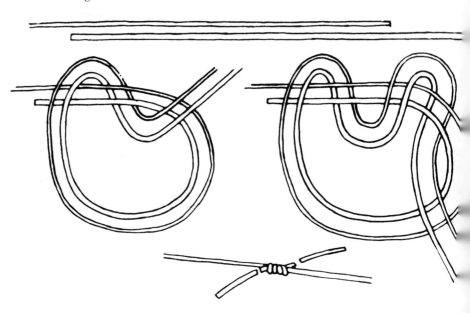

Lay line and leader side by side and overlapping at least 8 inches for ease of tying.

Treating the parallel pieces as a single line, tie an ordinary overhand knot, but don't draw it down. Instead, take the same ends and go through the same opening again, and in the same direction as before (in other words, don't backtrack the line, or it would untie the knot).

Grasp both pieces on both sides of the knot and draw down tight. Excess ends can be trimmed very close.

ALBRIGHT SPECIAL

Application: To tie a monofilament leader directly to monofilament line. Preferable to Surgeon's Knot when the leader is exceptionally thick. Also can be used to tie line to cable-type wire leader, or to nylon-coated wire.

Double back a couple inches of the heavy leader. Insert line between the doubled strands and pull through about a foot of line for ease of handling.

Hold line and both leader strands between thumb and forefinger at about the position of the arrow in top drawing.

Albright Special.

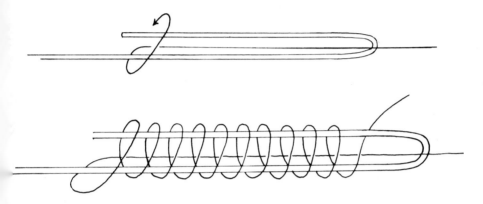

Make 10 or 12 wraps back toward standing line. You must wrap the line back over itself and over both strands of the leader, as shown in lower drawing. As you make these wraps, you will have to keep slipping your thumb-and-finger grip gradually upward to hold them in place.

Finally, insert the end of the line back through the leader loop once more at the point of original entry. Don't release grip on wraps.

This knot must be tightened slowly, and in stages. First, pull on the standing line to remove slack; then pull gently on the short end of the leader to close loop; then pull on short end of line to tighten things a bit more.

Only now can the thumb-and-finger grip on the wraps be released.

Finish tightening with opposing pressure on line and leader. Trim line, leaving about a ⅛-inch stub.

END-LOOP KNOT

Application: To loop a lure to the end of the leader. Virtually all lures develop more action if looped, rather than knotted tightly, to the leader. However, don't use this particular knot with light line—only with heavy leader, as it weakens the line to about 60 percent of strength.

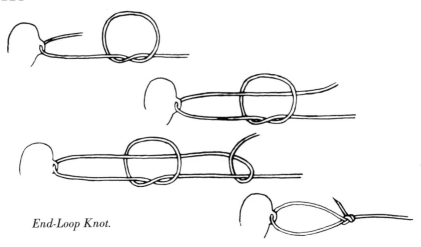

End-Loop Knot.

Before attaching the lure, tie an overhand knot near the end of the leader, but don't draw it closed.

Insert the end of the leader through lure eye, turn, and go through the overhand knot.

Make a half hitch around the line, above the overhand knot.

Hold end of line to keep it from slipping out, and tighten knot with opposing pressure on lure and line.

With practice, you can adjust the final loop size to your liking. Do this by pulling the overhand knot close to the lure eye before making the half hitch.

NAIL OR TUBE KNOT

Application: To tie a fly-leader butt directly to the end of a fly line. Cannot be used for monofilament-to-monofilament ties.

Nail or Tube Knot.

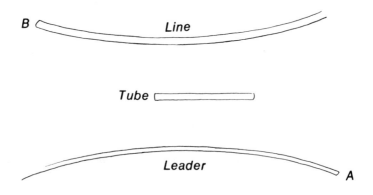

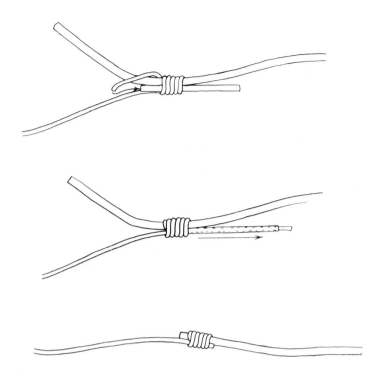

Though this knot can be tied by using a nail, it is much easier with a small-diameter tube, such as a hypodermic needle, or the discarded ink tube from a ball-point pen.

Lay out the fly line and leader as shown, with overlapping ends and with the tube in between them. Grip all three with thumb and finger of left hand.

Grasp end of the leader (A) with right hand and begin wrapping toward end of fly line (B). Make the wraps as close together as possible, and wrap five or six times.

Turn the end of the leader and run it completely through the tube, then gently slide the tube out in direction of the arrow.

Tighten with opposing pressure on the short and long ends of the leader only. The leader wraps must bite firmly into the coating of the fly line.

Once the knot is tight, the excess ends of both fly line and leader can be clipped short, leaving very slight protrusions.

BLOOD KNOT

Application: To join monofilaments of nearly equal diameter. Especially useful when adding additional line to a reel spool.

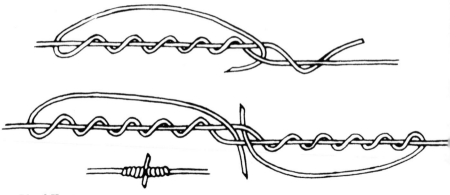

Blood Knot.

Overlap ends of the line, giving yourself plenty to work with.

Wrap one line around the other five times, then turn the end back and insert it between the lines, below the first wrap.

Now wrap the second line around the first one, also five times but in the opposite direction. Turn the second end and insert it through the same center opening, and in opposite direction to the first.

The two ends must be held while the knot is being drawn down, as they slip out very easily. Trim, leaving a ⅛-inch end on each piece.

HAYWIRE TWIST

Application: For wrapping wire leader to hook or swivel, or simply for making a loop in the end of the wire.

Haywire Twist.

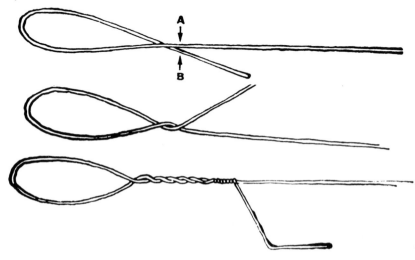

If leader wire is wrapped merely by twisting one strand over the other, the resulting connection can be trusted only for very light fishing—and even then might fail if subjected to prolonged stress. The haywire is made by twisting *both* strands of wire at the same time. Though it is finished off with a few regular overhand wraps, these do not contribute to strength, but serve only to lock the haywire twists in place.

Procedure is the same whether making a loop for later attachment to a snap, or fixing a swivel or hook to the wire.

Once the loop is formed, it must be held firmly with the fingers of the left hand while you wrap with the right. Pliers may be used to hold onto the loop while wrapping.

Cross the strands as shown. Using right hand, press *down* at point A with the forefinger, while simultaneously pressing *up* at point B with the ball of the thumb. Twist as far around as you can in a single rotation of the wrist. This leaves the position shown in the middle drawing.

Remove your right hand, assume the same thumb-and-finger position as before, and make another full twist. The right hand must be removed and a new grip taken for every twist—and all the while, the loop must not be allowed to rotate.

Once you have made six or seven twists (ten or twelve in the case of Monel trolling wire), start the finishing process by wrapping the short end around the leader three or four times—making sure that the wraps lie close together.

The final stage is to break off the excess wire. It should never be clipped off, as this leaves a sharp edge that can cut you severely if the wrap is handled later.

Bend the excess wire to about a 90-degree angle in relation to the standing wire. Then bend the end of the excess wire to form a handle as shown in lower picture.

By rotating the excess wire with this handle, you cause it to break at the point of the last wrap. You may have difficulty breaking the wire at first. If so, it is probably because you are making the circular motion in the same direction as you made the wrap. You must let your circular sweep run parallel to the standing wire.

SECURING CABLE LEADER

Leaders of multistrand or cable wire cannot be wrapped with a haywire twist. Such leader material can be purchased plain, or with a nylon coating. In either case, the most common method of securing such wire is with crimped sleeves.

Sleeves can be purchased at the tackle store. Make sure the sleeves you buy are the right diameter for your particular size of cable. The crimping tool can be bought at the same place.

To use a sleeve, slide it onto the leader, then run the end of the leader through the eye of hook or swivel. Then turn the end and insert it into the sleeve again. Pull the loop down to the desired size before crimping the sleeve.

The three illustrations show a single-sleeve arrangement for fishing with spinning or other light line; a double sleeve for extra protection against failure; and a double sleeve with circular wrap, which is generally used only with heavy cable for big-game fishing.

To make the circle wrap, run the end of the leader twice through the hook eye. Pull the resulting circle down to the desired size, then run the end in and out of the circle as many times as is necessary to bring the short end around close to the standing leader.

Crimped sleeves: single crimped sleeve, double sleeve, and circle wrap with double sleeve.

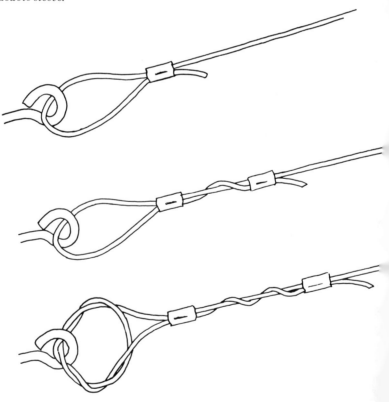

FIGURE-EIGHT KNOT

Application: Can be used in place of a sleeve to tie hook or swivel to cable or nylon-coated cable wire.

Figure-Eight Knot for wire.

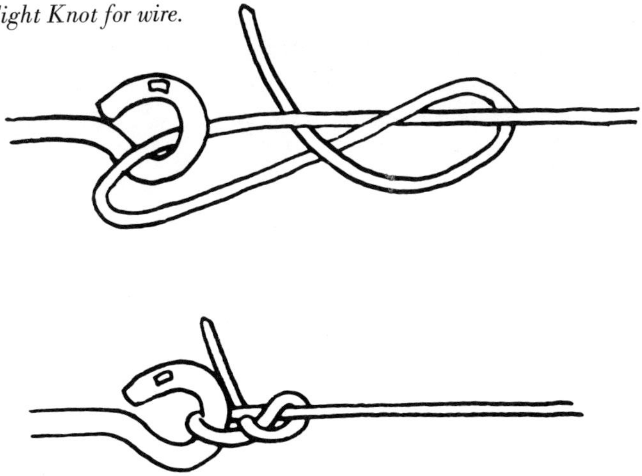

Run the wire through the eye, turn it, and wrap once around the leader.
Insert the end in the space between eye and wrap. Hold end to keep it from slipping out, and tighten by pulling on wire and hook. Use pliers to hold hook while pulling.

HEAT-FUSING NYLON-COATED CABLE

Application: To attach a hook, swivel, or lure to nylon-coated cable wire. Looks flimsy, but is 100 percent.

Steelon is twisted with gaps between the twists and fused with a flame.

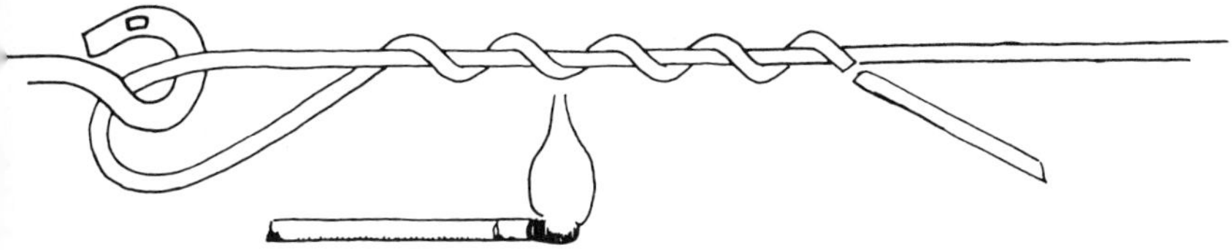

Insert end of cable through eye, turn, and make four or five rather widely spiraled wraps around standing wire. Hold with fingers of one hand at point of final wrap.

Now pass the flame of a cigarette lighter or match quickly along the wraps, keeping the flame moving until the nylon coating melts and fuses. It turns a dull white.

If flame is applied too long, the coating will start dripping away. So long as this doesn't happen, your attachment is secure.

Clip excess as close as possible to last wrap.

10

MAKING LEADERS
AND TERMINAL RIGS

Leaders are a must in just about every kind of saltwater fishing. They guard against fraying or cutting by the fish, and also absorb some of the punishment meted out to terminal tackle by rough bottom, such as rocks or coral.

The simplest of all leaders is nothing more than a length of heavy monofilament tied directly to your line. And not only is it the simplest but, being simple, is also the best for all-round saltwater use. In leader selection, you always strive for the lowest possible visibility that is consistent with the protection needed.

Despite the wide variety of leader lengths, strengths, and makeups, dedicated light-tackle anglers are coming more and more to a single basic arrangement that can be used as-is for much of their fishing, and easily adapted for any situation they might face. Definitely, this arrangement is unequaled for use with all kinds of casting tackle—surf, plug, spinning, or fly. And it offers many advantages, as well, with trolling or general tackle in light-line classes.

Let's look at this setup carefully.

First you form a double line at the end of your fishing line, using the Bimini Twist, or in a pinch, the Spider Hitch (see Chapter 9). The double line need be only long enough to permit tying a knot.

Treating the double line as a single line for knot-tying purposes, tie it directly to a piece of heavy monofilament, as long as your rod. Make this tie with the Surgeon's Knot or Albright Special. Both knots retain only about 85 percent of test, but when tied to a *double* line, then the actual test will exceed the test of the line. That's the reason for double-lining. You could, of course, tie the leader to your single line, but with resulting loss of strength. While 80 or 85 percent sounds like a pretty good mark, you should look at it the opposite way and realize that you're losing 15 to 20 percent of your line's strength!

Why such a long piece of leader? Well, the exact length isn't critical. And the rod-length suggestion is only for a handy guideline. But a goodly length is advisable for a couple of reasons. First, it allows the leader to be cranked inside the rod guides, so that when you cast, the strain and friction is taken by the heavy leader—not by your light line. Second, the long leader also protects against an extra-large fish wrapping itself in the line and breaking it with its tail.

So far we have a long monofilament leader tied directly to the line. This is commonly called a shock leader, and will be referred to as such from here on.

What size monofilament should you use for a shock leader? That, of course, must vary according to line size and the protection needed. With lines up to 15-pound-test, and for all-round inshore angling, a good choice would be 30- or 40-pound leader material. For heavier demands with the same lines, such as deep jigging, 60-pound mono is usually selected.

Suppose you need a wire leader for protection against sharp-toothed fish. In that case, you retain the shock leader and simply add a short length of wire to the end of it. If you wish to use straight wire, tie a swivel to the shock leader and wrap the wire to the swivel. If you choose cable or mono-coated cable, it can be tied to the shock leader with an Albright Special knot. In either case, you would not need more than a foot or so of wire.

In some cases you might wish to use *very* heavy monofilament of 80- or 100-pound test as protection against the raspy jaws of big tarpon or grouper. Again, you retain the basic shock leader, but add a foot or so of the heavier stuff to the end—using either a swivel or an Albright Special knot to make the connection.

All this may sound like a great deal of trouble. Until you become thoroughly familiar with the knots and setups, it might be, but thereafter it's a breeze. In any event, the shock-leader arrangement is a virtual necessity if you're the adventurous type who goes after extra-big fish with small tackle. Even if your ambitions are more modest, you'll experience a lot fewer break-offs if you rig that way. However, less elaborate rigs are satisfactory in most cases.

Now let's look at leaders and rigs for specific applications.

OFFSHORE LEADERS

Long wire leaders are standard for offshore trolling. These often are made up in advance and coiled for storage.

Make a loop in one end of the wire, using the Haywire Twist. Rig your hook to the other end—leaving a "pin" if you plan to use the leader with balao or strip. Or simply leave the end without anything on it if you plan to rig mullet baits or attach lures later.

The wire loop is fashioned so that you can slip it on a heavy-duty snap-swivel which is left permanently attached to the end of your fishing line.

Length of the leader should be at least 9 feet, for fish up to the sailfish and white-marlin class. If larger species of marlin are a possibility, length should be 15 feet. International Game Fish Association rules allow a maximum of 15 feet of leader with lines of 50-pound test or less, and 30 feet of leader with 80- and 130-pound lines.

Offshore leader—wire.

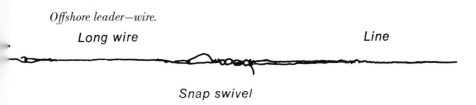

An alternative offshore setup is to make all but about 2 feet of the long leader out of heavy monofilament—80- or 100-pound-test. The short length of wire is ample to protect against teeth or bill near the bait, while the monofilament is more convenient to handle than long, springy wire.

You can make up the short tippets in advance—again with a loop in one end for affixing to a snap swivel.

Offshore leader—monofilament and wire.

Short wire   **Long mono**

Snap swivel

SINKER RIGS

SPLIT SHOT. These tiny sinkers are handy for adding just a bit of weight—perhaps to keep a bait farther under the surface while drifting, or add a little extra distance for casting a light bait. Simply press on the shock leader or line several inches above the hook.

Split shot crimped to line.

CLINCH-ON SINKERS. When you want to add weight without bothering to unrig or change your other terminal tackle, press a clinch-on sinker to line or leader. They're available in several weights.

EGG SINKERS. Best for wary biters, the egg sinker slides freely on your line. When a fish takes, it pulls line through the sinker and so feels no spooky resistance. To rig, slide the egg sinker on your line or shock leader, tie a swivel below it, and add a couple feet more leader to the swivel.

Also, you can press a split shot to your shock leader in order to stop the sinker from sliding down to the hook.

Egg sinker—standard rig.

Egg sinker rigged with split shot instead of swivel.

Split shot

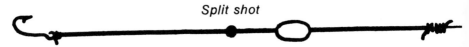

SURF RIG. Shown here with a pyramid sinker for holding power in sand, this can also be rigged with a bank sinker. Tie line or shock leader to a three-way swivel; tie short length of leader material, with sinker attached. to one remaining swivel eye; tie leader and hook to the last eye.

Standard surf rig.

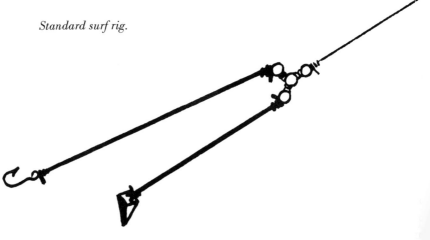

SURF FISH-FINDER RIG. In this setup, the pyramid or bank sinker is fixed to a snap-swivel or a nylon sinker slide (which you can buy in tackle stores). Thread your line through the eye of the sinker slide, then tie on a leader and hook.

This rig works like the egg sinker in that it allows line to be pulled freely, without resistance of the sinker.

BOTTOM RIG. This can be used with heavy sinker and large hooks for offshore bottom fishing, or lighter sinker and smaller hooks for bay fishing.

Tie a three-way swivel to shock leader. Suspend sinker below it on short length of leader. Tie longer piece of leader and hook to third eye of the swivel.

If you keep your line taut, the sinker will rest on the bottom, while the bait stays clear.

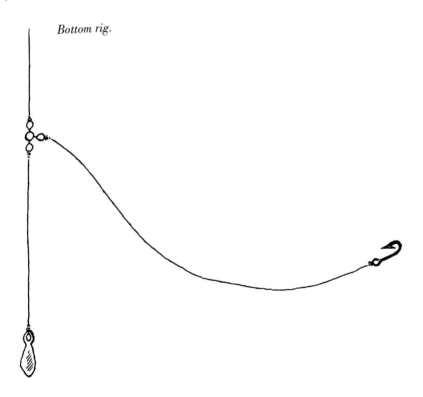

Bottom rig.

DOUBLE-HOOK BOTTOM RIG. As you can see (next page), this is made the same as the preceding rig, except two swivels are used with two lines. Space between the swivels should be long enough so the two baited lines can't tangle together.

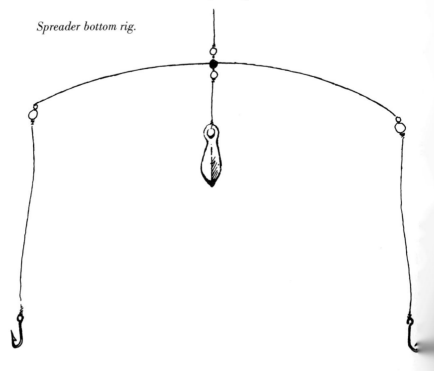

Double-hook bottom rig.

SPREADER BOTTOM RIG. This rig employs a horizontal spreader wire and a bank sinker to hold two hooks apart right on the bottom.

Spreader bottom rig.

FLOAT RIGS

STATIONARY FLOAT. Some floats can be clipped directly to line or leader, but most must be threaded onto the line, then held in place by a peg. The popping cork illustrated here is one such design that has a two-fold use. Not only does it support the bait and signal a strike, but it actually attracts fish to the bait. You pop the cork by jerking your rod. It makes a noise like that of a surface plug. Fish come to investigate, spot the bait, and nab it.

Popping cork rig.

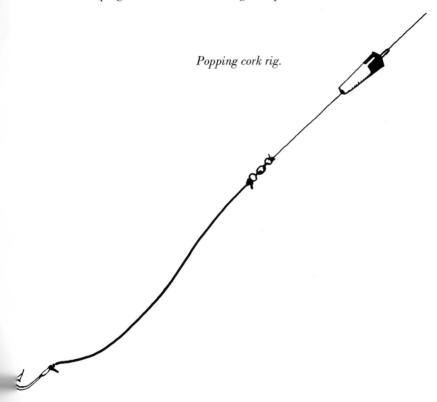

CASTING FLOAT. A stationary float several feet above the bait is awkward, if not impossible, to cast with any accuracy. The answer is a float that stays down at the swivel while casting, yet stops at the desired depth once in the water. To achieve this, you need not only a float, but a small plastic bead. Slide the bead on your line first, then slide on the float. Beads can be purchased in tackle stores, and you should get the very smallest that your line will go through.

Determine the position at which you want the float to stop, then wrap a bit of fine sewing thread around your line at that point and tie it tightly.

After your cast is completed, the little lump of thread will stop the travel of the bead, and the bead, in turn, will stop the float.

You could accomplish the purpose by tying a knot in your line to stop the bead, but that would severely weaken the line.

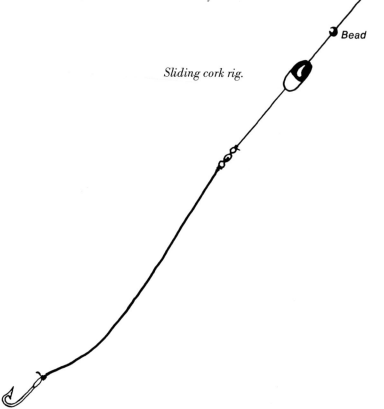

Sliding cork rig.

Bead

FLY-FISHING LEADERS

LIGHT TIPPET. This type of leader is used for bonefish, weakfish, permit, or the general run of saltwater fish for which no heavy tippet is usually necessary.

Start with a 36-inch butt of 30-pound monofilament, tied to the fly line with a tube knot. Join the specified lengths of progressively smaller diameter to each other with the Surgeon's Knot.

Tapered saltwater fly leader.

36"	30"	12"	24'
30-lb.	20-lb.	15-lb.	12-l

HEAVY TIPPET. With most large saltwater flies, elaborate tapering of the leader is not necessary. Start with a 6-foot butt of 30-pound monofilament, tied to the fly line with a tube knot.

This diagram indicates 12- or 15-pound test for the light material. Those are the most commonly used sizes in saltwater fly-fishing, but you could use 10-, 8-, or 6-pound. In any case, take a piece of the light material and use the Bimini Twist to double-line each end of it.

Tie one doubled end of the light material to the 30-pound butt. Tie the other to the 1-foot heavy tippet. These ties can be made with the Surgeon's Knot or Albright Special.

Heavy saltwater fly leader.

6 feet	2 feet	1 foot
30-lb.	12 or 15-lb.	Heavy

The heavy tippet may be of monofilament or nylon-coated cable. If monofilament, 30- or 40-pound-test is normally used for inshore fishing (snook, striped bass, channel bass, etc.), and 80- or 100-pound-test for tarpon fishing.

11

HOW TO LAND FISH

A surprising number of anglers become pretty darned efficient at hooking and playing fish long before it sinks into their skulls that methods and techniques of landing their catch are every bit as important, and require every bit as much skill and disciplined action.

Undoubtedly, more fish are lost at boatside than during any other phase of battle—not just trophy fish, either, but fish of quite ordinary dimensions. Even with good landing equipment properly used, you're going to lose a fair percentage of your fish after they come within reach. So don't stack the odds any higher.

Familiarize yourself with all the practical ways of getting a catch safely to your icebox or stringer, and learn some of the impractical ways, too, in case of emergency.

Let's look at several procedures:

HOISTING A FISH WITH YOUR ROD

This method can safely be practiced only with panfish. Even with fish weighing as little as a pound, lifting them from the water greatly increases the chance of pulling your hook, breaking the line, or possibly even breaking the rod if it's an especially light one. This is why bridge fishermen should use rods and lines heavier than would be required for the same type of fishing from boat or shore.

LIFTING A FISH BY THE LEADER

Grabbing your leader and flipping a fish aboard isn't too bad a landing method—that is, if you don't particularly mind losing a fish occasionally. At least you won't break your rod or line. The worst that can happen is the hook pulling out. On those happy days when you're catching a lot of fish, lift the ordinary ones aboard by the leader to save time and bother. Use net or gaff for the outstanding ones you don't wish to risk losing.

Of course, some species are easier lifted than others. Snapper, grouper, and redfish, for instance, have tough mouths and aren't apt to shake loose unless very lightly hooked. Weakfish, on the other hand, have very soft mouths and therefore tear free quite often.

BEACHING A FISH

When fishing in the surf, or from a shore with any sort of slope to the bank, landing a fish is pretty easy. But, believe it or not, I've seen people try to heave their fish through the air rather than simply sliding them up the bank or beach.

If you're wading from a beach, start backing toward shore as soon as you have your fish turned toward you. Continue backing away until you're a short distance up the beach. This is much better than merely standing at the edge of the surf and trying to beach your fish with a short line. The longer line affords added protection against breaking off or pulling the hook. Slide the head of your fish gently onto shore; time your pressure to take advantage of wave action, if any.

If the fish seems pretty heavy compared to the test of your line, don't try to pull it too far onto shore. Instead, try to get its head and "shoulders" up on the sand; then run forward immediately, grab the leader, and drag (don't lift) the fish all the way to dry land.

If you hook an unexpectedly large fish from a dock, seawall, or even a bridge, it's quite likely that your best chance of landing it will be to lead it (after it's well tired) to the closest shelving shore, and then beach it in the fashion just described.

LANDING FISH FROM PIERS AND BRIDGES

Anglers who fish from high structures encounter special problems in landing their fish. A couple of possibilities along those lines already have been covered (using pretty heavy rods and lines so ordinary catches can be cranked through the air; and leading a big one to the closest level shore).

If you fish regularly from seawalls, it will pay to rig a net or gaff with a handle of the length needed to reach the water. On commercial piers, special landing equipment—long-handled gaffs and hoop nets lowered by ropes—is generally provided, along with attendants to handle it.

Nets and gaffs with handles long enough to be used from a high bridge, however, are just too unwieldy to carry around, and it's a rare bridge fisherman who totes along such a device. Instead, the bridge specialist who seeks heavyweight fish relies on a "bridge gaff," which is a large weighted treble hook (around 10/0 size) attached to a length of small-diameter nylon rope. When a big one—maybe a black drum or jewfish—is hooked, beaten, and lying still atop the water, the bridge gaff is lowered, and jerked into the fish's jaw or head, and then the rope is used to hoist it to the catwalk.

USING THE LANDING NET

By far the most widely useful of all landing devices for freshwater and light saltwater fishing is the landing net. Really, no boat should be without one. Most modern nets have aluminum handles and framing, with mesh of nylon, plastic, or, in some cases, rubber. While diameter of the hoop and depth of the bag vary widely, it's a good idea to use as large a net as you can comfortably handle and easily stow. A good all-purpose choice would be a net with a 3- or 4-foot handle, and a hoop diameter of 18 to 24 inches.

Good netting form. Net is placed in water while angler leads fish toward it—head first.

Fish should be netted with a quick motion, but not a wild splashing one. If possible, put the net in the water, lead the fish close, and net it with a fast sweeping motion, head first. If you touch a fish's tail with the net and it has any life left in it, it will scoot away.

Of course, if the fish is so thoroughly beaten that you can control it without trouble, then you can net it any old way.

After you net your fish, it's always a good idea to swing it aboard without delay. Fish have been known to jump out of a net. Then, too, they sometimes will tear through a net. It doesn't occur often with modern synthetic net materials, but it can still happen—maybe because of an unnoticed hole or a spot weakened by accident. A pretty big fish can slip through a surprisingly small hole. All of which leads to the observation that you should inspect your net frequently. Any holes discovered should be repaired by tying them with braided nylon or Dacron line or, in a pinch, monofilament.

Treble hooks have a way of tangling up in a landing net so wondrously that your entire supply of patience and your whole vocabulary of picturesque phrases are used up before the hooks are out. For a big snook or some other

Torn mouth of this weakfish shows why these fish—and most others—should be netted. To avoid tangling treble hooks in mesh of the net, the fish can be lifted aboard by the leader, after the net is placed under it for protection in case it tears loose.

choice catch, the trouble is well worth it. But you can avoid the problem with trout and other lightweight catches by using the net as a safety device rather than a landing instrument. When your small fish is beaten, just hold the net under it while you lift it in with the leader. Should the hooks pull loose, your fish falls safely in the net and saves you the trouble of removing the hooks yourself.

USING A GAFF

Sticking a gaff into a fish sounds like a simple procedure, and in most cases it really is, but anglers sometimes goof up on their first few tries, and get the idea that some kind of mysterious "trick" is involved.

Like tying a knot or casting a lure, the how-to of gaffing is easily explained, but in order to pull it off successfully you must practice until the act becomes routine. Confidence is the main factor.

Basically, you need only shove the gaff hook into the water, get the point underneath the fish, and then heave upward sharply. Early failures can usually be attributed to one of two things: either the gaffer gets excited and begins flailing wildly, or he pussyfoots and tries to take things too easy—simply probing around with the gaff instead of sinking it home with authority.

Don't dilly-dally when the fish comes within range. Get the point underneath the target and jerk! Then, with the fish on the gaff, continue hauling and bring it aboard right away. Many species are good at jumping or twisting off the gaff, and it's always best to swing them in as quickly as possible— directly into the fish box.

Even the best of gaffers miss occasionally. Should you fail to connect, remove the gaff from the water immediately, and wait for another good shot. Don't go jabbing around in pursuit. An active fish that eludes the gaff might easily wrap the leader around the gaff hook and break off.

The most useful gaff to keep on hand, for most anglers, is one with a 2-inch hook of stainless steel (2 inches referring to the "bite," or the straight-line distance from the point across the gap to the shaft). Larger hooks are difficult to sink into smaller fish, such as average-size kingfish, because their bodies are so slender you might end up merely cradling the fish in the bend of the gaff instead of getting the hook into him. At the same time, a 2-inch hook is capable of holding much larger fish.

In short, with the small hook you're much more likely to get that point imbedded on the first try.

Of course, if you do a lot of offshore fishing you should have a larger gaff as well. A 4-inch model makes a good complement. Larger hooks usually are carried only by folks who plan to use them for specialized work on particular kinds of big fish.

What about handle length? The only strict requirement is that the handle be long enough to reach the water. Handles 3 or 4 feet long are average and entirely adequate for small fishing boats and many cruisers with low cockpits. The maximum handle length allowed in most competitive angling is 8 feet.

As to handle material, tubular aluminum is the best available in finished gaffs. It's light and easy to work with. Some anglers prefer to buy the hooks only, and fit them to handles of Calcutta cane or tubular fiberglass.

It goes without saying that gaff hooks should be kept sharp. Stainless steel is rather soft, and the point will dull or blunt easily. Check it often and keep it sharp with hone or file.

Gaffed fish should be lifted into boat without delay and deposited in fish box.

Also, the point should be protected at all times—both to prevent sticking holes in your leg accidentally while moving around the boat, and to keep the point from getting blunted through contact with hard objects.

Perhaps the best point guard is a large cork or cork ball. You can buy a coil spring of stainless steel, one end of which stays mounted on the shaft, while the other can be slipped on and off the point at will. This is an excellent protective device, but there is one risk involved. After the point is bared for action, the spring simply dangles. It doesn't interfere at all with gaffing, but if you miss, there is the possibility your leader will become entangled in the spring.

Short release gaff goes through lower lip of a tarpon. Hook will be removed, or leader cut. The jaw is all cartilaginous tissue, and so the tarpon is not injured.

Several different specialty gaffs are in common use. One is the release gaff—a hook with a handle just long enough for a one-hand grip. Some release gaffs, in fact, have no handle at all, but only a thong to go around the wrist. Though used primarily for tarpon, the release gaff can be worked with many fish you plan to let go. To use it, you must first play out the fish thoroughly, and after it is under good control at boatside, you slip the point into its mouth and through the lower jaw, thus enabling you to hold the fish while the hook is removed or the leader cut.

The release-gaff design is utilized by surf fishermen for nonreleasing purposes. Being small, it can hang at the belt until needed for sticking into a good-sized surf fish that has been played into shallow water. Then, of course, it provides a convenient handle for dragging the catch up on the beach.

Actually, a true surf gaff, or "pick," is a modified design in which the hook has been opened to almost a 90-degree angle, so it can be imbedded with a downward chopping motion. Surfing regulars make their own picks, or have them made up. But the simple release gaff does an adequate job.

Tarpon fishermen, using medium to heavy tackle, commonly use the release gaff even for boating their fish. A *whipped* tarpon is easy to lip gaff, and can be held in the water while a rope is threaded through the gills and tied. Or a lip-gaffed tarpon could simply be hauled aboard—but it might have enough kick left in it to necessitate a wrestling match in the cockpit.

In the Florida Keys, light-tackle tarpon fishing with fly, plug, and spinning tackle has become such a popular sport that a different kind of tarpon gaff now nestles inside all guide boats and many private craft as well. Far from being a little one-hand device, the Keys tarpon gaff is a monster—a 6-inch hook mounted on a very stout 6- or 8-foot handle. Moreover, the hook is not a conventional round-point model, but one with a flattened, barbed point that is sharpened to a knife edge—like the hook of a big-game flying gaff.

When attempting to land a giant tarpon on 10- to 15-pound line or fly leader, you don't play with it around the boat until it turns on its side and allows you to sink a lip gaff; not unless you're planning to release it, of course. Instead, the guide reaches out at the first opportunity with the big gaff and attempts to skewer the tarpon with it somewhere around the fish's middle. Obviously, this requires a stout heart and a strong arm—and sometimes the ability to swim. Usually the tarpon is tired enough so that the guide has little trouble controlling it on the gaff. However, if the fish is a big one and the people involved are particularly anxious to get it for a tournament or a record, there is the temptation to gaff it a little "green." Rare is the light-tackle guide in the Keys who hasn't gone overboard for his customer at one time or another.

Here a marlin has been impaled on a flying gaff—in the muscular "shoulder" area. After the hook is set, the handle of a flying gaff separates and is set aside while the fish is held by a rope tied to the gaff hook.

The flying gaff—a standard weapon in the arsenal of big-game angling for marlin and giant tuna—is sometimes used for smaller species, both inshore and offshore, when extra-light tackle is involved. The head of a flying gaff is fixed to a stout rope or line, and the handle is fitted to the head with some sort of temporary fastening—either a friction fitting, or else a tie with light line. Once the hook is in the fish, the handle comes loose and is set aside, leaving the quarry hooked up to the rope. The rope, quite obviously, is firmly fastened to a boat cleat.

A fairly recent addition to the lineup of specialty gaffs is one which looks like an ordinary long-handled gaff, but has a swivel fitting in the handle. You can hold onto the upper end of the handle while the hook and lower end freely revolve. Its application is for sharks, and perhaps some other husky species such as cobia, which usually cannot be hauled directly into the boat. You must attempt to control them on the gaff for a while, and the swiveling feature prevents them from twisting the gaff out of your hands. Sharks are especially notorious for twisting, but a variety of other big fish are not backward in this department.

Marlin on a flying gaff is pulled by rope until it can be killed and boated..
The flying-gaff rope, of course, is secured to a stout boat cleat.

HOW TO BOAT SAILFISH

Average-size sailfish and white marlin are easily handled at boatside by gripping their spears. A gaff is seldom used because a great many of these fish are
released—and also because the potentially dangerous bill would not be under
much good control.

But the "billing" procedure can be dangerous too, unless certain important
guidelines are followed.

First, gloves must be worn to protect the hands from both wire and the
raspy bill.

When the leader comes within reach, take the upper end of it firmly in
both hands, and hold tight. More often than not, the fish will thrash or jump
as soon as it feels this added pressure. Hold on until this activity quietens.

Next, you start "hand-lining" the leader to bring the fish within reach.
This is the part that could be dangerous. You shouldn't lead the fish directly
toward your person. Instead, stand in the corner of the cockpit and make

After sailfish is pulled within reach, it should be grasped firmly near base of the bill.

your pulls sideways—keeping the bill pointed toward the bow and drawing the fish alongside your position.

When the bill comes within reach, grab it with one hand, near the base, if possible. Don't let go of the leader with the other hand until sure your first grip is solid. Then take the bill in both hands.

The fish will struggle again at this point, perhaps violently. Just hold on until it settles again. No sailfish is apt to "overpower" a person of even normal muscular physique. If you plan to release the fish, remove the hook or cut the leader very close to it. Otherwise, haul the fish over the gunwale and into the boat.

12
NAVIGATING FOR FISH

There are countless small-boat anglers who never take the trouble to learn even the most basic elements of navigation, or familiarize themselves with a few simple tools, instruments, and procedures that could make their outings not only more efficient and enjoyable, but far more productive of fish.

Navigation basically serves only three purposes for a small-boat fisherman: (1) to get him to spots or areas where he plans to fish; (2) to get him back to his launching spot without undue sweat or search; and (3) to enable him to pinpoint and *return to* good holes, spots, or wrecks which he may himself discover while fishing.

The simplest of all navigation systems is to stay constantly in sight of identifiable landmarks or navigation markers, and steer your courses by sight alone. Just keep from running aground and everything is hunky-dory. Obviously, this is the system used by most coastal anglers most of the time—duffer and master boatman alike. But its limitations are also obvious. For one thing, when you hit new territory—either by launching at a new spot or by traveling farther abroad than usual from your old one—you must familiarize yourself with, and orient yourself to, a new set of visual references. This takes time and must be done carefully. Otherwise, you might turn for home and then start asking yourself, "Do I head for that buoy or the other one? Which one of those islands did I come around?"

USING CHARTS

Whether an angler navigates by sight or instrument, the first essential piece of equipment is a nautical chart of the area he fishes. These charts, published and distributed by the National Ocean Survey, are sold at marine stores. Most useful for purposes under discussion are the Small Craft charts, designated by the letters "SC" after the number. However, SC charts are not yet available for all areas, so you may have to use the regular Coast charts, which, of course, are equally functional though larger and a bit harder to manage in cramped space.

Note too that your SC chart may not range as far offshore as you might wish to go—say to Atlantic-side reefs or to banks out in the Gulf. So you might well wish to keep both types at hand even though the covered areas overlap.

For visual navigation, you merely consult the nautical chart as you would a land map. Note your starting point and proceed to the chosen destination—or simply explore—by identifying the markers, islands, and other reference points you see according to your chart. And your chart also indicates water depths. This *helps* you keep from running aground in shallow-water areas, but you can't depend on it entirely. For one thing, the printed depths indicate *average* low water. On spring low tides, the water is shallower than indicated. Also, bottom conditions can, and do, change in many coastal areas. So always use the latest charts available (publication date is printed on each chart) and stay alert!

By studying a chart at some length before making the trip, you not only can save yourself some trouble in getting around, but also pick out potentially productive fishing spots—such as bar edges, deep areas surrounded by shallow ones, creeks and runoffs, small channels, rocky shoals, reef patches, or whatever conditions suggest fish in the particular inshore or offshore area you have targeted. All these and more are shown on the charts—not because the charts were designed for fishing, but simply because they affect navigational procedures.

Nautical charts, of course, are far more than just "road maps" for anglers who ramble about by sight. More experienced boatmen use them for plotting courses, determining position, computing distances and even boat speed, and many other purposes.

Some of these uses will now be touched on in a fundamental way. They can be extremely valuable in finding fish and in getting about on the water. Familiarity with these basics may also give you incentive to study boatmanship more carefully in boating books and manuals.

COMPASS AND COURSES

Every coastal fisherman should have a reliable compass installed on his boat and should learn to plot a simple course. This advice holds, even for an angler who "always" travels by sight. Following are just a couple of instances in which steering by compass can be helpful—or downright necessary—even over completely familiar routes in your regular waters:

1. You're 2 or 3 miles offshore, or out in the open stretches of a large bay. You lose sight of shore because of fog or rain. It's possible to lose sense of direction entirely, especially if the wind dies or shifts. Without a compass, the only sensible thing to do would be to wait for visibility. With a compass, you can set out in full confidence that you'll end up close enough to look for landmarks, when they become visible, to bring you in.

2. You want to travel a course you've traveled a hundred times before—always by visually proceeding from marker to marker. Only this time circumstances compel you to travel it in the dark, or under visibility conditions so poor that you can't see from one marker to the next. You never thought about it before, but the marked route isn't a straight line. Without compass headings, the result could be anything from prolonged bumbling about to actually getting so disoriented that you have to wait for daylight.

The easiest way to obtain compass courses between points that you travel a lot by sight is simply to look at your compass while running the courses, and jot down the headings in a notebook. Or you can sit down at home with a chart and plot your courses and enter all of them in the notebook at once (or mark them right on the chart).

The other obvious reason for a fisherman to plot courses is to find his way between points on a chart which are too far apart to permit sight-steering. Let's say you want to go from a buoy near shore to another buoy offshore. To plot the course, you need only a straightedge and a protractor. Here's how to do it:

With the straightedge, draw a line on the chart from the starting point to the target point, which in the example mentioned would be from one buoy to the other. If this line does not cross either a meridian (vertical line on the chart) or a parallel (horizontal line on the chart), extend it with the straightedge until it does cross the closest such meridian *or* parallel.

Now place the center of the base line of the protractor directly over the point where your penciled line crosses the meridian or parallel line. Align the base line of the protractor exactly over the meridian or parallel line.

Your penciled line will cross the arc of the protractor, and you read the heading in degrees right off the protractor scale at that point. Write down the heading alongside your penciled line.

This simple method requires only a stationery-counter protractor, which is widely available and very cheap. If you wish, you can get a course protractor or parallel rules at your marine supply store. Both are as simple to use but cost more money.

In any event, the result is the course you take to reach the desired destination. But let's stress again that we are talking only in the most basic of terms and in regard to travel between points a relatively short distance apart—no more than a few miles. And the target must be a prominent *visible* object that you'll be able to pick up by sight once you get to the general vicinity.

In other words, this course will be good enough to get you within sight of the destination. Then you steer visually the rest of the way.

Why can't you depend on your plotted heading to put you exactly on course and keep you there?

There is a long combination of reasons: compass variation and deviation; the fact that it's difficult to steer an exact course in a small, fast-moving boat anyway; influences of wind and current.

All those factors can be ignored for the purposes we've talked about so far (provided your compass is not *sadly* out of whack). And the reason you can ignore them is that you're only trying to get within eyeshot of your destination and then head for it.

Navigating over long distances, or to reach a precise unmarked position, is a horse of another color. All the factors mentioned above must be carefully evaluated, and more besides—especially boat speed.

TAKING BEARINGS

Now that we've talked about some of the ways to get from one place to another, let's look at another important consideration for the fisherman—how to pinpoint a fishing spot and return to it on the next trip.

Let's say you've found a great spot. Maybe you don't even know what's down there—ledge, rocks, wreck—or maybe you have a depth recorder and you do know. Either way, the important thing is to get to the place again.

If fairly close to shore, you can look for cross bearings. This means you'll have to line up two prominent objects in one direction, and two more in another direction. Let's say, for instance, that you look over the bow and see that a certain buoy lines up with a power pole on shore. Over to the right, you line up a small cottage (or one side of it) with a water tank farther back on shore.

Next time out, go farther offshore than normally, then line up the buoy with the power pole and run slowly on that line toward shore until the cottage on your right lines up with the water tower. This simple cross-bearing system is amazingly precise. And this is one time you can give at least halfhearted thanks for the clutter of man-made objects crowding most of our shores. They make it much easier to take cross bearings.

Be sure to write down your bearings (in that same little notebook you use for your courses and other navigational notes). And don't skimp on the written details. Be sure there's enough information to denote exactly *which* power pole; exactly *which* cottage on the beach. Draw crude sketches if you think they will help.

If possible, avoid using trees as reference points, as their appearance can easily change because of leaf growth or storm damage. Of course, a lone tree in an open area does make a handy bearing.

If it is impossible to line up two objects in one or both directions, or if you're so far offshore that only the most prominent objects are visible, you can use a compass to take a pair of bearings on two *single* separated objects, say a large smokestack and a tall building.

Your boat compass, however, is a poor instrument for this. You should have a hand-bearing compass, designed so you can aim and sight it, much like sighting a gun, and take the reading directly from the sight picture. Again, write down the two bearings.

Bearings taken with the compass are not apt to be so precise as visual cross bearings, but should get you close enough to the spot so that you can drop a marker and search it out. Sometimes, too, the "spot" is really a fairly large area, and your two bearings with the hand compass will land you in good fishing even though truly accurate readings with a hand compass are difficult because of wave motion or strong current.

If you wish to find a charted but unmarked wreck or reef offshore, and with no visible landmarks at all, it will require far more study time than simply reading this little essay, and far more information than is contained herein. I will only outline what must be done, not how to do it.

1. Locate the position of the wreck on the chart, and plot a course to it from the closest lighthouse or other fixed navigation aid. This is called a true course.

2. Correct the course for *variation,* and correct your own compass for *deviation.* Your compass reads a magnetic course rather than a true course; the difference is called variation. Deviation is an error within the compass, usually caused by metallic influences near the compass mount.

3. Determine the exact distance between the wreck and your starting point.

4. Determine the speed of your boat at various RPM.

5. Figure the exact time it will take, at your known speed, to cover the exact distance to the wreck.

6. Begin your run well behind the starting point so you'll be running at the prescribed speed when you pass it. You'll also establish your course at the same time. As you pass the starting point, put your stopwatch in motion, then time the exact number of minutes and seconds it should take, according to your previous computations, to reach the wreck.

Now, even with all those careful preparations and procedures, chances are remote that you'll hit the wreck on the nose, because of human steering error plus unavoidable slight variations in boat speed caused by a number of subtle influences.

So all your study will have been in vain *unless* your boat is equipped with a fathometer with which to conduct a final search. In other words, if you don't have a fathometer, don't bother to look for remote wrecks, even though they're precisely charted.

Here's how to proceed if you do have a depth sounder. When your stop-watch ticks off the last second of computed running time, throw over a marker—which need be nothing more than a bleach jug with line and some sort of small anchor. Continue running the same course and speed another few seconds, and then toss over a second marker.

One marker might be enough, but now you have two which line up your original course, and thus provide a more accurate visual reference for the search pattern you begin with your fathometer until you locate the wreck.

No need to be terrified at the thought of correcting your compass or of computing distances and boat speeds and running times. The methods are fairly simple, but must be explained in more detail than is possible here. You can find the information in various boating articles and books.

Perhaps I should apologize to the many angling boatmen who take pride in their seamanship and who have long since zoomed beyond the simple navigation plateaus outlined here. But let's face it. The majority of us fish-oriented types consider our boats as just another item of necessary fishing tackle, and we're interested in learning only those elements of boatmanship which will get us out and back safely—and put us over some fish.

Part III
Fishing Systems
and Techniques

13

TROLLING

Drag a bait behind a moving boat long enough and you're bound to come up with a fish. All too many boaters do take this casual approach to trolling. They toss over a spoon or feather, set the rod in a holder, and wait for something to happen.

But to the serious saltwater angler, trolling is something else entirely—a dedicated system where skill and planning and alert procedures are needed to pay off in the satisfaction of ambitious goals attained. There are as many trolling specialties as casting or bait-fishing specialties, and the angler who masters his chosen type of trolling is no less an expert than the one who gets his thrills from casting plugs or flies.

OFFSHORE SURFACE TROLLING

With few exceptions, surface trolling is the standard system of big-game fishing throughout the world and, whether by choice or accident, is the producer of many lesser gamefish along with the glamor species, which are marlin, sailfish, swordfish, and giant tuna.

It's referred to as surface trolling because the popular baits used ride either atop the water or no more than a few feet underneath, but—in theory, anyway—many of the fish taken rise from considerable depth to investigate these topwater baits, being attracted by the surface disturbance created by boat turbulence, splashing teasers, and, to a lesser extent, the action of the baits themselves. While all veteran offshore trollers have their pet ideas as to what makes fish respond, and from how deep they can be attracted, nobody really knows too much about these subtle factors. But there's no doubt that propellers, teasers, and wakes do catch the attention, and pique the interest, of oceanic gamefish. Whether the fish come from somewhere far below or quite near the surface is immaterial. Anglers refer to "raising" the fish, regardless.

Often enough, fish definitely are at the surface to begin with and needn't be "raised" at all. They can be spotted feeding in schools of bait, or free-jumping, or riding the crest of a swell, or simply "tailing," which means lying

Boats in the 20- to 24-foot class may not have the comfort or luxury of big sportfishing cruisers, but they do offshore work very well, and have been used to capture all the major big-game fish.

at the surface with their caudal (tail) fins exposed, and sometimes their dorsals as well.

It is generally agreed that fish are more likely to roam near the top when the water is choppy, or even rough. And there is some scientific opinion, backed by observations of skippers and offshore fishermen, that billfishes tend to feed near the surface in the early-morning and late-evening hours, retreating back to the depths during the middle of the day.

A striped marlin takes a skipping bait. A watchful angler can almost always identify a striking billfish because the bill or dorsal fin, or both, will clear the water before or during the strike.

The studious angler must consider these things, and play the odds as best he can. But they are not to be accepted as rigid rules. Many trophy fish have been caught on skipping baits during conditions of flat calm; and it certainly isn't unheard of to see or hook a billfish on top of the water at high noon.

Selecting Offshore Baits

Only rarely will you encounter a situation where one particular bait is so obviously superior to all others that it should be used exclusively, and on every line. Normally, the offshore troller should present a selection of baits—at least two different ones and perhaps three or four, depending on how many lines can be fished in comfort from the particular boat.

As noted in Chapter 8, offshore baits are rigged either to skip the surface or to swim just underneath the surface. It's a good idea to have both types out— emphasizing one style or the other, according to your own evaluation. Skippers are the primary weapons in most situations, particularly for billfish. Members of the tuna and mackerel family show a preference for swimmers, though they hit skipping baits readily at times, and they might easily be attracted to a skipping bait, only to choose the one swimming nearby. Even billfish frequently select a swimmer when given a choice, and if several fish come up at once they may well gobble every bait in sight.

The only conclusion that can be reached from all this is to keep a variety of baits working. You can always cut down the menu if a strong preference on the part of the fish becomes evident.

The size of the baits must also be considered. For fish in the sailfish-dolphin class, primary skipping baits are balao or baitfish of similar size, such as finger mullet and cigar minnows. Swimmers could be finger mullet with a chin sinker, strips, or feather-strip combinations.

Standard baits for marlin and giant tuna are larger mullet and mackerel—some rigged to splash and others, leaded, to swim. Many species can be substituted, according to availability, including bonito, dolphin, bonefish, and barracuda. Those generally are rigged as splashers.

Some artificials fit right into an assortment of rigged baits. A simple feather is a deadly device for most kinds of pelagic fish, and if you're after action or variety you might wish to put one out. On the other hand, billfish are seldom caught on a slow-trolled feather, and for that reason you might not care to include one in your lineup.

A live blue runner goes on the hook for slow trolling offshore. The sailfish tail sticking out of the fish box proves the effectiveness of live-bait trolling.

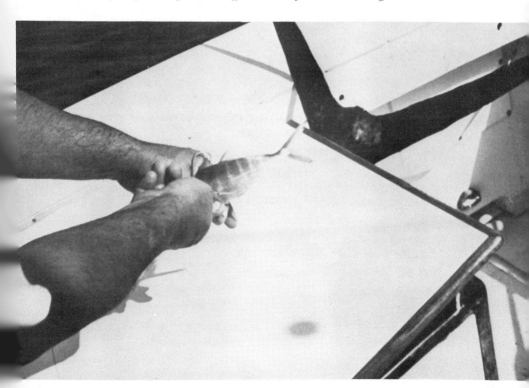

Certain soft plastic baits, especially squids, are productive of sails and mar-lin, and of other kinds of fish as well.

Natural squids are deadly, but infrequently used except in situations where they are vastly more likely to produce strikes than are the more quickly rigged baits—baiting swordfish, for example. And while white marlin might accept a number of different offerings, squid is the demonstrated best bait off the Maryland and New Jersey coasts.

Every angler must evaluate and select his own assortment of offshore baits in given areas and situations.

Line Spacing and Bait Position
The number of lines that can be trolled efficiently depends on the size of your boat, whether or not it is fitted with outriggers, and how many anglers you have aboard to keep track of them. Small sportfishing cruisers generally can handle three or four lines—one from each outrigger and one or two fished "flat" directly over the transom. Large cruisers often fish two lines from each rigger, plus two flatlines.

For those who fish from trailered boats up to 24 feet or so, normal practice is to put out two rigger lines, with optional flatline. On small craft not fitted with outriggers, two flatlines are used.

The important point is that flatlines are every bit as effective as rigger lines. Whether your boat has riggers or not, you can troll offshore with confidence.

How far back should the baits ride? One bait, by all means, should be posi-tioned short—just aft of the boat's wake and as close to the transom as 25 or 30 feet. This, obviously, should be a flatline. If another flatline is employed, it should be kept fairly close as well, but slightly farther back than the first one, to help avoid tangling. Lacking outriggers, this would be the standard two-line setup—one bait 30 feet away, another 40 or 45 feet away.

Those distances can be estimated; they are not critical. And be aware that it's virtually impossible to troll a bait too close to the boat. Of all the major offshore species, only certain of the tunas seem to be consistently boat-leery.

Two outrigger baits, used in combination with one or two flatlines, can both be positioned approximately 20 feet farther back than the longest flat-line; or one can be put at that distance while the other goes back to perhaps 80 feet.

Boat Speed
Trolling speed is important, but certainly not precise as to miles per hour. Neither is it always constant. To begin with, remember that open-ocean game fish are pretty swift—therefore, you'll be trolling faster than you probably are

Two flatlines and two outrigger lines can easily be trolled from an outboard boat that is equipped with outriggers.

used to for inshore fishing. The approximate average is 6 to 10 knots, but more important is the effect of your speed on bait action. Your skipping baits should skitter along the surface, occasionally digging in and swimming a short distance, but always popping back to skip some more. Swimming baits, conversely, should stay underneath the water and not pop up at all, except once in a great while when they catch a wave just so.

When your skipping baits stay under more than they should, then pick up speed slightly. And if your swimmers are jumping out of the water all the time, slow down. The proper speed, once attained, may not stay proper. Frequent adjustment of the throttle may be necessary because of changing sea conditions, or direction of boat travel in relation to the waves.

There are two situations in which "average" trolling speed differs sharply from the foregoing. One is trolling with live baits; the other is trolling *exclusively* with certain artificial lures.

Live baits generally require slower speeds, again based on how the baits are being pulled. Live balao are trolled at not much more than idle, large and frisky bonito at a rate approaching rigged-bait speed, and blue runners somewhere in between. Watch the baitfish carefully to see that they are swimming in pretty much normal fashion, and not being pulled awkwardly through the water. Yet there must be *enough* boat pull to keep them tracking reasonably well, and to allow you to cover some territory in your trolling pattern. And if you proceed too slowly with blue runners, in particular, they have a habit of running under the boat and hiding.

Some artificial lures are effective when trolled at rigged-bait speeds, and can successfully be used in combination with rigged baits. But it's also true that feathers, spoons, plastic squids, and other artificials commonly used offshore will produce even more strikes at higher speeds. So if you are fitted up with artificial lures exclusively, you can increase average speed to 12 or 14 knots. And don't discount the possibility of hitting good fish at speeds as high as 20 knots!

Granted, the idea of dragging lures at such rapid paces has not yet been wholeheartedly accepted throughout the offshore fishing community, but it has proved deadly effective for both billfish and other ocean gamesters wherever it has been seriously tried. The system has reached its greatest acceptance in Hawaii and California, and is spreading to other Pacific areas. It has been used mostly for marlin fishing, and with quite large lures similar in design to teasers. However, in scattered trials many different kinds of fish—sails, bluefin and Allison tuna, white marlin, and wahoo, to name a few—have fallen for this approach in many different waters and with a variety of lure styles, including plastic squids and eels, big pork rinds, and even plugs.

The heart of the system is not the lure style, but the fast speed itself. Rigged baits could even be used, but are impractical because they would go to pieces quickly at such speeds.

The theory is sound and results so far seem to be supporting it. Hark back to what was said earlier about *disturbance* in the water being considered the key factor in raising fish. A faster-moving boat and a crazy, bouncing lure figure to attract attention. Never fear that a marlin or sail is incapable of catching up to the lure should it become interested. Even the big ones could hit twice that speed in a race for food.

Certain potential benefits to the angler become evident. Fast trolling covers a lot more ground in search of big fish; and when a strike does come, it's always a "crash" strike. No need to concern yourself about dropping back.

Still experimental—or even untried—in many top offshore fishing areas, this kind of fast trolling will one day become a standard system everywhere. Certainly it will not replace trolling with rigged or live baits, but will complement it, and should be particularly useful at times and places where marlin and other gamesters are sparse and scattered, and wide searching seems to be the ticket.

Where to Look for Offshore Fish

Aimless wandering about over the ocean may produce an occasional good catch, but not many. Fishing areas must be picked with some care, and within that area there are almost always many signs and conditions that the attentive troller can read to his advantage.

Selecting a general area usually is not too difficult. In many coastal locales, the productive territory has been well established over the years, and you need only do a bit of homework, or talk to local anglers and guides, to get on the right track.

These productive broad areas may lie as near as a mile or so offshore (as along portions of the southeast Florida coast), or as much as 40 or 50 miles out (as is the case along much of the Middle Atlantic and Gulf coasts). Sheer distance has nothing at all to do with it. The one great key is the contour of the ocean bottom—deep dropoffs, canyons, seamounts.

When trolling the selected area, always be on a sharp lookout for conditions or situations which might tend to attract free-roaming ocean gamefish. Some favorable signs are rips, eddies, weed lines, and floating debris.

Weed lines and floating objects are famous for harboring of dolphin. But they should be explored thoroughly by the seeker of billfish as well.

A clump of sargassum weed on the leader indicates that this dolphin was hooked near an offshore weedline—the best conditions of all for finding dolphin.

Find a floating log offshore and you're apt to find dolphin, and perhaps other fish as well. If birds are sitting on the log, it may be an extra-good sign that gamefish have lately been feeding on bait sheltered by the log.

An active concentration of birds is, of course, a well-known sign, but don't fail to investigate even one or two birds if they seem to be particularly excited about something going on in a given area. The birds may be working directly in a surfacing school of feeding gamefish, such as dolphin, bonito, or tuna; or their attention may be directed at a school of small fish feeding on still smaller minnows. But regardless of whether the ruckus is being caused by fish which you would like to hook, you should troll your baits methodically around the edge of the action, because much bigger game may be in the area as well.

Frigate birds (also called man-o'-war birds) are considered by most offshore veterans as an especially likely indicator of big fish. A lone frigate bird will sometimes hover for long periods over a single sailfish or marlin or shark. But the bird may also simply be soaring and searching. For sure, though, if you see one or more frigate birds dipping to the surface, you should get over there fast. Something is bound to be there—maybe dolphin, but quite possibly a billfish.

A single frigate bird (also called man-o'-war bird) is often a better indicator of larger gamefish offshore than a whole flock of gulls or terns.

At times you may spot flushing baitfish without any birds tipping you off. If you see balao scattering, or flying fish (and if you're sure it wasn't your own boat that spooked them), then clear for immediate possible action.

Any kind of "edge" merits investigation, whether it be the meeting place of two different colors of water, or two different currents, causing a rip.

Remember that on the Gulf Stream coast of southeast Florida, most sailfish are caught not too far out in blue water, and a great many just inside the blue water. Roam farther into the blue for marlin, dolphin, and tuna.

The Strike and Dropback

Most fish which take a trolled bait are hooked (or lost) immediately and almost automatically. The motion of the moving boat sets the hook, and even though the angler may make an additional strike with his rod, this is mostly a "make sure" reaction.

The one jarring exception is in the case of billfish. Once in a great while you may get a "crash" strike from a marlin or sail—one in which he takes the bait so forcefully and deeply that it virtually hooks himself—but this is the rare exception. Hooking a billfish almost always requires execution of a technique known as the "dropback," which simply means giving slack line instantly when the fish takes the bait.

The dropback may be accomplished mechanically, by means of an outrigger or other line-releasing device; or manually, by allowing line to slip from a free-spooled reel under only enough thumb resistance to prevent back-lashing. Even when outriggers are used, additional manual dropback is gener-ally advisable.

The technique is easy to describe, but more difficult to execute—not be-cause of any great manual dexterity required, but because timing is the im-portant thing, and the timing must be judged individually with every fish.

Anyway, here's how it's supposed to work: A billfish takes the bait and snaps the line from the outrigger pin. The line goes slack immediately, but of course will tighten again as soon as the outrigger-provided slack is removed. If you're holding the rod, make sure the reel is in free-spool and with your thumb held lightly on the spool to guard against overrun, so that you can con-tinue dropping back directly from the reel. If the rod is in a holder at the time of the strike, you must move fast to take it out and clear it for the free-spool-ing process. There's always the chance that an outrigger's automatic dropback alone will result in a hookup, but odds are greatly increased if you continue

In some areas, billfish can be spotted as they "tail" at the surface—partic-ularly striped marlin and broadbill swordfish.

dropping back—at least long enough to feel that the fish is really moving hard with the bait.

When you decide (or guess) that it's time to set the hook, lower the rod tip and throw the reel into gear. Wait just a moment until you feel a strong pull on the rod, then hit it! That moment's delay is only to make sure you don't strike against slack line.

Should the strike come on a flatline, you will not, of course, have outrigger slack to assist you, but must accomplish the entire dropback directly from the reel. This is no special disadvantage, particularly if you are holding the rod at the time of the strike and already have the reel in free-spool.

Sadly, nobody can say just how long you should drop back, despite the oft-heard advice that you should "count to 10." The size of your bait, as compared to estimated size of the fish, may have a lot to do with the time. If a blue marlin gobbles a balao, for instance, you won't drop back nearly so far as if the same fish strikes a large mullet. General guidelines may be helpful, but not entirely dependable.

In the end, all you can do is try your best to judge, or "feel," or guess, when that fish has a solid hold on the bait and is moving with authority.

With white marlin and to a lesser extent with sailfish, there's more danger in waiting too long than in striking too soon, for if you miss on a quick strike you at least have a good chance of keeping your bait intact and drawing the fish back for another shot at it. You do this as follows: As soon as you strike and feel no hookup, crank your reel rapidly while holding the rod tip high. This action brings the bait back to the top of the water and moves it once more. The fish, more often than not, thinks its prey is escaping and will grab it again. Many whites and sails have been hooked on the second, or even the third, try.

Considering the importance of the dropback and its quick and proper execution, you can see how helpful it is to identify the fish at the time of the strike. It always pays to watch the baits faithfully, because a billfish usually gives itself away before it hits. You may see its dorsal fin slicing behind the bait, or see its bill clear the water on the strike. If you have the height advantage of a flying bridge, you may see the entire fish just under the surface behind a bait.

INSHORE TROLLING

There is no strictly definable boundary line between "offshore" and "inshore" fishing areas. The fellow who fishes so far out that he is barely, if at all, in sight of land might take exception to being referred to as an "inshore" fisherman, even though he be fishing for species—bluefish, for instance—which are usually considered inshore types.

For purposes of this discussion, "offshore" trolling will refer only to blue-water activity, and "inshore" trolling to everything else—from outside reef areas to the coastline, bays, inlets, and estuaries.

Reef trolling overlaps blue-water fishing in many areas, particularly Florida, the Bahamas, and other tropical and subtropical territories. Offshore fishermen often swing into the reef while working such areas. They may do so

Mackerel of several species are among the favorite inshore trolling targets of virtually every coast. Here, Baltimore Orioles first baseman Boog Powell unhooks a 5-pound Spanish mackerel.

simply to drum up some strikes from barracuda, kingfish, mackerel, or jack on days when action is slow in the deep. Or they may do it because sails, wahoo, and other prestigious gamefish types may well be found there along with the typical lineup of reef-huggers. The regular menu of blue-water rigged baits is entirely acceptable to predatory reef fish, but if you're trolling any hard-to-rig baits it's best to crank them up before hitting the reef. Otherwise you'd risk losing them to 'cudas and such. Balao and strips will work just as well, and are the surface baits of choice (along with mullet, another not-too-expensive bait) if you go out to troll the reefs specifically, without thought of big-game trolling. Shallow-running artificial lures that produce well over the reefs are spoons, feathers, and small plastic squids.

Trolling for shallow-water fish generally calls for slower speeds than you would use for offshore or reef varieties. A few species of inshore fish, however, are indeed fast swimmers and like their lures moving accordingly. This is particularly true of mackerel, for which your trolling speed should be at least 6 knots. If you troll in protected waters for mackerel from a small boat with 5- or 6-horsepower motor, you might have to open up to nearly full throttle to keep your spoon or jig moving fast enough.

There is an alternate solution, but a tiring one. You can troll at a much slower speed, if you continually whip your rod to keep the lure darting.

Many fishermen troll fast, without rod action, while searching for mackerel or king mackerel. Once they locate an apparent school or concentrated fishing area, they throttle back to a much slower troll, then work in a circle or a figure-eight. This allows them to stay much more easily in the selected area, and they then start whipping the lures in order to compensate for the slower boat speed.

Other major inshore trolling targets include striped bass, bluefish, channel bass or redfish, weakfish, snook, and tarpon. Many other kinds of fish are taken with trolled lures, of course—some desirable, some undesirable.

All are relatively slow-speed targets, meaning that you need only select the slowest boat speed that brings out the best action of your lure. The closest thing to an all-purpose lure for inshore trolling is a spoon. Most spoon models "telegraph" their action to the angler via a definite throbbing of the rod tip. If you don't see the tip throbbing—or feel the vibration—either you're not moving quite fast enough, or the spoon is fouled.

Judge the proper speed for swimming-type plugs by letting them ride in view, close to the boat, until satisfied with their action. After the pace is set, let them go back to regular trolling distance.

If your trolling rig involves any sort of natural bait—such as the spinner-and-seaworm combination for stripers and weakfish—only enough boat speed to barely keep the spinner turning is necessary.

Lefty Kreh, outdoor editor of the Baltimore Sun, *trolls for mackerel. White wa
ter in the boat's wake hints at the fast trolling speed required.*

As in offshore trolling, it's always a good idea to keep one lure fairly close
to the boat—just behind the wake. A second line can be positioned farther
back. Troll as many lines as you can comfortably handle. Two usually are
enough. Wide-beam boats can get by with three, if the outboard anglers hold
their rods well to either side, and the center rod is directly astern. If two or
three lines are used, stagger the distances. This will help keep from tangling
during turns, and may also determine the best distance for getting strikes. I
one line consistently gets more hits than others, adjust the distance of the
others accordingly.

As a rule, you'll do better to keep the rod tips as low to the water as pos
sible at all times in order to make the lures run their deepest. But raise the
tips if your rigs start bouncing bottom or getting fouled. You can, of course

place the rods in holders—as long as the depth and action of the lures suit you in that mode.

Though hook-setting is generally no problem with a trolled lure—the motion of the boat being enough to do the job—you can hit back for safety's sake. Should you fail to connect on a strike, it often pays to start jigging the rod, thus causing your bait to move erratically. If the striking fish hasn't been stung too badly, it may hit again when the lure suddenly starts acting wild.

In addition to being a good angling system in itself, inshore trolling can be of great benefit in locating good spots or learning a new area. As a learning system, it can be used in two basic ways: (1) Troll until you get a fish, then troll the same area several more times. Should you drum up additional action, chances are the spot is a likely one. You can stop immediately and work it over by casting, or live-baiting, or whatever your chosen method. (2) Devote an entire day to trolling in an unfamiliar area. Troll all the likely-looking spots or stretches, and some of the not-so-likely-looking ones. When you get a strike or a fish, retrace the route, of course, and try to get more action there. But after the spot is thoroughly tested—with good or bad results—move on to another. Take notes throughout the day, and mark your charts. Regardless of how many fish you catch, a project such as this will give you a good look at a new area, and provide many clues to help you catch fish by other methods, on other trips.

Line twist can become a serious problem when trolling. Though spoons and spinners are the chief villains, some other types of lures may also twist the line on occasion. If your line gets twisted, try using two swivels instead of one—the first at the spoon (a snap-swivel) and the second between line and leader.

To remove twist from a line, simply take off all terminal tackle and troll the twisted length of line behind the boat for a few minutes.

DEEP TROLLING

Presenting a trolled bait *far* below the water's surface can be a demanding job, calling for some sort of special equipment. Adding a few ounces of extra sinker weight may send your bait plummeting to bottom when the boat is still, but as soon as you start trolling, up comes the rig to a near-surface position. When lead is used as a *primary* means of attaining great depth, it is measured in pounds, not ounces. However, several ounces of lead—usually in the form of a specially designed trolling sinker—can achieve a moderate depth when used with ordinary lines, and can help you get down really deep in combination with metallic lines.

Husky amberjack are among the common prizes taken by deep trollers.

Following are descriptions of the popular approaches to the challenge of deep trolling, listed in approximate order of depth-probing capability, from shallowest to deepest.

Diving Plugs

The only type of artificial lure that will travel fairly deep on a troll, by virtue of its own design, is a deep-diving plug. As noted in Chapter 4, this design is characterized by an oversized planing surface at the head—usually in the form of an extended metal lip of large dimension. These can be trolled effectivel at depths up to 30 feet or so. The lips also give them a vibrating or swimming motion, and by and large they are excellent strike-getters on a great variety of fish.

In many areas, trollers are not fully aware of the diving plug's fish-catching capability. They go to all the trouble of rigging up special deep-trolling equipment of one sort or another—which is perfectly all right when really necessary. But why bother if you could do the required job with nothing more than a common plug—especially if you don't troll at 20 or 30 feet all that often?

You may be well aware, for instance, that deep-trolled plugs work well on such inshore types of fish as stripers, snook, and tarpon when they are in deep channels, passes, or rocky cuts. Yet you might not know that these plugs are equally attractive farther offshore for king mackerel, grouper, snapper, and other reef and pelagic species.

Trolling Planers

Obviously, trolling planers work on the same principle as deep-diving plugs. While they are weighted with lead, this has little to do with their diving capability, but serves only to keep the planer in proper attitude.

Offered in several sizes, planers are most useful for taking rather light or small artificial baits down to depths they could not attain on their own. Examples of the common lures used with planers are spoons, feathers, feather-strip rigs, and jigs. Small natural rigged baits also can be employed.

The vast majority of planers probably are used along the Atlantic Coast for mackerel and king mackerel, and in Pacific Coast areas for salmon and stripers. Of course, they would be equally efficient in deep trolling for Atlantic-side striped bass, but habit has a lot to do with angling styles, and Easterners are much more likely to go for wire lines instead.

A planer exerts considerable pressure on line and rod, which must be considered—along with depth requirement and size of the bait—when choosing planer size. The smaller planers work well with, say, light spoons at depths up to 30 feet; larger ones with bigger spoons or other baits to perhaps as much as 50 feet, or more.

Manufactured planers are designed so that once a fish is hooked the trolling attitude of the planer changes instantly. You are not forced to wage the fight against the same pressure your rod felt while trolling; in fact, the new attitude helps plane the fish upward in the water.

Metallic Lines

Though metallic or wire lines are not considered "legal" by the International Game Fish Association and other groups which oversee record or competitive fishing, they are widely popular and undeniably effective in trolling up good catches from deep water. But with their effectiveness can come some problems, as we'll see shortly.

Three types of metallic lines are currently in popular use—lead-core line with a braided nylon or Dacron coating; stainless-steel wire cable; and single-strand wire line of Monel, which is a nickel alloy with handling characteristics similar to those of copper wire.

Lead-core lines are used almost exclusively on fairly light trolling tackle and for inshore species, such as blues and stripers.

Monel is used for the same purposes, but also for offshore deep trolling or reef trolling in heavier tests and with much stouter tackle.

Cable is not so commonly used as the other two, being considerably more expensive and not so efficient as Monel in gaining great depth. It is sometimes chosen, however, for heavy-duty deep trolling because it is less subject to kinking, weakening, and breaking.

All the metallic lines are available in a variety of breaking tests. Lead-core is most popular in the 20- to 40-pound-test range; Monel is used in similar tests inshore and in 80-pound test for heavy work offshore.

In sinking efficiency, Monel is far and away the best, but for many applications the lead-core is entirely adequate. Cable falls in between. While no strict formula is possible, a 300-foot trolling length of lead-core line will go down some 50 feet, as compared to about 65 feet for cable and 100 feet for Monel.

But actual depths are quite variable, of course, depending on such factors as bait design and weight, actual diameters of the particular lines, and boat speed.

Trolling sinkers may be used in combination with wire lines, but in many cases are not necessary. A sinker does contribute something to getting down and staying down. Also, you can maintain a faster trolling speed, while keeping the bait in the desired depth range, by adding a sinker.

Because of the variables involved, you will have to do some experimenting on your own in regard to how much line you must let out to get down where you wish. It is almost essential that your line be marked—starting at 100 feet, and then at 100-foot intervals, or 50-foot intervals, over as much length of line as you are ever likely to put out.

If your deep trolling is somewhat routine as to fishing areas and required depth, one or two marks may be enough.

The braided coat of some lead-core lines is varicolored and keyed by the manufacturer to help you determine how much of it is out. In any event, you can mark lead-core lines easily with nail polish. Dental floss, wrapped and tied tightly, then colored with nail polish for visibility, is often chosen as marking material for cable or Monel line.

As to the problems hinted at earlier, they relate to handling and spooling characteristics of metallic lines. Obviously no metallic line is going to lie as snugly on a spool or behave itself nearly as well as soft lines. Lead-core comes pretty close. The others must always be treated with extreme care, particularly Monel.

A backlash is bad enough in monofilament, but in wire it's almost tragic— not only from an untangling point of view, but because snarls easily kink Monel to the breaking point. And any severe kink must always be cut out and the wire spliced. Tangles do not necessarily weaken cable, but the untangling job is no easier.

Original spooling of wire line on your reel should be done under heavy hand pressure, using gloves. Always guard against overruns while letting out the line by slowing up the spool with hand or thumb. And when cranking in the line—unless there is a fish or substantial weight on the end of it—you should also apply hand tension. With heavier wire lines, it's always best to wear gloves while fishing, so that the line can be handled as necessary.

Downriggers

The most effective device of all for trolling at extreme depth is the downrigger, or underwater outrigger. And it also provides the *only* deep-trolling setup that permits the use of what we think of as "regular" fishing tackle—no wire line, or heavy sinker or planer.

Underwater outriggers have been around for many years, but only in homemade versions used by a handful of anglers. Nowadays, there is a wide array of factory-made downrigger outfits, and this approach to deep trolling has become pretty much standard in many areas, while continuing to gain ground in many others.

The downrigger itself can be described as a large reel fitted with wire line. Attached to the wire line is a very heavy weight. Either integral to the weight, or closely attached to it, is some sort of clip or pin to which the fishing line can be attached—in the same way that a line is clipped to a regular outrigger.

In use, the fishing line is fastened to the pin, and then the heavy weight is lowered away from the downrigger to the desired depth, while line is allowed to slip from the fishing reel at the same rate of speed. When a fish hits the bait, the line snaps free from the pin, and the angler is free to wage war. Meanwhile, the downrigger weight is hoisted back up—out of harm's way and ready for another bait.

Simple, eh? Well, yes and no. The procedure is simple enough, but putting it into practice can be—not difficult, maybe, but certainly painstaking.

You should give serious thought to a downrigger if deep trolling figures strongly in your angling plans over much of the season. For those anglers who troll deep only on occasion, thought must be given as to how much value it would be to them—and whether or not they might meet the occasional deep demands by drift fishing or deep trolling with less expensive gear.

Another reason to buy a downrigger is simply to experiment with it, and find out just what new deep-fishing avenues might open up in your area.

Downrigger outfits are sold in various sizes—the differences being mainly in the size of the reel, how much wire line it can handle, and the weight of the sinker. Some models, particularly those scaled for heavy-duty offshore work, offer motorized retrieve. Some even have built-in thermometers for testing temperatures at various depths and selecting bait position accordingly.

Most units can be installed by means of a mounting bracket bolted to transom or gunwale. This allows the downrigger itself to be removed quickly when not needed, though the bracket need not be unbolted.

Smaller units, used with light tackle and, usually, spoons or other artificial lures, are quite easy to use and firmly established for such work as salmon fishing in the Pacific and Great Lakes, and striper fishing. They also are very good for reef trolling in quest of such gamesters as amberjack, grouper, snapper, and king mackerel.

The largest—hence strongest and deepest—of the downrigger outfits are designed for use over deep reefs, wrecks, or the kind of places often referred to as "monster holes." And they also open the door to the most intriguing deepwater adventures of all—big-game fishing. It's well established that swordfish, marlin, and tuna spend more time down deep than near the surface. Many big-game anglers have been entranced, over the years, by the idea of fishing for those species down there where they live. A few have even done some experimenting in the far past—using homemade downriggers, in which the weight was lowered from a regular wire-line fishing rod and reel.

While success was never overwhelming, there have been a few isolated incidents of outstanding hookups and catches—enough certainly to offer great encouragement.

One example was that of Doc and Helen Robinson aboard Capt. Louis Schmidt's *Caiman* at Pinas Bay, Panama, in 1960. Fishing the downrigger around the famous Pinas "reef" (actually a seamount rising from about 55 fathoms to 20 fathoms), Helen caught a women's world record amberjack of 106½ pounds on 80-pound line—a record which still stands at this writing, fourteen years later. She and Doc took several other hefty amberjack, and Doc also hooked four black marlin which he described as "among the biggest we have seen in Panama," meaning in the 600- to 800-pound range. But he lost all four of them due to tackle failure traceable to the downrigger setup, principally in the release-pin arrangement—such things as line twist, or the leader tangling in the line after breakaway. Solutions to the problems were eventually worked out, but the Robinsons never spent much time at down-rigger fishing thereafter, for the simple reason that surface fishing was so productive most of the time.

One boat here and there, experimenting with big-game downrigger fishing rarely and briefly, really doesn't shed much light on the possibilities.

Now that modern downriggers, with more highly sophisticated release mechanisms, are being installed on more and more offshore fishing boats, knowledge is bound to increase rapidly, and the full potential of this un-tapped sportfishing resource may be close to realization.

14

STILL-FISHING

Fishing from an anchored boat is sometimes looked on as an easy approach, but in fact, it can be one of the most demanding, for the simple reason that as soon as the anchor goes down, your prospects become limited to whatever fish might be reachable from that single boat position.

Thus, the still-fisherman must either go where the fish are, or else contrive to bring them close to the boat. There are three basic approaches to this problem, though all three can frequently be worked together.

Flounder, fluke, and other flatfish species are pets of bottom fishermen everywhere.

1. Anchor in a spot where fish tend to congregate. This usually means a reef, rock patch, a depression in shallower surrounding water, or some other sort of attractive bottom condition. Bluefish, king mackerel, and other roving species, however, will sometimes take up temporary or seasonal residence in a certain area, which either becomes well enough known locally to put you on the right track, or which you find on your own by trolling or drifting.

2. Anchor in a "fish thoroughfare"—that is, some sort of place where fish might be moving through. Many such places can be spotted by an attentive angler. Examples include passes and inlets, small channels that cut through flats, the edges of oyster bars or sand bars that gradually deepen with a rising tide, and eddying points of coastal streams, especially where a smaller flow joins a larger one. This type of spot usually requires a moving current. Gamefish may simply move with the current, on their way someplace else, or they might lie in the current and wait for an easy meal to come their way. Therefore, if you can manage to combine a "thoroughfare" condition with a "holding" condition—perhaps a channel bend, hole, or rocky bottom—you have a double-barrel chance.

3. Attract fish to your anchored boat position by judicious use of chum. Chumming doesn't free you entirely from the problem of choosing a good spot. After all, the juiciest chum in the world won't lure fish if there are none close enough to respond. But *exact* positioning becomes far less critical. The happiest setup of all, obviously, is good chum in a good spot.

HOW TO USE CHUM

Chumming is the trick by which a fisherman hopes not only to *attract* fish, but at the same time to sharpen their appetites and dull their sense of caution. Though chumming can be helpful to a slow-drifting angler in some situations, it primarily is a still-fishing technique.

Many chums and systems are in use. Some are elaborate and—let's face it—messy; others are simple and inoffensive.

A party-boat crew, for instance, may collect piles of unwanted fish from the docks, grind them into mush, and take the stuff out to the fishing water in cans or barrels. They also use great quantities of commercial or selected chum, such as mossbunker, either exclusively or in combination with any trash fish that might be available. In any event, they toss the goop overside by the cupful or bucketful at determined intervals, creating a chum slick that extends out of sight.

That's chumming on a grand scale, and is done to attract blues and other schooling types from long distances. The private boater needn't take such a

Though king mackerel can be caught by various angling methods, chumming from an anchored boat generally is the most action-packed of all.

massive approach, nor is it advisable in most cases. Some restraint has to be shown. If you dump huge quantities of chum overboard, letting it drift hither and yon, the fish won't have much incentive to come in close to your boat.

Those aforementioned party boats, once they bombard their way to the attention of the fish, reduce the flow drastically—tossing over smaller amounts and not so frequently—in order to keep the fish interested, but close.

The most practical approach to chumming for the small-boat angler is to buy his chum in frozen blocks (you can find frozen, packaged chum at many bait dealers and commercial fish houses). After anchoring, the chum is removed from the package and placed in a chum net, or simply wrapped in any kind of netting that can be tied and hung over the transom. Gradually the frozen chum melts, creating a slick and surrendering small bits of flesh through the netting. The angler shakes the bag from time to time, releasing occasional flurries of solid particles. If you have any choice at all in the matter, the frozen chum should be of mossbunker or other very oily fishes. Bunker chum is sometimes sold in cans or plasticized packages that need no refrigeration before opening. These generally work very well—the system being to punch a couple of small holes in each end of the package and hang it in the water in much the same manner as the frozen chum. The package can be placed in a net, or tied on a line.

If you have unfrozen ground chum and don't wish to keep ladling it out of a bucket, this too can be hung over in a net or wire-mesh chum pot. But you'll need more of it, since its goodies will dissipate much more quickly than if frozen.

Many types of desirable fish respond directly to the appetizing aroma of ground chum. With other species, the chum has an indirect magnetism in that it coaxes forth quantities of baitfish, such as balao, pilchards, pinfish, and others—depending on which baitfish might be present in your neck of the woods. Obviously, a raft of excited small fry rings the dinner bell for predators.

If balao or other baitfish do start working in your chum line, you can catch them on tiny hooks. This is a possible side benefit—instant live bait. And, by the same token, when you go out specifically to catch live bait, chumming often makes the task much less time-consuming.

Sardines and similar small fish, used as both chum and bait, lead to action on schooling gamefish on both the Atlantic and Pacific coasts.

There are many specialized chums, and specialized methods. Chumming with live bait is a standard style off the Southern California coast, and is practiced in other isolated situations. Sardinelike small fishes are used. Because of the quantities required, and the elaborate bait-keeping equipment needed, this kind of chumming is largely confined to charter and party boats. You may, however, be able to work a productive compromise. Should you have a more-than-adequate supply of pilchards or other small live baitfish on hand, toss out one or two of them occasionally while chumming with ground chum. At times, too, dead sardines or pilchards can be almost as productive as live ones when fed into a chum slick—as can scoops of dead glass minnows or other tiny fry. Obviously, when live chum is used, your hook should be baited with the same thing.

Another kind of specialized chumming is called "sand-balling." While practiced mostly in Southern waters for yellowtail snappers, it works with any fish that will readily leave its usual bottom hangout and rise in the water to feed. You need a bucket of sand and a bucket of chum. A bit of chum is folded into the sand and formed into a ball, then dropped overside. This allows the chum to sink before the sand dissolves and releases it. The hope is that by using smaller and smaller clumps of sand, you gradually entice the fish into roaming higher, until finally you can fish them with straight chum and a free line.

The sand is more than just a sinking mechanism. It clouds the water and contributes to attracting fish, which often come to investigate any sort of unusual disturbance.

Sand-balling is a pretty sloppy process. As an alternative, the chum-bag user can simply weight his bag to get down deep, then raise it by stages. And for fish that simply don't, or won't, come up, the chum should *stay* deep. A most practical method of assuring that your chum flow stays at, or near, bottom is to tie it to the anchor line.

Almost any bottom fisherman can use chum to his great advantage, inshore or offshore. The seeker of fish in calm and shallow water can turn an ordinary can of sardines into a fish-getter. Punch a few holes in the can and toss it over to lie on bottom and ooze out its oily lure. Another fine type of emergency or always-at-hand chum is canned cat food—and the cheaper brands with higher oil content work best. This may be used like the sardines, or you might want to open the cat food and dispense small blobs of it to hold fish around the boat.

Crustacean-feeding fish, such as sheepshead, drum, tautog, hogfish, and redfish or channel bass, respond readily to chum, but it should be of shellfish rather than ground scale-fish. Shellfish chum, or scraps, is not widely sold at bait stores. Since the fisherman generally has to gather and prepare the stuff himself, not too many go to the trouble. But be assured that if you're catching some of those fish now, your luck will probably double or triple if you take the pains to chum.

This kind of chum is where you find it—shells and legs of crabs and lobster; shrimp heads scrounged from shrimp boats or packing plants; fiddlers or other small crabs rounded up on special outings; snails, clams, mussels, or oysters put in a sack and crushed with a hammer.

Incidentally, a measure of broken clam or oyster shell is a valuable contributor to your chum mixture, even if you prefer to retain the inside goodies for yourself. Shellfish-hungry bottom feeders can even be drawn by nothing more than throwing over handfuls of the bare shell, though of course they react much better if there is something tasty to boot.

However you may chum, or with what, your baits and angling methods must be tailored accordingly. There's no point in preparing a lovely surface slick and then dumping a cut bait on bottom. Nobody is apt to miss the mark that far, of course, but still you must learn to recognize the things that are happening, and experiment for things that might be happening, as a result of your chumming. Sometimes you must make your presentation just so, catering to the whims of one species. On other occasions you may drum up several different prospects and be called upon to make a decision as to the most attractive.

Fish that work your chum line near the surface, or at mid-depth, are most likely to take a free-drifting bait. Live or dead, the bait should be drifted out in as natural a manner as possible—without undue weight or drag. Ordinarily you try to get by without any sinker at all, but if your bait doesn't seem to be getting far enough under the surface, then add weight sparingly.

Any fish which is actively feeding in your chum probably can be caught on cut bait or dead bait, provided it drifts along in an unsuspicious manner. If you're sure fish are present, but refusing your bait, chances are you'll have to trim terminal tackle—use lighter leaders and hooks, and hide the hook better in the bait.

Remember that bigger types of predatory fish may well come around, even though they are not directly interested in your chum. Thus, it's never amiss to put out a live bait or two, either on a free-line or a float. The live-bait rods can be stuck in holders while you continue to fish lighter rigs with cut bait.

If you prefer casting, or if you run out of bait, artificial lures frequently work extra well around chum, since fish are excited, feeding with abandon, and may strike reflexively. Cast and retrieve in the chum slick, of course, but try other routes, too. For instance, cast off to the side and let your lure sweep around toward the chummed area as you retrieve. Mackerel, blues, and other active fish may be near, and darting in and out of the chum.

Bill Hegle, manager of the Metropolitan Miami Fishing Tournament, found this 4-pound mangrove snapper willing to take a cut bait fished in his chum line.

Jigs and swimming plugs are most often used for this kind of work, but don't overlook noisy surface plugs. A jig can be particularly useful because you can let it sink and then work it up to test various depths.

It certainly isn't unusual to actually see big fish in the chum, or cruising over to investigate, in which case you can toss a lure directly to them. In this manner, many a trophy has been nabbed by fly-fishermen, or by spin-fishermen and plug-casters.

It's true that the best chances for surprise and variety occur when you chum offshore, but it can happen in protected waters as well.

When practicing one of the deep-chumming systems described earlier, try both sinker-rigged bottom baits and—if possible—baits drifted along near bottom. By using a light sinker, and lobbing the bait toward the bow of the boat, you can often get it down deep enough to cover a fair range of territory. Another good device is to use a shrimp or strip of bait on a jig. This can be bottom-fished as effectively as a sinker rig, and can also be moved along slowly. Experiment to see which approach works best. And if you lose the bait, you still might catch a fish by retrieving the bare jig.

Again, your bait should pretty much match the chum—cut baits for use around ground fish, shrimp or crab if chumming with shellfish for crustacean feeders. Most fish-feeding predators will happily gulp a shrimp, but the reverse may not be true. A lot of crustacean feeders ignore cut fish.

INSHORE STILL-FISHING

Chum can make a good spot even better, and in many instances will produce fish that you otherwise would not get at all. But, as was said earlier, a great deal of productive still-fishing certainly does not require chum. The emphasis is on anchoring in the right place, but baits and methods must not be underrated.

Inshore bottom fishing is probably the most widely practiced of anchored specialties. Some people like the potluck approach; others fish selectively for species that range from panfish all the way to biggies like giant drum and jewfish. A few of the "super-sport" fish—for instance, bluefish, tarpon, and channel bass—can regularly be caught by bottom fishing with dead baits. There are

A whole blue crab fished on bottom produced this 45-pound black drum for Al Pflueger, Jr.

times, too, when a live bait, fished on bottom with a sinker, does the best work on sportsters such as snook, striped bass, and cobia—even though they more often respond better to a free-drifting bait.

Selection of a bottom rig is no cause for anxiety. Several different ones are described and illustrated in Chapter 10, but that doesn't mean you have to bite your fingernails over making a choice. It's just that certain rigs become "standard" by virtue of long use in different regions. Those labeled "bottom rigs" in Chapter 10 are more likely to be chosen by Pacific and North Atlantic coast fishermen, while the ones called "egg-sinker rigs" are the pets of bottom fishermen along South Atlantic and Gulf shores. If those anglers swapped territories, they could use their home rigs to equal effect in the new waters.

Regardless of the rig, it must be scaled to the bait you choose and the fish you are after. The rule of thumb, as always, is to use the lightest sinker that will reach and hold bottom. Your tackle, though, will have something to do with this selection, since inshore bottom fishing is practiced with every style and size of tackle imaginable. A spinning outfit with thin line dictates a smaller sinker than would be used with a boat rod and heavy line—even though the same baits and hooks are being fished by both.

Bait selection, however, can be quite important. Many bottom feeders gratefully accept any morsel that comes their way, whether it be cut fish, shrimp, seaworm, squid, or crab. For the potluck approach, use whatever is available or economical. Certain species, though, can be very selective. Local bait dealers, and other customers you meet in the store, can be helpful in making determinations. Shrimp and squid seem to be the most universally accepted baits, if you're in doubt.

When live baits are fished from an anchored boat they are usually, but not always, presented off-bottom. They may be free-lined out from the boat or fished below a float. Live shrimp, crabs, worms, or baitfish can all be treated in this manner. Often you might find it advisable to get down fairly deep, but not all the way to bottom. Light split-shot or clinch sinkers are helpful here, as they can gain you the necessary depth without hindering bait freedom all that much. This approach is often a killer on seatrout or weakfish, among others, even though the same fish will at times hit anything from a surface plug to a bottom bait.

When a fairly large live baitfish is presented smack on bottom—as in snook fishing in Florida passes—the egg-sinker rig is much to be preferred, because the bait doesn't have to lug around the weight.

Bottom fishing often requires patience, and it also requires practice. For one thing, you should learn to keep your line taut, and this isn't always as easy as it might sound, because of current or wind conditions. Then you must learn the proper response when a fish bites. Most often, you should ignore little taps and nudges—setting the hook only after you feel a strong pull. But with a few bottom species—sheepshead and tautog among them—all you *ever* get is a little tap or two. Delay setting the hook, and the fish is gone with your bait.

Usually it's best to hit back at once when a fish takes a live shrimp or small minnow, but delay the strike if something grabs a larger type of baitfish. Give the fish time to get it well in its mouth.

OFFSHORE STILL-FISHING

"Big baits for big fish" is an old angling axiom that was never more true than in offshore bottom fishing. Even out there in deep water, small fish usually outnumber big ones—and the little fellows are less cautious. Give them half a chance and they'll devour your bait greedily before a lunker makes up his mind.

So if you hope to nab bragging-size bottom fish—fat snappers, groupers, and others—think first of hefty baits like mullet heads, half a fish, or a whole

Big groupers like big baits. A fish head, whole dead fish, or big chunk of cut bait is needed to fill a maw this size.

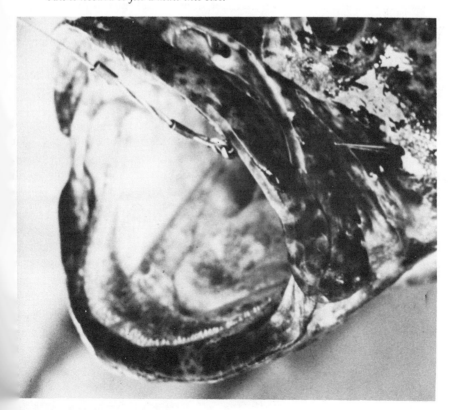

dead fish of reasonably small size. Bait-stealers may nibble away, but they seldom destroy the bait before a lunker gets a shot at it. If live baitfish are at hand, they are even more attractive and durable.

It's true, though, that smaller pieces of cut bait will take big fish. And in some cases you're fishing with the hope of mopping up on modest-size prey—say red or gray snappers averaging a pound or so—and thus are committed to rather small baits. In that case it probably will help to let your rig hit bottom, then turn the crank of your reel a couple of times to raise the bait a few feet. This is a good idea, anyway, since it minimizes hangups. Snapper, grouper, cod, and most other primary bottom-fishing targets don't mind going up a short distance for their dinner, but many kinds of tiny bait-stealers are reluctant to get that far away from cover.

You also have the option of fishing small baits on one rig, while tossing out a mullet head or live bait on another rod that you set aside in a holder. That system doesn't work out too well on crowded party boats, or any other boat where the odd line keeps getting in the way.

For getting baits down in deep water, the bank-sinker bottom rig is much to be preferred over an egg-sinker arrangement. Being rigged at the tail end of your leader, the bank sinker dives straight and true, carrying the baits along obediently behind.

If you must use a sliding egg sinker—and they come in sizes plenty large enough for this work—you'll have to let your line out more slowly, and with pauses on the way down. This is because the egg sinker is *above* your leader. Being heavier, it will sink first—maybe running far up the line, and causing the leader and hook to double up and tangle in the line.

Should you have only egg sinkers at your disposal, you can save a lot of headaches by simply tying them to the end of your rig, in bank-sinker fashion, rather than letting them slide above the leader.

Locating a good area of reef, bank, or rock bottom is the toughest problem the offshore bait-dunker faces. Commercial skippers, with the aid of depth recorders and electronic navigation equipment, have little trouble getting to the promised land. For private boaters, the process can be long and tedious, but it's necessary.

Off southeast Florida and other tropical reef areas, the problem is somewhat simplified in that the fisherman has quite a broad expanse of at least potentially productive territory in which to mount his search. A simple trial-and-error process of anchoring and reanchoring a few times may hit paydirt. Also, the water is clear and variations in bottom color can be spotted in depth ranging up to 80 or 100 feet on occasion. Further visual checking, with glass-bottom bucket or diving mask, can disclose whether dark coloration of the bottom is rocky or merely grassy.

In most coastal areas, however, the productive banks, rock patches, or reefs are usually more isolated and there is seldom any hope of using visual checks. You'll have to inquire as to the approximate locations of popular bottom-fishing areas. Such information can be obtained at marinas, docks, and some tackle stores. The best you can hope to find out is how far, which direction, and approximate running time.

Obviously, that skimpy information is completely useless if it refers to a really limited spot. But it can be valid as a starting point if it refers to a broad area over which stretches of good bottom occur.

Once you reach the broad area, as nearly as you can determine, a search must start. Even if you have a fathometer, the hunt might be a long one, and it will pay to stop and check any small lumps or ledges that show on the graph. Some reaches of the ocean and Gulf simply don't have any really imposing bottom structure. Any deviation from surrounding flat bottom can harbor some darn good fish.

Lacking a fathometer, about the only thing you can do is drift while dragging baits along the bottom, hoping to catch a species of fish that normally sticks to reef or cover. Small trash fish that you might run into on sand or soft bottom don't count. But if you capture even a small fish of a variety that likes rough habitat, anchor and start fishing. Chances are the larger and more desirable fish are there too.

Whenever you do find a good fishing spot, take bearings, if at all possible, so you'll be able to come back again (instructions for taking cross-bearings are given in Chapter 12). If you can't see any shoreline landmarks at all, then at least return home in as straight a line as you can steer, taking note of your speed or RPM, and approximate running time. You'd never be able to return to the same exact spot, of course, but you could get back to the area, and perhaps run across another one.

15
DRIFT-FISHING

By allowing his baits to trail behind a drifting boat, the fisherman can cover a lot more territory and bring his offerings to the attention of more fish. For this reason, drifting is almost always a good approach when testing unfamiliar waters, but at the same time it is a standard system that is often practiced by careful design.

When viewed as a potluck system, there is no better way to assure that something will frequently be tugging at your line. This is especially attractive to any youngsters aboard, who may share your enthusiasm over landing a fat bluefish or seatrout, but demand in the meantime to be engaged in a battle of wits with the various kinds of panfish and bottom fish that roam many drifting areas.

Even when undertaken selectively and with particular targets, drifting produces pleasant surprises more often than not.

Some other considerations may recommend drift-fishing among alternate possibilities available to you. For one thing, more anglers can fish more comfortably, since an entire length of the boat can be utilized—rather than having all lines bunched over the stern, as is the case when trolling and often when anchored. For another, boat movement gives action to your baits, meaning that dead baits may work as well as live ones on some choosy types of gamefish.

Broadly speaking, drift-fishing covers three areas of operation—inshore drifting over fairly shallow flats; inshore drifting in deeper waters, principally channels and passes; and offshore drifting. A number of specialized offshoots have been developed. Some of them, such as deep jigging and kite fishing, are the subjects of separate chapters.

Any kind of drifting, however, requires attention to certain basic considerations. One of the most important is recognizing when to crank up and *redrift*. When you start picking up good fish, you should immediately become alerted to the possibility that it might shortly be advisable to motor upwind and go over the same route once more. On the other hand, you don't want to leave a productive stretch of water too quickly. Give new customers a reasonable chance to bite, but when response definitely declines, go back to where the action was. And at this point, take care to avoid the one big mistake so often made by inexperienced drift-fishermen—that of running your motor over the productive area. Make a wide circle when returning to the head of the drift.

You may not realize that both the attitude and direction of a free-drifting boat can be influenced to your advantage. Few boats will drift absolutely broadside to the wind, because of motor drag and variations in hulls, to say nothing of any effects of water current. A broadside attitude is generally the most desirable, since all lines trail straight and clear of each other. In an outboard boat you can "square off" most efficiently by tilting the leg of the motor entirely out of the water. If the lower unit of either an outboard or inboard-outboard motor must be left in the water, some correction is possible by simply "steering"—that is, should you wish to square off by swinging the bow to the right, turn the wheel to full-right steering position. Seldom will this achieve a full broadside attitude, but it can improve things.

Even when no currents are involved, few boats drift directly downwind either. You may have the impression of a straight drift, but the boat actually is tacking slightly, favoring the direction in which the bow is pointing.

Let's say the wind is out of the north, and the bow of your boat is pointed west. You drift toward the south, but at the same time you keep easing westward. If there happens to be a strong east-to-west current flow, you head westward more rapidly.

What has all this got to do with drift-fishing success? Only this: When you find a productive stretch of drift, and wish to go back and drift it again, chances are you won't be able to get there by running straight upwind. Thus, it's very important to keep orienting your position to stationary reference points—shoreline landmarks or nearby navigation markers, if any. And the time to do this is when the fish are biting. Difficult as it is, take time to look around and judge your position as best you can.

Offshore, this kind of orientation is usually impossible, which is why you should throw out your own marking buoy when you run across a hot spot. See Chapter 6 for how to make such a buoy.

INSHORE DRIFTING

Throughout the South, probably the one most popular form of saltwater fishing from boats is drifting across fairly shallow and grassy flats. The target is speckled trout, or spotted weakfish, but bluefish and Spanish mackerel are often caught, as are jack, ladyfish, sea bass, and a wide array of panfish. And the good drifting areas are usually within easy reach of rental skiffs with low-horsepower motors.

Essentially the same system is employed in virtually every coastal area, and with different goals in mind. Much drifting is done over sandy or soft bottom for such fish as fluke, flounder, and kingfish (whiting).

Tackle choice is of little consequence. Spinning gear is most often used, simply because more people own it. Bait-casting gear is equally effective, and even boat rods can be used, because casting is not really a necessity. You can simply peel line off the reel and allow it to drift away from the moving boat.

Working a bucktail over grass flats of the Florida Keys produced this 5-pound spotted seatrout for Bill Porter.

Many trout fishermen use no leader at all. However, a monofilament leader two or three times the strength of the line always affords an extra safeguard. And if blues or mackerel are in the area, a light wire leader is not amiss.

Most "trout flats" are in water averaging 4 or 5 feet deep and seldom more than 10 feet. Ideally, the baits should stay well below the surface, but above the grass to prevent constant fouling. With a moderate breeze, the baits normally trail just right without a sinker. A fast drift will bring the baits up, and dictate the addition of a split-shot or a light clinch-on sinker a foot or so above the hook—just enough to keep it under the surface, not on bottom. Conversely, when the drift is so slow that even an unweighted bait keeps fouling, it's best to use a float. Many anglers habitually use a popping cork anyway.

Of course, if your main targets are bottom-hugging fish over grass-free bottom, you should use a sinker rig regularly.

By far the best baits for use over grass flats are live shrimp and small strips of cut fish. The strips do not have to be carefully tailored, but merely rough-cut in elongated style rather than chunked. Spotted trout take a strip just as avidly as a shrimp, which means that your bait bill can be lowered.

Those same baits will produce fish in just about any area and over any kind of bottom, but, as always, local preferences as to baits for different fish should always be heeded, though not necessarily adhered to religiously.

More and more drifting fishermen, particularly over the grass beds, are using artificial lures. Some have gone to fake baits exclusively, while others like to drift a natural bait in regular fashion while they use another outfit to cast on the downwind side of the boat.

Trout hit just about any kind of artificial, but the one most productive type seems to be a plastic-tail jig, also called bait-tail. Close behind are mirror plugs, and other shallow, darting designs. Surface plugs can be quite productive, and, of course, are the most exciting. It goes without saying that all these lures are attractive to other predatory fish as well as trout.

When used as the primary weapon of a drifter, the bait-tail jig, or even a bucktail, should be fished in much the same fashion as a natural bait, and often catches bigger fish, if not more of them. Toss the jig upwind and let it drift like a bait. You'll probably be surprised at how many fish grab it on a straight drift—junk fish as well as gamesters. However, you should work the jig by lifting or twitching the rod tip from time to time. Don't try to keep the lure dancing continuously. Let the line straighten out again between movements of the rod.

On a fast-to-moderate drift you may not have to retrieve the jig at all while working it in the manner described. And even if the drift is not brisk enough to keep your lure off bottom, the same movements, combined with a slow retrieve, work just as well.

Downwind casting can be productive too, but here you will have to retrieve pretty fast even to impart normal action to the lure. That's because the boat is drifting in the direction of the cast and making it tougher to keep a tight line.

A very good casting direction is either straight off the bow or straight off the stern. This has the effect of swinging the lure, much as if you were fishing across a river current, giving it an extra lifelike appearance and covering a bit more ground than with a regular straight-line retrieve. This type of cast is especially attractive if you happen to be a fly-rodder.

Going back now to jigs that are simply trailed behind the moving boat, let's point out that they can also be a most useful vehicle for natural-bait drifting—perhaps the best of all. Instead of using a hook, or a hook and sinker, you simply stick a strip of bait, or a piece of shrimp, to the hook of the jig.

Sweetened in this manner, the jig provides both the smell appeal of bait and the extra action of a lure. Basically, you just let the combination drift along. But occasionally you might give it some short twitches. If you get a good bite but fail to hook up, jig the lure sharply a few times. The fish may slug it again, even though it got the bait on its first whack.

By changing jig size you should be able to adjust for the desired depth—using perhaps a ¼- or ⅛-ounce model for a slow drift in shallow water, and a ⅜- or ½-ounce size for deeper demands.

In addition to being a great coaxer of predatory fish, a baited jig is greedily accepted by bottom feeders as well. I don't think there's a better setup going for nudging a drifted bait along clear bottom for flounder.

DRIFT-FISHING IN CHANNELS AND PASSES

All the advice in the preceding section applies equally to inshore drifting in shallow water and deep—the only obvious changes being in the weight needed for your baits or lures to attain the proper depth. Now the subject turns to drifting techniques in channels, passes, inlets, and tide rips—not because the water is generally deeper, but as a specialized approach to fishing certain game species which love to romp and feed in such places.

Among the best-known examples of this particular endeavor are tide-rip jigging for bluefish on the Atlantic Coast, and jigging or live-baiting for tarpon in passes along Florida's Gulf shore. But the same conditions under which those fish are found are equally attractive to many gamefish in many different parts of the country—snook, striped bass, and mackerel, to name just a few.

The fishing area is usually well defined and, to some extent at least, limited. More often than not, it's the current or tidal flow that moves your boat, regardless of wind direction.

In some places—as at Boca Grande pass in southwest Florida—the productive depths have been so well established over many years that little or no experimenting in this regard is necessary. Most Boca Grande guides present their tarpon baits at 60 or 42 feet, depending on their position in the pass. It's not that critical, and many a tarpon has been nailed at other depths, but strikes at those two levels are so dependable that the regulars stick to them.

Most other fish, in most other deep-drifting spots, aren't at all predictable. Your first challenge is to determine the feeding strata. This can be done by making repeated drifts with live baits, sending them to different depths each time. Or it can be done by jigging.

A drifted live herring was the downfall of this nice striped bass.

Al Pflueger, Jr., caught this 8-pound bluefish while drifting and jigging deep near a jetty.

The most common approach by tide-rip bluefishermen is to use a flashy metallic squid or jig, sometimes sweetened with a small strip of real squid. This is dropped to bottom and then the rod is lifted up and down—jigged—several times, with pauses in between so that the jig can dive and wobble downward. If there are no takers, then a slightly higher level is probed in the same manner. This might be done by simply cranking the squid upward a few turns, but usually the drift is so fast that it's best to bring the lure all the way back and drop it once more—this time letting it hit bottom, but retrieving a few feet before starting to jig. Once the fish are found, then every effort is made to continue jigging at the proven depth.

Pacific Coast fishermen use similar jigs for similar work, but the Southern angler—though he doesn't change the system much—will replace the metal squid with his own regional version of a jig, which is a lead-head hook trimmed with bucktail or a plastic tail. Many a Northern fisherman uses both bucktail jigs and metallic squids. Maybe this indicates that Southerners are just more stubborn, because either type is productive anywhere.

Jigs weighing no more than 1 ounce will reach bottom in most cases. Occasionally, a combination of extra-deep channel and strong current will require a jig weighing 2 to 3 ounces. Should the fish-producing depth be fairly shallow, of course, lighter jigs can be used more comfortably, and will also be better for smaller fish, such as mackerel and lightweight blues.

Both tarpon and striped bass roam various levels, even as the bluefish do, and may be striking best near bottom one day, near the surface tomorrow. On the other hand, almost all snook and channel bass in passes or deep channels feed down deep.

Live bait for deep drifting should be selected in accordance with natural forage if at all possible. In many another kind of angling, a variety of live baits might work equally well, but fish that collect in rips and passes are usually there to munch on something in particular. They can be quite selective. Tarpon, for instance, habitually feed on small crabs that flow through passes with the tide, but at times crabs seem to be in short supply and live baitfish get more hits.

Sometimes, unfortunately, you must experiment to find out not only where the fish are feeding, but what kind of bait or lure they prefer.

OFFSHORE DRIFTING

Weekend skippers may be excused if, at first, they tend to think of offshore angling only in terms of surface trolling. After all, skipping baits across the top of blue water has been the bread-and-butter of charter cruisers for many years, and there's no denying the effectiveness of the system for sailfish, dolphin, tuna, and many other free-roaming ocean gamefish.

But, like any other angling method, surface trolling has its ups and downs—and over the course of the entire season there may well be as many downs as ups. Charter captains realize this. Progressive skippers are constantly seeking other methods of putting fish in the boat during days (or weeks) when surface trolling just doesn't provide sustained action. This approach has led to many fine innovations such as deep trolling, slow trolling with live blue runner or balao, anchoring and chumming, and using a kite.

I feel it is even more important for the private boater to regard surface trolling not as a religion, but merely as one of several offshore specialties to be considered when the time is right. In the long run, various types of drift-fishing will probably produce just as many sails and other pelagic fish—and beyond any doubt will provide many more catches of fish in general, from bottom fish to surface acrobats.

The reason, of course, is that you can cover various depths of water when drifting. Also, you can fish more lines at once, and even practice two or three different fishing methods, with different types of tackle, simultaneously.

Live baits, rigged baits, and artificial lures can all join in the act, but serious drifting efforts should always, by choice, center around live baits, with the other used as supplements.

An extra-big bait, sent deep with a heavy sinker, is used by offshore drift-fishermen seeking amberjack.

The first consideration, therefore, is to obtain a goodly supply of live bait and have provisions for keeping it frisky. Never depend on catching your live bait on the spot. Map plans to collect the bait on your way out to the fishing grounds. From many launching spots you'll have to cross shallow areas of grass or rock to reach the outside, and in such places you can fish for bait. Grass flats are especially good for pinfish—one of the most-used offshore baits, and one of the hardiest in a live well. And while fishing for pinfish, you might well pick up some blue runners or other types of small jack, which are even better than pinfish in the estimation of most anglers. Sock away any other little fish you might catch—pigfish, grunt, snapper, yellowtail, spot, croaker porgy. Those are "eatin' fish," true, but the ideal bait-size specimens are smaller than you'd normally want to put on the table. Besides, you're after big stuff.

For baitfishing, try No. 8 or 10 panfish hooks baited with small bits of shrimp or cut fish. One or two split shot complete the rig. Or fix up a standard bottom rig with two or three dropper lines above a terminal sinker (see Chapter 10), and you might haul up baitfish a couple at a crack.

As noted, blue runners are especially desirable bait, and in areas where they occur it will pay you to scout for places where they can be caught with some regularity. Certain navigation markers generally attract runners. When fishing for runners at a marker, the best rig seems to be a small nylon jig tipped with a piece of shrimp. Cast it toward the marker and let it sink to bottom, then jig it upward.

Few baits are better than live balao, which can be caught in the Keys and some other southern Florida areas by anchoring and chumming, and fishing with tiny hooks and cut baits once balao start responding to the chum. Any ground chum will attract balao, but an especially convenient one is dry oat

Once you see balao in the chum line, cut way back on the amount of chum used, because you must lure the little fish within reach of your line.

If worst comes to worst in your bait procurement, you can go ahead and try to pick up some grunts or something out in deep water.

By now you may have the idea that getting live bait is not always so easy, and right you are. Still, you shouldn't resent the time put into the job, because once you start drifting such baits offshore your reward can come quickly.

If offshore drifting is to give you a shot simultaneously at billfish, bottom fish, and most things in between, then your drifting area has to be located in billfish territory—or rather at the edges of it, where bottom can be reached by some of your rigs without too much difficulty. In southeast Florida and the

When the fishing area is reasonably well known, small-boat anglers can take more sailfish by drifting with live baits than by trolling. The same system also provides a simultaneous crack at both reef and pelagic gamefish. With one sailfish already in boat, angler Bob Lewis gets set to release another off Miami.

Keys, best results on a full range of species can be expected in the vicinity of the outside dropoff, in water ranging from approximately 80 to 200 feet deep. That same depth range is the most desirable anywhere, though in other areas of the country it may be located much farther offshore than it is in southern Florida.

Two baits definitely should be used—one at the surface and the other down deep, quite near bottom. The surface bait may be either free-lined or used with a float. A toy balloon, inflated and tied to the swivel between line and leader, makes the best float, though a piece of scrap plastic foam can also be used.

For the deep bait, rig a stationary trolling sinker, weighing 4 to 6 ounces, at the top of your leader. Let the weighted rig down all the way to bottom, if you can reach it. Engage the gears of the reel and the drift of the boat will lift your rig far enough off bottom to prevent hanging. However, if you notice any bumping as you drift into shallower water, give the reel handle a few cranks.

With both the surface and deep baits, you should use one of the offshore leaders described in Chapter 10, and about 9 feet long, as sailfish are among your possible catches.

The deep bait must necessarily be hooked through both lips, since a hook positioned on top would pull the baitfish in an unnatural attitude through the water. For the float bait, try a back hookup at first. Unless there is an exceptionally strong drift, the bait should be able to swim freely. If it starts to drag change to the lip hookup.

With those two rigs alone, you're pretty well covered. But now—depending on your ambition, the length of your boat, and the number of anglers aboard—there are several other things you can try while waiting for something to find your drifting live baits.

You can deep-jig.

You can fish a dead bait down deep for snapper or grouper—not that you deep-fished live one won't take the same fish.

You can free-line a rigged balao.

Just be careful that whatever you choose as a supplementary offering doesn't keep fouling up either of your two live-bait lines.

There's a perfect way of avoiding such trouble—use a kite. Since the kite flies to the *downwind* side of the boat, it enables you to fish your surface live bait (or baits) completely out of the way. Fly one or two live baits from the kite, and you have that much more room to operate on the regular or upwind side.

Kite fishing is explained in detail in Chapter 19.

Let's review just three of many different angling combinations that are possible:

1. Use *all* live baits—one below a float, one down deep, and, if you have a kite, two more off the other side of the boat. A more alluring invitation to billfish, king mackerel, and other pelagic gamesters could scarcely be imagined. And the deep bait might also cause you trouble with grouper, snapper, and amberjack.

2. If you lean more toward bottom action, but wouldn't mind the chance of getting a sail or something at the same time, use just one live bait at the surface—on a kite, preferably, but with a float if you have no kite—and then concentrate on fishing deep with either live or rigged baits, or by deep jigging.

3. If your bag is casting artificial lures, put out a surface live bait anyway. Then deep-jig while the live bait acts as a decoy. It might well attract a prize fish. And with prompt action and a little luck, your buddy might be able to yank the bait away in time for you to get a lure to the fish.

We could go on and on, but the point is simply that you drift from one to four live baits, and easily work other styles of angling around them.

Adopt this approach as a steady diet and over the course of a few offshore trips you'll probably get as many sailfish as your trolling pals, and a lot of other action to boot.

Be careful, though, not to bite off more than you can chew. It takes constant attention and effort to monitor several lines at once, and even then you may have trouble keeping up—or doing what needs to be done at the right time.

A logical approach when there are two anglers aboard is for each to fish one line, while a live bait is kept out on an unattended rig that either fisherman can get to when necessary. With three anglers, two unattended lines might be used.

16

FISHING FROM BEACH BRIDGE, AND SHORE

Excellent opportunities for the shorebound fisherman exist in all coastal areas—so many, in fact, and so varied, that a lot of anglers remain shorebound by choice, not economic necessity.

There isn't a single species of inshore sport fish that can't be taken from one shoreline station or another—surf, jetty, bridge, pier, dock, seawall, or wading flat. This includes all the "glamor" fish of saltwater circles, as well as the many different fun and food fish that blanket our Atlantic, Gulf, and Pacific coasts. Nor can any be considered as only rare or freak catches. Striped bass, tarpon, channel bass, permit, bonefish, corbina, snook, bluefish, weakfish—all are ready prospects.

Moreover, some gamesters that normally are considered "offshore" fish can be taken, in proper season, from ocean piers and jetties in certain areas.

Specialists abound among onshore anglers, even as they do in boating ranks. There are folks hooked on surfcasting for stripers; bridge fishing for snook; wading for seatrout and redfish; working the surf for corbina or pompano. And you'll find specialists of broader scope as well—people who prefer the surf, say, or the piers, but who are happy with whatever their stomping ground might produce, whether a 30-pound lunker or a mess of whiting.

But it's no secret that the host of shorebound fishermen stands willing and ready to take each opportunity as it arises, and to toss a bait or lure from any spot offering access to the water.

SURF-FISHING TECHNIQUES

Say "surf fishing" and your first mental image probably will be of crashing breakers, of long and rugged rods, of 4-ounce sinkers or 6-inch lures sailing far over the foam. That's the classic picture, of course, and one that's true enough. But it's far from complete.

Surf conditions vary tremendously, not only from one section of the cou try to another, but also within the same section. On some beaches the waves boom and roar. On others they rumble or merely sigh. On some they are entirely still and quiet. Thus there is at least an occasional niche in the surf-fishing world for even the lightest kinds of casting tackle, including fly rods. In some territories, very light gear predominates—the mainland Gulf Coast, for example.

Where the surf is well behaved, extremely long casts may not be necessary. In fact, distance tossing can often work to your disadvantage, because many kinds of both large and small fish habitually cruise right up to the edge of the sand, looking for baitfish or crustaceans tumbling in the wash.

Many an inexperienced surf fisherman has spent a fruitless day heaving his baits as far out as he could manage, when he might well have made a good catch by pitching them much closer to shore.

Surf scene—Cape Hatteras National Seashore.

Beaches of the Florida Gulf Coast turn up snook regularly. Since surf is calm and fish are close to shore, light rods and small lures can easily be used.

On the other hand, there can be times when the longest cast you ca muscle, with the stoutest surf gear available to you, just doesn't quite reac paydirt.

The sum of these observations is that surfing tackle must basically I scaled to the conditions an angler most often faces—and the serious surf fisl erman will then go on to add other outfits as he recognizes the need for the in meeting specific jobs.

In popular terminology, the term "surf tackle" is bestowed on either co ventional or spinning outfits designed to deliver extra-long casts with fair heavy sinkers and lures. In skilled hands, and with terminal rigs in the 4- 6-ounce range, the longest casts of all are obtainable with conventional ge Such an outfit consists of a very stiff glass or Calcutta rod, averaging about feet in overall length, and fitted with a smooth-running surf or ocean casti reel, spooled with 36-pound braided nylon squidding line.

Rods as long as 14 or even 16 feet are seen on occasion, but the majority of surf experts feel that a 10- or 11-footer is long enough.

Somewhat lighter conventional gear is the norm for throwing artificial squids and plugs, or sinkers weighing 2 to 4 ounces. The rods are as long, perhaps even longer on occasion, but with more casting action. And to improve distance with lighter weights, line test generally is dropped to 27- or perhaps even 18-pound.

Although spinning tackle is more often chosen for lighter surfing needs, conventional outfits can be optionally used—say a light 8-foot rod, smaller surf reel, and 12- or 15-pound line.

There is spinning tackle, of course, to cover all the heavier surf-fishing applications as well—long-butt rods reaching 12 feet in length, and wide-drum reels that handle monofilament line of 15- or 20-pound test. There are even giant-size spinning reels that can take suitable capacities of 30-pound line.

Be advised, however, that no matter how heavy your spinning tackle might be, casting 5- and 6-ounce weights is a rugged proposition. Your poor little forefinger, holding the line for a cast, simply may not survive the job, even if heavily taped. Best leave that kind of work to the big conventional rigs.

By far the most popular bottom rigs for surf fishing are the pyramid-sinker setups, two of which are shown in Chapter 10. No other sinker style does half as good a job of holding to sand bottom in the face of constant surging of waves and backcurrents. On occasion, though, and especially in more gentle surf, it is desirable to have the bait moving around so that it has a better chance of coming to the attention of a hungry fish. Therefore, a bank sinker of equivalent weight can be substituted for the pyramid.

Sinker size seldom is dictated by the kind of fish you hope to catch, but only by what is needed in order to cast as far as you want to, and to hold bottom with fair efficiency in a particular surf condition. Small hooks and small baits are routinely used with just as heavy sinkers as big hooks and big baits.

For close-in fishing with light spinning tackle and in calm surf, the sliding egg sinker is quite a good choice.

Among many productive surf baits are cut mossbunker or mullet, seaworms, shrimp, squid, clams, and sand fleas. All of them are as attractive to panfish (and trash fish) as they are to larger game species, and it can be a never-ending struggle for the surfer to keep a presentable bait on his hook.

Quite obviously, the initial step is to match bait size (and hook size) to your ideas of what you would like to have inhale the offering. A large bait doesn't necessarily mean you won't be troubled by unwanted interlopers, but it's a start. With very soft baits, it's always worth the time it takes to secure the bait to the hook with thread.

Without doubt, the most versatile family of artificials you can use in surf-casting is the lineup of metallic lures variously called squids, jigs, or wobblers. They are described in Chapter 4. These lures cast like a bullet, and their erratic, flashy action imitates the silvery baitfishes on which so many surf-roaming predators feed. Certain designs can be obtained that more closely imitate particular bait species, such as sand eels. And the popular lines of metallic squids come in weights to suit all sorts of tackle, from 1 ounce or less to as much as 3 or 4 ounces, and sometimes heavier.

Except when you're casting to preselected spots, a good approach to squid-fishing is to cast as far as you can, and then try several different retrieves on succeeding long casts, covering a lot of water each time.

Two lures with nearly equal results. Bass on left went for a plastic worm rig; one on right chose a slender-minnow plug. Both hit in the surf at Nags Head, N.C.

Metal jigs, like the one that fooled this big bluefish, are among the best of surf lures because of the variety of productive retrieves they afford.

Unless a pattern is already established, varying the retrieve is extremely important, because fish sometimes go for a slow-to-medium retrieve right down on bottom, and at other times prefer a fast-moving lure near the top. Nor can such preferences be broken down by species. Today's striper might be feasting on fast-swimming baitfish; tomorrow's might be forced to search the bottom for anything that comes along. The versatile metallic squids can fool it in any case.

Hold your rod tip high and crank fast. The lure will stay up and wobble with extra enthusiasm. Lower the rod tip and crank slowly. The lure will sink down, yet still maintain an enticing slow wiggle.

But no one lure is perfect all the time, and so big surf plugs can be used to complement the squids—topwater models to splash and gurgle and perhaps draw fish from longer distances; underwater swimmers for several purposes, but especially if you want a big lure that will run *both* deep and fairly fast.

Another honored member of the surfer's lure kit is an eelskin, sometimes rigged right onto a metal squid, but also used with a weighted head to allow for casting. The skins fill with water on the retrieve for a natural look and action. In recent years, plastic eels and worms have come along to make things easier.

Once again we have to consider that in the many stretches of coast where heavy surf tackle isn't needed, all the popular saltwater artificials become "surf lures." Mirror plugs get a big play in those areas, as do bucktail and bait-tail jigs, and smaller metal squids or spoons.

A bucktail or bait-tail jig, nudged *very* slowly along bottom, is usually a killer for snook, seatrout, and redfish (small channel bass) on Gulf beaches. But those fish, too, have their wilder feeding periods and may, at times, insist on surface plugs or darting underwater plugs and spoons.

How do you find fish in the surf? Any way you can. That wasn't really meant to be a smart-alec statement. There are many promising things you can look for, as we'll see in a moment, but even the most knowledgeable of surf men often put in long hours of searching and trial-and-error—cruising the shore in beach buggies or four-wheel-drive vehicles, listening to the surfer's "grapevine," or simply waiting it out in a spot that should be, or has been in the past, productive.

Along many areas, especially where the water depth drops off gradually from the surf line, you can often do wonders by exploring the beach at low tide and making note of runs or sloughs. These are simply trenches or channels dug out by the action of wave and current. Few are deep but they are at least deeper than surrounding waters and fish use them as natural pathways when coming in to feed. Spot the sloughs on low tide; fish them when the tide starts to rise.

Some of the sloughs are close and obvious at low tide. Others may be farther out and not easily definable, yet the alert angler can identify some of those as well, through such clues as color changes in the water, or wave action that is different from surrounding patterns.

By the same token, be alert for any waves that continually break in one area, farther out than the rest of the breakers. A fairly long line of such breakers might indicate a deep slough on one side or the other of the breaking line itself (which is shallow). A small area of breakers usually indicates a shoal, or perhaps a rock pile, around which fish might well feed. Be aware

Waders can find good fishing for spotted seatrout just about everywhere along the Gulf Coast. And this nice string, caught at Carolina Beach Inlet near Wilmington, N.C., proves Atlantic anglers aren't left out of the picture. Best trout-wading country of all is the Indian River waterway of east-central Florida.

however, that many beaches—particularly in certain areas of the Pacific Coast—are so shallow for so far out that several lines of whitewater waves may generally be present. Clues to fish conditions, if available at all, will be much more subtle and hard to read.

Rocks are always good prospects, and more so if flanked by stretches of sand beach. Most of the desirable surf fish like to explore for food around rocks, and some types *require* such a habitat.

Points and capes are almost invariably good surf-fishing areas because of rips, eddies, and crosscurrents that usually are found around them.

FISHING THE OCEAN PIERS

Each fishing pier seems to be its own little angling world, frequently complete with tackle and bait shop, restaurant, "mates" or attendants, and maybe even a sheltered place in which to take a nap. And, more to the point, an angling menu that would surprise anyone not accustomed to visiting the piers.

Much pier fishing is highly seasonal, but during the long periods between "runs" of mackerel, bluefish, or whatever, something is always going on. Usually it's many things. Not that all of them are exceptionally productive, but the opportunities are there.

If a run happens to be going on, everybody will be ganged together, flailing away in common fashion. But at other times, pier fishermen separate into various groups, concentrating on a particular interest, and often are oblivious to the activities of other groups.

Seasonal runs of fish, such as blues and mackerel, make ocean piers a hectic scene. Here the angler on left hustles to clear his line while an attendant moves up with long-handled landing net.

At given periods, and depending, of course, on season and pier location, here are some of the specialties that attract attention:

Fish the surf, by staying close to the beach end of the pier. Almost every-where, northern kingfish or whiting can be taken in this manner, along with flounder, surf perch, croaker, and the special prize—pompano. While shrimp and similar baits will take most of them, pompano specialists always prefer sand fleas.

The middle reaches of the pier are usually worked by people seeking most of those same species of fish, along with spot or other popular panfish types. Here too, just outside the surf, you may find a corps of anglers using off-bottom baits below a float in quest of weakfish. The "middle pier" folks are aware that the fish they're after might be caught out on the end of the pier, but the middle is as good as any, and they are generally content to leave the end to more adventurous anglers after big stuff.

Meanwhile, there's a fellow over here dropping a crab straight down by the pilings, where he hopes a sheepshead is waiting; and another over there bumping a lure slowly along bottom in quest of flounder.

Really big fish are an ever-present hope on many piers. In the South, tar-pon frequently come around, and sometimes, the only tarpon ever taken in a given area fall victim to pier anglers. When you reach Florida, tarpon become regulars and are joined by snook.

Among deepwater fish that roam within reach of piers are king mackerel, bonito or little tunny, cobia, and big barracuda.

Big sharks can be caught from piers, while smaller ones are common. Some piers boast shark-fishing regulars.

Being little structures in a huge sea, piers must be content with what the ocean gods might send their way. But if pier fishermen lack the range of a boater, or even a surfer, they help make up for it with one obvious advantage. Personnel at the commercial piers are able to give *precise* information as to what's going on. They can tell you exactly what rigs and baits have been tak-ing certain species, and on what tides and times. Besides that, they can usu-ally sell you what you need on the spot. It's impossible to keep all the spe-cialty baits on hand at all times, but the piers try.

Ideal tackle choice for a pier-fishing specialist is a surf outfit, either con-ventional or spinning. Such a rig allows you to make long casts when called for, and is also a potent weapon for controlling big fish once they reach the vicinity of the pilings.

Even when going after small fish, rather stout tackle is a good idea, since you'll have to crank your fish many feet through the air. Light spinning rods can handle the fish all right, but are severely strained when it comes to lifting a couple of pounds of dead weight out of the water. If you do use light rods, you might try fitting them with heavier-than-usual line—say 12- or 15-pound-test instead of 6 or 8—and then hand-lining your fish to the deck after they reach the surface. This will avoid risking rod breakage.

For landing really large fish, most piers keep a long-handled gaff handy, or a hoop net that can be lowered by rope.

BRIDGE FISHING

Though the catchable species, and many of the techniques, are not much different from pier fishing, bridge fishing does open up a lot wider range of prospects. For one thing, there are a lot more bridges than piers, and they give access to a much greater variety of waterways. Also, most piers sit atop gradually deepening water, whereas one long bridge often crosses flats and shoals, submerged grass beds, bars, and channels—which variations may occur almost anywhere along the way.

Bridge-fishing scene.

While this means you will have to take some pains in order to learn the layout at a selected bridge, it also means the menu of fishy prospects is likely to be a broad one—possibly ranging from weakfish over the flats and bar edges, to bottom feeders in the deeper spots, and free-roaming gamesters of several types running through the channel.

As in pier fishing, stout tackle is advisable, though not strictly necessary. If you were to choose an outfit especially for all-round bridge fishing, a good choice would be a middleweight spinning rig, featuring a 7½- to 8½-foot rod, intermediate-size reel and 15-pound line; or a light conventional surf outfit.

While specialized bridge fishing takes many forms, bottom fishing always will be the most popular because it's the most dependable for steady action. This does not mean, however, that bottom fishing produces only small stuff. A great variety of medium-to-large species can fall to bottom baits. They include bass and bluefish, seatrout, drum, sheepshead, snapper, and grouper—even tarpon.

A big tarpon rolls near the old Bahia Honda bridge in the Florida Keys. Bridge and pier fishermen throughout Florida tangle with tarpon. In summer, they sometimes are taken from piers in other East Coast states.

Any standard sinker rig is entirely suitable, but for the sake of convenience, a sliding egg sinker is preferable. Ofttimes you'll be using the same leader and hook for either bottom fishing or free-floating. When you want to swap from top to bottom, you need only slip on the sinker.

Artificial lures pay off consistently but, because of the height involved, casting from a bridge is not so easy as casting and retrieving from boat or shore. New techniques may be necessary. For instance, if you want your lure to travel deeper than a strong current—combined with bridge height—will allow, then switch to the upcurrent side of the bridge and retrieve with the flow of the tide. This isn't a bad approach anyway, since snook, jack, tarpon, and other gamefish like to lie or cruise on the upstream side, looking for food being swept toward the bridge.

Also, the casting specialist may well be able to work his lures from the approaches to a bridge, rather than the bridge itself, thus reducing the problem of high retrieve angle. Yet another approach to lure-fishing is to "troll" as you walk along the bridge, simply keeping the lure almost directly below you in the water.

The bridge fisherman is always tempted to fling his cast a long way, or let his bait ride to distant reaches on a strong tide. When using strip baits or live baits on free or lightly weighted line, this may be all right. But if bottom fishing, the farther out your bait goes, the harder it will be for you to feel bites—and the greater your chances for snagging on bottom.

Even if it requires unusually heavy sinkers, try to keep bottom baits reasonably close. Of course, there is no problem when fishing shallower areas where the effect of current may not be severe. Make some long casts now and then in order to test new spots.

Remember, though, that a lot of different fish are actually attracted to the bridge and its pilings. The bridge is not only a fishing station but also a sort of artificial reef. Shellfish feeders, such as sheepshead, tautog, and cunner, like to hang around the pilings crunching barnacles and small crabs that might be there. You'll never catch them by trying to set distance-casting records. To the contrary, you drop your bait as close against the pilings as you can manage.

Other fish that are primarily bottom feeders might not be quite such piling-huggers, yet they like to stay under the bridge for the shelter and other types of food that might be there. Again a close drop is to be preferred.

As stated before, many game species like the shade of the bridge too. Therefore, it isn't amiss to patrol a swimming live bait—shrimp, crab, or small fish—close to the pilings, or at least inside the bridge's shadow. But this can be very tricky indeed. Give the bait too much swimming room and it'll hang you up, or drag your line against barnacles and damage it. You have to keep

Bridge approaches often turn up good fishing, and are easier to work than the bridge itself because they are lower to the water.

the bait under reasonable control, and often you are required to keep pulling it up and re-presenting it.

A live shrimp is probably the single best bait that can be used around most bridges in the land, for the simple reason that it is a delicacy to almost anything that might be in the neighborhood—from bottom fish, up through weakfish and channel bass, to surface and near-surface cruisers like snook and tarpon.

Night fishing from bridges (piers and docks, too) is often the most productive. Especially appealing are the spans with street lights or some other illumination that casts a glow on the water. The glow attracts baitfish like moths, and these, in turn, attract predators. Ambitious bridge fishermen regularly bring gasoline lanterns along and lower them down near the water's surface to heighten this effect.

Snook and tarpon always feed better at night around bridges and docks. Weakfish or seatrout frequently do. Bottom fishing is generally as good as in daylight, and for many kinds of fish even better.

WADE-FISHING

Since the wading angler must—for obvious reasons—practice his art in shallow water, this form of angling has reached its greatest popularity along Gulf of Mexico shores, where shallow, protected waters are virtually boundless, and where trout, redfish, snook, and tarpon regularly romp the shoals.

But good wading areas are by no means confined to the Gulf Coast. Extensive inland waterways dot the Atlantic shore as well, offering a good variety of prospects. Certain sectors, in fact, can boast a corps of wade-fishermen as avid as any on the Gulf. Florida's Indian River country, for instance, is a mecca for anglers sloshing their way toward the country's biggest spotted seatrout. And rockfish (striped bass) lure fishermen of similar bent to various stretches of Chesapeake Bay.

While natural bait is used by many waders, and with undisputed success, here is a field where the light-tackle casters can really make hay. Certainly there is no better training ground for a saltwater fly-fisherman, nor a more action-packed one for an angler already skilled at fly-tossing. The angler can set his own route, favor the wind, and fling his fly in any direction without having to worry about boat partners, or room for back-casting. Moreover, flies retrieved across fairly shallow flats often draw as many—or more—blind strikes as do spinning lures. In most other instances, blind-casting with a fly rod can be dull indeed.

It's the same sense of freedom and personal command that appeals to spin-fishermen and plug-casters—searching, and being able to cast freely in any direction, and with no boat-handling chores to interfere.

Sound fishing practices, however, must still be followed, and one of the most important of all is *how* you wade. Move slowly through the water, sliding your feet along instead of picking them up and putting them down noisily. Even then, if you move too fast you will create a surface disturbance that scares fish. Take things easy, though, and you'll be able to move much closer without alarming your prey than would ever be possible in a boat.

Sliding your feet makes for safety as well. It reduces chances of stepping suddenly into a hole or unseen channel, and virtually eliminates any threat of sting-ray stabs. If your foot should touch a ray, it will scoot off. But step on one and you give it the leverage—and the motivation—to use its sticker.

While blind-casting is the standard style, especially on expansive grass flats with little bottom variation, it pays to be ever alert for indications of fish. You may spot boils or bulges of water, or see small baitfish breaking the surface. And if visibility permits, be sure to aim a cast toward any spot that seems at all different from its surroundings. Most fish like to hang around any sort of hole or edge on the flats.

Reasonably small bays or coves can be excellent areas—particularly if they are drained by small runs or channels, and contain an oyster or sand bar that is awash at low tide.

The pattern in such places is for fish such as trout, snook, and reds to move into the cove through the little channel, then spread out over the flats on rising tide. During high water, you work the main body of the flat, along with bar edges and shorelines. As the tide falls, fish will start dropping back toward the edge of the channel and you should concentrate your casts along that edge. Work over the channel itself on low tide.

A wading fisherman must be a self-contained unit. Often it is inconvenient to go back to shore for any reason, so you must take along a basic assortment of lures, spare leaders and rigs, a fish stringer, and maybe a landing net. Some species of fish can safely be landed by hand, but others have sharp spines or slashing teeth to make handling difficult. An adequate landing net with aluminum handle can be hung comfortably on your back.

Surface plugs, shallow-running plugs, and light jigs are the flats fisherman's mainstays. Surface plugs should be rather quiet models—perhaps

Actor David Wayne waded for his 8-pound bonefish on the flats near Great Harbour Cay in the Bahamas.

dancing plugs and slender-minnow types of floater-divers. The latter can also double as subsurface runners. Mirror plugs are very popular among waders. Jigs are often used as the primary lure, but should be on hand in any case so you can test the bottom of deeper holes and channels.

If live bait is your preference, you will, of course, need a bait container, which should be a perforated floating bait bucket lashed to your waist with a reliable line. Best of all bait-fishing rigs is the popping-cork setup (see Chapter 10). Indeed, this is the kind of fishing for which the popping cork was developed.

In warm weather you can comfortably wet-wade in old trousers and sneakers. Shoes always should be worn because of shell and litter on almost any bottom. Waders will be needed in cold water, and a lot of fishermen prefer to wade dry regardless of weather. Best protection is afforded by chest-high, boot-foot waders, but light stocking-foot waders are ample for most use in open and sheltered water.

Along the Overseas Highway in the Florida Keys, a wading fisherman has the chance to go after bonefish, permit, and even tarpon by walking the clear, extra-shallow flats and looking for them. Whether fishing from a boat or afoot, techniques are the same, and are described in Chapter 17.

Even the fabled permit is a potential prize for wading fishermen in the Florida Keys.

Part IV
Modern
Specialties

17

STALKING THE FLATS

No other arena in saltwater fishing provides so fascinating an array of light-tackle challenges as a thin and crystal flat, where fish are hunted by sight. Here is where spin-fishermen and fly-fishermen and bait-casters can really put their skills to the test, and where both the variety and size of potential targets are virtually limitless.

Bonefish are by far the most famous, and the most widespread, of flats-roaming gamesters. They started the whole thing, in fact, and remain the undisputed star attraction. But today's cast of shallow-water characters includes a great many others—some less challenging than the bonefish, some even more so.

Permit outshine bonefish in size, rarity, and finicky response to baits and lures. When big tarpon can be found in a sight-fishing situation, bones must pout in the background.

If he chooses, the flats fisherman can also go after redfish (channel bass), barracuda, snook, small tarpon, bar jack, crevalle jack, big and little sharks—and even, at times, husky mutton snapper.

It's no secret that *all* the good flats-fishing territory in the United States is jammed into extreme southern Florida—from Miami's Biscayne Bay through the Keys, and around into Florida Bay, south of the mainland.

Many foreign spots in the tropics attract stateside anglers by the drove—among them, the Bahamas, Belize (British Honduras), southern Mexico, and various islands in the Caribbean. At all those places bonefish, and possibly permit, are the chief attractions, although other sight-fishing opportunities may be at hand.

The practical way to go about stalking the flats is with a professional guide—not in order to reach hidden territory but simply because the guide keeps tabs on the fish, poles and positions the boat, helps with the spotting, and may provide valuable angling instruction. But note the word "may." Most guides in the Florida Keys are outstanding instructors. Foreign guides generally are not, even though they do their own job very well.

If you choose to go out on your own—because of pride or a slender purse—you have a good chance of connecting if you school yourself in the basics.

load up on local advice, and set out with patience and determination.

Naturally, Florida residents have the best shot, since a lot of them own outboard boats that are at least adequate for flats duties, and they have more opportunities to explore and experiment. But many a vacationer and camper in Florida lugs along a small boat—perhaps a bass boat, a cartopper, or other light freshwater craft. Such vessels are not only adequate for the flats, but absolutely ideal—as long as they stay in shallow, protected waters. The flats themselves, of course, always fit that description, but care must be taken while crossing deeper basins or channels en route to the stalking grounds.

There are always rental boats, too, and many liveries in the Keys are located within a stone's throw of bonefish territory.

One big hitch for a newcomer attempting to go it alone is boat poling. It does take a lot of practice before you can get that darn boat to move where you want it to. But even this can be overcome. In the beginning, rely primarily on drifting, and use the pole for minor corrections of course and attitude.

Though it's easier to control the boat when poling from the bow, practiced polers can operate from the stern—an obvious advantage for a fly-caster.

Control develops with practice as you discover just where pushing force must be applied to get the boat response you want.

It's easier to pole a boat from the bow, since you have better control if the heavy end goes through the water first. Also, there is more elbow room at the bow—the motor doesn't get in your way. A boat can be poled *faster* from the stern, and with less effort, but only a skilled poler can maintain control.

While learning to pole, try to remember that your own end of the boat (the bow) moves *away* from the direction of force. This means that the leading end (the stern) will swing toward the *same* side on which poling force is applied. To turn left, stick the pole on the left side and push. To go forward, push directly behind you. It will take plenty of practice.

Another approach is wading for the fish. A number of flats in the Florida Keys can be reached by wading directly from the Overseas Highway. You don't need a boat at all. And even when you fish from a boat, you may choose to get out and wade at times, or do so out of necessity—when your boat draws too much water to reach attractive-looking places, or to avoid a long siege of poling upwind.

Before climbing out of the boat, make sure the bottom is hard enough to permit wading. Flats of marl or mud might suck you in up to your knees. And

One way to lick the poling problem—take your boat to the edge of a flat, then get out and wade.

always, before leaving the boat, anchor it securely so it will be there when you get back.

At last we come to fishing techniques and procedures. The following section concentrates on bonefish, but it should be studied no matter what your flats-stalking aims may be, since basic techniques are much the same for all other thin-water fish as well. Succeeding sections will take up some of the other popular species, plus angling variations which may be required.

BONEFISHING

Spinning tackle is the most effective all-round gear for bonefishing, and extremely sporting. An ideal spinning rig features a rod of one-hand design, 7 feet long, and with very light action. The open-face reel should hold at least 200 yards of 8- or 10-pound-test monofilament, although for smaller bonefish, and in practiced hands, 6-pound line can be used.

Many bonefish specialists prefer an extra-long rod, measuring 8 or 9 feet and with a longer butt. Rod action, however, remains extremely light. Seldom is such a rod available in manufactured lines, but must be custom-made or home-built, generally using a fly-rod blank. The advantage is in longer casting with unweighted shrimp or tiny jigs, and in being able to hold more line out of the water when a bonefish runs.

A 15-pound-test monofilament leader is the heaviest needed under any conditions. A lot of bonefishermen use no leader at all. Others double their line, using the Bimini Twist, and tie hook or lure to the double line.

Bonefish feed primarily on crustaceans and mollusks. Any shellfish, whole or cut (depending on size), makes good natural bait. Live shrimp is regarded as best of all, but if it's unobtainable, the choice should be dead shrimp, pieces of crab, whole small crabs, or chunks of conch.

Hooks are usually 2/0 and 3/0 sizes with offset point. Use no sinker unless a weight is absolutely necessary for casting. Then pinch on a split shot or two.

Whatever bait is used, the idea is to spot the fish—or a school—then send your cast well in front, not too close or you'll spook it to the middle of the ocean. Let the bait lie still as long as the fish continues moving in its general direction. Bones have a keen sense of smell, so give them a chance to use it.

Should the fish definitely change direction, and you feel you can retrieve the bait a short distance into better position, then do so very slowly, as any sudden movement will alarm the fish. And if it seems impossible to improve the lie of your bait, crank it up and make another cast.

While bonefish are ready takers of properly presented jigs and flies, the beginning bonefisherman should stick to natural baits until he catches a few and becomes acquainted with the game. Then he can move on to artificials, which are a bit more demanding, both in casting accuracy and retrieve techniques.

Lures and Presentation for Bonefish

Leading lures are bucktail jigs weighing between ⅛ and ¼ ounce. Flathead types, or skimmers (see Chapter 4), are preferable on most flats because they are less prone to fouling in the short grass that often is present. Round-head jigs are very productive when conditions permit their use over sand bottom, or atop flats slightly deeper than the norm. Whatever the jig design, popular colors are white, pink, and tan, although many different colors and combinations take fish. It's a rare day when bonefish are really color-conscious. Plastic-tail jigs in the aforementioned sizes have lately been employed more and more by bonefishermen. Whether they work better than the traditional bucktail or feather jig remains a matter for dockside debate, but they certainly do work.

Fly patterns for bonefish are many and elaborate, especially in the Keys. But simple flies—nothing more than bucktails tied to No. 1 or No. 1/0 hooks—have captured literally thousands of bones. Colors are the same as for jigs. In my experience, plain bucktail flies are always dependable for small bonefish, and for any size bonefish on flats that are not subject to constant

Flat-head or skimmer-type jigs should be chosen for exceptionally grassy or shallow flats. They sink more slowly than other head designs, and tend to keep the hook upright.

Streamer flies are so effective on Florida Keys tarpon in shallow water that spin and plug casters use weighted versions of such flies as their standard lures.

The small round-head jig that accounted for this bonefish is a popular type in sand-bottom flats territory where grassy foulups are no problem.

traffic. But in some areas of the Keys—particularly on flats known to attract unusually large specimens and therefore worked religiously by numerous anglers—the fish shy away from those comparatively big flies, and must be fished with special patterns developed thereabouts and tied on hooks down to No. 4. Such flies are available in Keys tackle shops.

The shrimp fly is perhaps best-known of all bonefish flies and the most widely sold. It's very productive and comes in several sizes and colors, though pink is standard.

Many bonefish flies are tied in weedless fashion—either with a "chin whisker" of stiff bucktail to fend grass away from the hook, or on a Keel hook. A Keel hook is one in which the shank is bent so that the point rides at the same level as the eye. Though truly weedless, it is considered a poor hooker of fish. However, you can bend the point upward ever so slightly and improve the hookability dramatically. This also affects its weedless properties, but not that much.

Suitable fly-fishing outfits can be built around a No. 10 floating line or a No. 8 or 9, as described in Chapter 1. Light-tippet leaders always should be used (see Chapter 10).

Whether with a fly or jig, proper presentation of the lure is the most demanding part of bonefishing, since a delicate balance must be struck to cast close enough—and retrieve well enough—for the fish to see the lure, yet not hit so close as to spook it.

Just how close you can drop your lure without touching off the alarm varies with visibility and water condition, and also on how actively the fish are feeding. On rare occasions you can drop a spinning jig right on top of a bone and have it lunge for it immediately, but of course you never *try* to do it that way. Usually your lure should hit the water *at least* 10 or 12 feet from the fish—and much farther than that over very clear flats and extremely calm conditions. A small fly can hit much closer, provided the line doesn't splat down on top of the fish.

Despite such variables, pinpoint casting is not a requirement in bonefishing. Naturally, you have to shoot pretty well, but if you can throw your lure somewhere inside a target as large as your kitchen, you're in good shape. Don't worry about dropping it into a teacup.

Why? Because the retrieve is just as important as the cast, and maybe more so. All you aim for on the cast is to deposit your lure ahead of the fish and beyond him. Any guide will tell you that a lot of folks can't even do that, but anyone with considerable casting experience in other fields should have little trouble.

After the lure lands, your tricky work begins. The retrieve must be paced so that it crosses the bone's path at the right time. Retrieve too slowly and it may pass the interception point ahead of the lure. On the other hand, you may have to slow down or even stop the lure if it becomes poky, or pauses.

Too, the bone may change its course slightly, in which case you may be able to alter the course of your lure accordingly, by extending the rod tip far right or far left as you retrieve. A drastic alteration, however, calls for a new cast.

Searching for Bonefish
Always work a flat slowly, whether poling or wading. If in a boat, you can talk all you want to, but avoid heavy stomping or clatter.

Travel in the direction of best visibility, which will be with the sun behind your back. And *always* wear polarizing sunglasses.

Beginning bonefishermen should endeavor to work flats which are predominantly sandy, or which at least have many sandy spots scattered over darker, grassy bottom. Let the bottom coloration and depth help you decide what kind of visible clues to fish are the most likely. On very shallow flats, you generally look more *at* the water than *into* it. Be alert either for the tail of a bonefish sticking above the surface as it roots for food, or for its dorsal and tail fins cutting the surface as it moves along. On calm days, "tailing" fish can be spotted far away, but when there's a ripple on the surface, even a nearby tail can be tough to see.

Over deeper flats you may never see a tail or a fin at all, but there may be a wake to indicate the presence of fish. A school of bones makes a very impres-

Big bonefish are frequently found "tailing" in water barely deep enough to afford swimming room. Transparent look of the tail identifies its owner as a bone.

sive wake indeed. Even a single can create a sizable wake on a calm surface, but when the water is corrugated by wind, you'll have to look sharp. Be especially watchful for any ripples moving against the wind. There's no guarantee that wakes are caused by bonefish. Ordinarily, you make use of wakes by getting your first clue from them, then moving up and trying to actually spot the fish. However, if you can't make out exactly what's causing the disturbance, go ahead and cast.

A bonefish tail is triangular in shape and, in most light angles, whitishly transparent. Small sharks frequent most bonefish flats and forever are causing the heart of a bonefisherman to jump. But a shark usually moves along steadily, waving its tail from side to side all the time, and the tail is opaque. A tailing bonefish usually tips up its tail, waves it around, then lowers it. The tail may come up again in the same spot, or a few feet away.

If you see a high black fin that is crescent-shaped, you have full right to a fluttering heart—that's a permit.

Over soft bottom, feeding bonefish often put up little puffs of whitish mud which can help you spot them and track their movements. These "muds" are small and dissipate quickly when created by one or two fish. Should you spot a fast-fading puff of mud, scan the water all around, and you'll probably see a nice fresh mud well up, indicating the present location of the fish.

Big schools of bonefish can send up a large cloud of mud. This, however, occurs in somewhat deeper water than you find on a sight-fishing flat—although you might locate such a mud off the flat's edges. If you do, try to determine which portion of the mud cloud contains the brightest, hence the newest, mud. Cast to that area.

Despite the cooperative tendencies of bonefish to "tail" and "mud," your searching may very well need to be aimed at spotting the fish itself, entirely underwater. This is the toughest task of all for the newcomer, most especially over dark or grassy bottom.

The fish most commonly mistaken for bonefish is the barracuda. Remember that 'cudas often lie still, whereas bonefish are constantly on the move, except for brief moments when they stop to dig for food. Also, the barracuda is frequently seen lying at the surface, or hanging in the water, while bonefish almost always hug bottom.

A bonefish underwater looks very much like an arrow, with a pointed nose and a sharply forked tail. If it is swimming toward you, its head and "shoulders" will appear quite broad, tapering to a much thinner tail section. By contrast, 'cudas have an overall slender appearance in proportion to their length.

There is no such thing as a best tide for bonefishing. Generally speaking, flats adjacent to deep water start producing early on the incoming tide. Fish move in as water depth allows. Flats located farther back from deep water—

such as in a cove or along shorelines—are productive on higher tide phases. When the tide starts falling, an angler can gradually move back toward the deep edges, because fish will be doing the same. Pay close attention to any runs or sloughs slightly deeper than the main body of the flat, since bonefish often use them as natural "trails" when the tide is ebbing.

Fighting the Bonefish

The storied fighting speed of a bonefish is not exaggerated, but neither is it always so. Those great, long, blistering runs occur when you hook your fish on top of a wide flat. The farther it has to go to reach what it considers safe water, the straighter and faster the run will be. Under such conditions, a 4-pound bone will often zip off 100 yards of line, and a trophy-size fish can reach or exceed 200.

When hooked over deeper flats, or along edges with close access to deeper water, the run may not cover half the usual distance, nor will it necessarily be straight and swift. But any bonefish, in any kind of water, is a tough cookie. It will put you through paces that most other fish two and three times its size couldn't manage.

The characteristic first run of a bonefish requires two basic reactions on your part. You should extend the rod high overhead, supporting it at arm's length above you, and keep the rod butt nearly vertical. The high angle holds

Holding rod high overhead during the first long run of a bonefish or permit keeps more of the line above water and reduces chances of line being cut by mangrove roots or shell on the flat.

much of your line off the water and reduces the possibility that it might be cut by dragging over a sea fan, shell, or mangrove shoot. The vertical butt, of course, means that the rod stays in its full-bend position.

Your drag should be set very light—certainly not more than 3 pounds, and preferably 2—because your spool diameter will drop rapidly and increase drag pressures. Under no conditions should you try to stop that first run. Once the run is over, you bring your rod down to ordinary fighting position and go to work—pumping smoothly and trying to get back line as fast as you can.

Usually you will indeed be able to recoup half or more of your lost line before the bone starts another argument. But at any time it might set off on another run, so be ready. It may, in fact, get off two or three additional spurts, but none nearly so long or breath-stopping as that first one. The final stage of battle generally is a bulldogging circle around the boat—and this may require you to move rapidly from one end of the boat to the other in keeping your line clear.

Jack Nicklaus conquered this 7-pound bonefish on a trip with the author to Great Harbour Cay, Bahamas.

PERMIT

While permit are frequently found on the very same flats as bonefish, and can be fished with exactly the same tackle and essentially the same techniques, several very important differences must be noted. The first one is a snooty attitude toward baits and lures, and most especially toward flies.

Permit are crustacean-feeders too, and they have been caught on live shrimp, dead shrimp, and cut crabmeat. But the only truly reliable bait is a live crab. Because they are more widely available, small blue crabs, about the size of a silver dollar, are the most popular. However, any species of small crab you might pluck from rocks or beaches will be acceptable. The hookup for blue crabs is shown in Chapter 8.

Just as spooky as bonefish and harder to fool with artificial lures, the permit is considered the most challenging target found on warm-water flats.

Unfortunately, many a bonefisherman gets an unexpected crack at permit while fishing with live shrimp. All is not lost. There's a vague chance the permit will accept the shrimp—and a very good chance if you present the morsel in a special way. Instead of simply tossing your shrimp in front of the permit and hoping it will gobble it up, try skittering it across the surface. This may fire the fish up, and when it starts moving toward the bait, you let the bait settle in the water.

A permit's patented reaction to any artificial lure that's properly presented—jig or fly—is to follow it and then turn away. Sometimes the follow is an out-and-out charge, mouth agape and with such ferocity that there seems no way it could change its mind. But often it does, turning away at the last instant.

If your lucky star is shining, a permit may actually grab your hopping jig, but not often will this happen. There is, however, one retrieve technique that works with considerable regularity. When a permit starts trailing your lure— when you know it has it spotted—stop your retrieve dead. The jig will go to bottom. If there is some grass on the bottom, or soft marl, the jig will settle almost out of sight. And that's what you want.

Apparently believing it has pinpointed the location of a hiding crab, the permit often will "tail" on your lure and suck it right out. Nor is it apt to spit the lure out instantly. The permit is used to picking up hard and horny critters, and you have ample time to set your hook before the fish discovers its mistake.

Unfortunately, there is no such ready advice to be given a fly-fisherman. Nothing in the way of fly pattern or technique has been discovered that consistently fools permit on the flats. Not that plenty haven't been caught on flies, but it's a rugged challenge. Many anglers have their own ideas as to which flies are "best," but there is no wide agreement. If there is even a slight trend in the matter, it is to use drab-colored flies of blacks, tans, and browns.

This may be the place to stop and explain that much permit fishing is done in deep water—particularly over submerged wrecks—and that deepwater permit are much more susceptible to both flies and hard lures than are the same fish on the flats.

Although many permit are caught on bonefish flats, the best territory usually is found where the flats are at least a couple of feet deep, and marked by patches of hard coral or shell. Permit are deep-bodied fish which need more swimming room than bones do. Those encountered in less than a foot of water are generally "small" ones of 8 to 12 pounds. By contrast, the slightly deeper permit flats can turn up prizes averaging 12 to 20 pounds, and sometimes going to 30 or more.

Lefty Kreh (left) and Capt. Bill Curtis show off Lefty's 20-pound permit caught on a live blue crab in Miami's Biscayne Bay.

Despite all that heft, permit fishermen stick mostly to tackle of bonefish proportions—8- to 12-pound-test spinning line and light-tippet fly leaders.

The permit delivers a bonefish-type run to start with, and after that the struggle really begins. As an underwater brawler, permit outclass even jack crevalle of similar size.

It's imperative that you move up on a permit as soon as possible. Pole if need be, but crank the motor immediately if you have running room. Bonefish accidentally cut your line, but permit try to do it deliberately. If you can stay directly over the fish, that's where you should be, for not only will it try to drag your line over ledges and around obstacles, but when you have to pump it toward the boat from far away, it will hug the bottom and keep rubbing the hook or lure in an effort to dislodge it. Often the fish succeeds.

SIGHT-FISHING FOR TARPON

Tarpon everywhere roll at the surface—a welcome signal used by fishermen in the placement of their casts. To that extent, *most* tarpon fishing is "sight-fishing." But here again we're talking about the search for tarpon—big ones—in shallow, clear water of the Florida Keys, and of making a presentation to the visible fish. The season peaks in spring and early summer, but lasts through fall.

The sport has been most highly developed at Islamorada, but is also widely practiced in the Lower Keys, from Marathon to Key West. There are just as many shallow-water tarpon in the Lower Keys—and often more—but not nearly so many guides who specialize in this type of fishing, nor so many private boaters who practice it.

Thanks to long and concentrated angling efforts, a great many consistently productive spots have been discovered out of Islamorada—places where an angler can station his boat on certain tides, and reasonably expect to get casts at tarpon swimming by within easy range. Most of the spots are located along edges of shallow banks (flats). Tarpon habitually move up from deeper water until they run out of swimming room, then turn and follow the banks.

Big tarpon are never "easy" to catch on fly, plug, or spinning tackle, but chances of a successful outcome are much better when fishing the flats. In channels, tarpon use muscle more than wild action, and are difficult to raise on light line.

Some banks are so reliable that every tide sees a lineup of open boats staked out along the edge—each with an angler or two standing high, ready to cast instantly.

Although it's largely a waiting game, shallow-draft boats still are necessary, and poling is prominent in the picture. More often than not, some poling is required in order to reach the stake-out position. Then too, some of the fishing is done by poling along certain bank edges, or by poling over shallow basins.

With the advent of 24-volt electric motors, capable of pushing boats up to 20 feet long, a lot of sweat was removed from tarpon fishing. An electric motor seldom is very useful in bonefishing, because most of the bonefish flats are too skinny to permit operation. But tarpon stick to water at least a couple of feet deep, allowing the electric kicker to do its job.

The good sight-fishing spots are scattered all over big Florida Bay, between the Upper Keys and the southern mainland. That's no country for a newcomer to be rambling in. And the Gulfside of the Lower Keys is even trickier. The sport is so demanding anyway that experienced guides are a virtual necessity.

Still, it's possible for a super-ambitious soul to get into shallow-water tarpon fishing on his own, from a personal or rented boat—not by traveling into the back country, but by sticking in sight of Keys bridges. The channels spanned by those bridges harbor great quantities of tarpon, and many of them get to the channels by following flats edges near the close Atlantic-side Keys.

Even the guides fish the Atlantic-side shallows regularly. Often, many more fish can be sighted there than in the back country, although it seems that fewer of them are willing to strike. But that shouldn't be discouraging, because some of them do indeed hit—and there are days when you might find a lot of takers.

Tackle for Tarpon

All these tarpon we're talking about are what any but the most jaded expert would consider big. They average 50 to 70 pounds, and 100-pounders are by no means uncommon. Devotees keep looking for 200-pounders. While they haven't found any yet, tarpon up to 170 pounds have been taken on the flats with spinning tackle, and nearly that large on fly rod.

Obviously, bonefish tackle has no place here. The best compromise between strength and castability is attained with an outfit that handles 15-pound-test line. And this is true whether the personal choice is fly, plug, or spinning.

Spinning rods should measure 7 or 7½ feet, with a combination butt and foregrip length of around 16 inches. Longer butts might be helpful in casting,

Carl Navarre (right) of Chattanooga, Tenn., set a record in the Islamorada Tarpon Fly Championship with this 147½-pounder. Keys guide Eddie Wightman offers congratulations.

but get in the way during the fight. Rod action must be quite powerful. An intermediate-size reel, holding at least 200 yards of 15-pound line, completes the rig.

Plug-casting (bait-casting) tackle features a rod 7 feet long, which might even be built from the same blank as the spinning rod. Though a 12-inch butt minimum is imposed by certain clubs and tournaments, a 16- or 18-inch butt is not too long for practical purposes, and will make casting much easier. Use a large-capacity plug reel with smooth adjustable drag.

Fly-rod fishermen prefer the heaviest outfit described in Chapter 1, and a No. 11 or 12 line. The slightly lighter outfit, with No. 10 line, is adequate for the general run of fish, but borderline for tarpon weighing 100 pounds and more.

Leader makeups are identical for spin and plug outfits—several feet of 40-pound-test shock leader, tipped with 80- or 100-pound monofilament. The same heavy monofilament is used as tippet material for the fly leader. Both are explained in Chapter 10.

Shallow-water tarpon are more receptive to large streamer flies than any other artificial lure—so much more that the popular spinning and plug lures are mostly weighted versions of big flies. Specialized lures of that type must generally be purchased from shops in the Keys, since they are almost never used elsewhere.

With flies, the standard retrieve is a series of short strips with definite pauses in between. Often the strike comes when the fly is still in the water. If a tarpon approaches the fly and you strip it suddenly away from the fish's nose, it is apt to run instead of pursue, so be sure that the pulls are gentle.

As nearly as possible, the same type of retrieve should be practiced with spinning and plug lures—a slow swimming motion through the water, punctuated by soft upward lifts of the rod. Never "jig" the lure sharply as you would for many other kinds of fish.

One other type of lure that shallow tarpon like very well is, believe it or not, an artificial worm, rigged exactly as for bass fishing, though with a stout 5/0 hook. Orange is the most widely used, though other colors work.

Presenting the Lure and Fighting Tarpon

Tarpon may be big and brawny—but they're still spooky when cruising the flats. Thus, the presentation must be made with as much care as with bonefish. With a fly, you can hit quite close to the fish, but care must always be taken that you pull the fly in front of the *leading* tarpon when casting at a small school or pod of them. If you drag the lure through a school, those in front will be spooked and cause the whole bunch to flush. Even though you lead the forward fish, it may not be the one that takes. Another may dart ahead and beat it to the punch. Also, after the fly crosses at right angles, a tarpon may split from the middle or rearward ranks of the pod and give chase.

Setting the hook in a tarpon requires effort and muscle. Sock it at least three times—hard. This is where many transplanted anglers go wrong. They have schooled themselves to strike once and sharply, but with no great stress. It works on most fish, but not on a steel-jawed tarpon.

Your fish will almost certainly begin an immediate series of wild jumps. Maintain as much cool as is possible under the awe-inspiring circumstances, and if using a fly rod, devote your attention to clearing loose line from hand or deck. About the only other thing you can do at this stage—regardless of the type tackle—is to extend your rod forward at each jump, creating slack line. This is referred to as "bowing to the fish," because you not only extend and lower the rod, but also lean forward as far as you can.

When a tarpon leaps it shakes its head violently. Unless the line goes slack, it can use the tension to rip the hook from its mouth.

Later on, when the fish is waging most of its resistance under the surface, you must be constantly alert for another jump, and ready to bow in response to it.

Other than "bowing," there are no special techniques involved in fighting a tarpon. Follow the procedures given in Chapter 7, and use as much pressure as you dare. There are two main reasons why big tarpon become fair game for light tackle in shallow water—they jump more than usual and so tire themselves more quickly; and you are not faced with the considerable task of lifting a heavy weight up from the depths.

Even so, fighting pressure should be exerted to the utmost at all times, or the fight could drag into hours. The longer you have a fish on, the greater your chances of losing it. If things are done right, a 100-pound tarpon on the flats can be conquered by an expert in less than a half-hour. A newcomer who has learned to handle tackle well in other forms of fishing will seldom need more than an hour. Of course, there are those occasional fish that brawl with seemingly endless energy, even against the best of fishermen. So don't worry about any timetables. Just keep the pressure up.

REDFISH, SNOOK, TROUT, AND SHARK

In Florida Bay, out of either the Upper Keys or Flamingo in the Everglades National Park, much flats-poling attention is devoted to redfish (channel bass). The red is sort of a junior-grade bonefish—sought and fished in exactly the same manner, but considerably less spooky and usually more greedy.

Some very good redfishing flats are located immediately in front of the marina at Flamingo. That's the best place to start for the private boater. Strangely, however, none of the guides at Flamingo go in for flats fishing. If you want to stalk redfish with a guide, you'll have to book him at Islamorada, or some other place along the Upper Keys.

Bonefish tackle is ideal for this work, and so are bonefish lures. But other lures can be added. A weedless spoon is one of the best, since reds hit it readily and it can be pulled through the shallow grass that's prevalent on most of the good redfish flats. Reds also will take surface plugs, provided they are

Stalking the flats for redfish or channel bass is regularly practiced only in waters of the Everglades National Park. But Al Pflueger, Jr., found this one on a flat inside Sebastian Inlet, Florida. It weighed 30 pounds. No doubt reds come into very shallow flats water in many areas, and future exploration may lead to wide expansion of this sport.

worked slowly and with only soft pops. Jigs are excellent once you acquire the knack of keeping them off bottom and leading them to the redfish's nose.

Reds, you see, will not move so far to take a lure as a bonefish will. Their eyesight is limited and, moreover, they are frequently absorbed in rooting on bottom, and might fail to notice even a close lure. Several casts may be necessary before you grab their attention.

You throw your lure past the red and then try to guide it right smack to its nose.

Reds do a lot of "tailing." The tail looks very dark, almost black, but is similar in shape to that of a bonefish. And, unlike bonefish, a red may stay in one spot and tail repeatedly for several minutes.

The natural bait of choice is live shrimp. Dead shrimp and pieces of crab also are good. Since redfish smell much better than they see, they will search out a natural bait thrown in their vicinity, but it should still be fairly close—within 2 or 3 feet.

Snook can be taken from slightly deeper "potholes" that dot the flats in Florida Bay, between the mainland and Upper Keys.

Snook, trout, and small tarpon may be spotted on the flats while you look for redfish. But you don't see nearly as many of them "lying up" on top of the flat. Mostly they stay in depressions, which are visible to the poling angler as white areas, or holes, surrounded by the grassy flat. Many flats contain a lot of white holes, and whether they're big or small you should cast a jig or surface plug to any you see. Even though the water may be very little deeper than the adjacent grassy area, some surprisingly large snook, trout, and reds manage to lie in the holes unseen.

Sharks are plentiful on most flats. While they don't appeal to many anglers, they can frequently be caught on lures, and they put up a stirring battle.

18

DEEP JIGGING

Fishermen in many waters and for many years have used fast-sinking lures on all sorts of tackle for dredging up bottom fish. Jigging for cod with handlines is a venerable example. But nowadays the term "deep jigging" denotes a highly refined offshore endeavor, with spinning and plug tackle, and one that takes aim at *all* gamefish, up to and including sailfish.

Deep jigging originally was developed as a "purist" system—a way for competition-minded anglers in southern Florida to capture certain types of prestigious fish while sticking to the rules of casting with artificial lure. They were after fish which could not really be considered casting targets under standard circumstances. And they got them.

Casting entries in Florida clubs and tournaments now bulge routinely with *big* grouper and snapper; with amberjack, African pompano, and king-size

A mixed bag of surface and mid-depth fish that fell for deep jigs off the Florida Keys. Catch includes rainbow runner, dolphin, blackfin tuna, bar jack, barracuda—and even an ocean triggerfish. The triggerfish often nips at the heavy jigs but is seldom hooked because of its small mouth.

king mackerel; with bonito, blackfin tuna, and sailfish. Not quite so routine, simply because they are rarer, are scattered catches of wahoo and yellowfin tuna, but both these species fall frequently to jigs in other waters.

Even though comparatively few anglers are all that ambitious about grappling with giants on a spinning rod, they can still give thanks to the corps of dedicated deep-jiggers for bringing one exceedingly welcome fact to light: namely, that deep jigging is an excellent system for just "catching fish." Only a small percentage of the prey qualifies for tournament trophies, but a good day of jigging can produce a wealth of excitement and offshore variety unequaled by any other single angling system.

Many's the day a deep-jigger returns to dock with more grouper than a bottom fisherman working the same general area. And, in addition, the jigger most likely has scored on king mackerel, bonito, and other pelagic species as well. All caught on the same lures.

That's because deep jigging is the only approach whereby you can fish every different water level with a single rod and lure.

Though most widely done in southern Florida, for obvious reasons, deep jigging has invariably proved deadly in any waters where a jig can be dropped to the vicinity of predatory fish.

Al Pflueger, Jr., gaffs a husky bonito (little tunny) for John Emery. On any given cast, a deep-jigger might get either a hefty bottom-feeder or a pelagic game species such as this.

DEEP-JIGGING TACKLE AND LURES

It would be possible to jig with a boat rod, but so exhausting that nobody could stand up to the task for very long. Deep jigging is a sport for spinning or plug-casting outfits.

Most effective in water ranging from perhaps 60 to a maximum of 200 feet deep, the system makes use of jigs weighing between 1 and 4 ounces. A workable basic assortment of jigs features at least three sizes—say, 1½-, 2½-, and 3½- or 4-ounce models.

Basically, you should use the lightest that will reach bottom, because heavier jigs are somewhat more difficult to manipulate properly. Some experimenting may be necessary, since the weight requirement is influenced by currents as much as by depth. You must try not only to get the jig down, but get it down in a reasonably straight path. If your jig hits bottom far from the boat, it will rise much too fast once you tighten your line and start to move it.

Through habit, deep-jigging enthusiasts in Florida stick almost exclusively to lead-head lures. But the heavy metal jigs that are favored in the Northeast and the Pacific will work too. Capt. Lefty Reagan of Key West is separating one of the latter type from the jaws of a 20-pound barracuda.

By tradition, most deep jigs are of white bucktail, with a few strands of silvery Mylar tied in for flash. Yellow has been proved an equally productive color, and better for some kinds of fish, particularly the jacks. I have taken many fish with orange, pink, black, and blue jigs. As with all lures, the chief consideration (if, indeed, it is important at all) is probably varying the shades between light and dark. Still, white has been so widely successful that you could scarcely go wrong sticking to that.

The addition of a 6-inch or 9-inch plastic worm to the bucktail jig makes it even more attractive. Most avid jiggers add the worm as habit, since it flutters with much the same action as a baitfish's tail. Clear worms, treated to glow in the dark, are often chosen, but any bright color works well.

In fact, a worm or other plastic bait-tail can be used with effect on a bare jig-head, no bucktail needed.

Head style can be pretty important in a deep jig. Those with flattened or arrow-shaped heads are preferred, because of their erratic, darting motion while sinking. Blunt or round-head styles sink on a straight path, and not quite so rapidly. But they will catch fish too, though perhaps not as many.

It takes a lot of rod to make a large jig move down there at 100 or 150 feet. Even a rod that would be considered heavy for most inshore purposes is probably too light for deep jigging. That's because when you jig, you're mostly bending the resilient rod shaft instead of moving the lure to any great extent. Deep-jigging rods, therefore, must be quite stiff.

The common choice is a fast-taper blank, 8 feet long, for spinning. Like all fast-tapers, the shaft diameter is quite large at the butt, although tapering down quickly to a small-diameter tip. Unlike other fast-taper models, however, the tip section of a deep-jigging rod is reinforced, and has little noticeable action when you wave it around in the air.

Plug rods are built from exactly the same blank, trimmed to 7 feet in overall length.

Even in Florida, deep-jigging rods are custom-made, or else built by small local manufacturers. A few rod shops in the East turn them out on order.

Despite their length, deep-jigging rods are fitted with butts that are relatively short—about 16 inches for spinning, 12 inches for plug-casting. Long butts are awkward for manual jigging.

If you can't get hold of a true deep-jigging rod, use the stiffest popping rod or boat-spinning rod you can find.

Competitive fishermen stick to 12-pound-test line for spinning, 15-pound-test for plug tackle—those being the limits imposed by most clubs. Even 8-pound and 10-pound lines have been used with success.

For practical all-round deep jigging, I feel that 15-pound-test is the best choice for either style of tackle. Spin-fishermen might even use 20-pound.

Deep-jigging spinning rod (right) seems of almost broomstick proportions. Stiffness is needed both to pump heavy fish from deep water, and to give necessary action to the jig.

since there are reels which will accommodate a sufficient capacity of that size. Few plug reels hold more than 200 yards of 15-pound line, and that would be considered the minimum practical amount.

The shock-leader arrangement described in Chapter 10 is perfect for most deep jigging, and the monofilament should test 60 pounds. If fishing where king mackerel are present, you can add a 12-inch length of nylon-coated cable wire to the shock leader for protection. Note, however, that many deep-jigging enthusiasts never use wire at all. They get some cut-offs from sharp-toothed fish, but insist that they *land* more in the long run because they get so many more strikes with straight monofilament.

RETRIEVE SYSTEMS

Your basic procedure is to let the jig sink until it hits bottom. Seldom will you be able to *feel* it hit. You must keep a sharp watch on the line, and lock your reel as soon as you see the line go slack for an instant. Because of drift and current, line would continue to peel from your reel almost as fast, even after the jig stops sinking.

When the line tightens, hold your rod tip near water level and then raise the rod to about a 45-degree angle. This will lift the jig off bottom, whereupon you lower the rod to horizontal once more, allowing the jig to sink back.

Repeat this two or three times, not retrieving any line at all. Those first few lifts should be rather slow and deliberate. The object: to keep the jig at bottom for a few seconds in hopes of attracting grouper. Grouper readily hit a slow jig, and the longer you can keep the lure close to bottom, the better your chances of nabbing one.

Following those first few slow-jigging motions, lower your rod tip again and proceed to jig in more authoritative fashion. Put some snap into it this time as you heave the rod sharply from horizontal position to nearly vertical. Then start lowering the rod immediately, cranking in line as the tip goes down. But be careful not to drop the rod tip so quickly that you allow slack to form in the line. Continue this series of upward jigging motions all the way to the surface—pausing noticeably after each sweep of the rod, to let the jig sink back a short distance while you retrieve some line.

African pompano is a special prize for deep-jiggers in Florida. Al Pflueger, Jr., caught this one off Key Largo.

Don't try to keep the jigging coming up rapidly by jerking and cranking as fast as you can. Not only will this tire you much more quickly, but it isn't as attractive an action for most fish.

What happens is this: The lure jumps sharply upward for a few feet with each jig of the rod. Then it heads back toward bottom on an erratic course, imitative of a baitfish fleeing for its life. Most strikes come as the lure is sinking back.

Watch for the lure coming through the water as it nears the surface. If you're not paying attention and yank when the jig is too close, you'll jerk it right out of the water and maybe conk yourself in the head.

Actually, you don't need to take the lure out of the water at all. When it comes within a few feet of the boat, open your bail, or push the free-spool button, and proceed with your next drop.

A strike can come at any stage of the game, and from any kind of fish. Even though grouper and snapper will nab a jig that's barely moving on bottom, they also will follow it up to mid-depth before striking.

When you feel any kind of strike, or tug, or even if you sense only an unwarranted interruption of the lure's sinking pattern—strike hard, while cranking the reel very fast to remove slack. And then strike two or three more times if you feel solid resistance.

If you fail to hook up, try jigging the lure rapidly without retrieving any more line. And if that doesn't bring a new hit, then open your bail, let the lure sink for a few seconds, and start jigging and retrieving once more.

Most strikes aren't hard to feel. Some will almost pull you off your feet. But it isn't unusual for a fish to take the jig and head upward, so that you feel almost nothing. Again, watch the line at all times.

Obviously, deep jigging can be pretty strenuous—especially if you jig for long periods of time without drumming up much action. If you don't have that kind of dedication, you can always combine deep jigging with other and more relaxing forms of offshore drifting, as suggested in Chapter 15.

WHERE TO JIG

Deep jigging is best practiced near outside reefs and dropoffs, or in certain limited spots of known productivity—such as artificial reefs and wrecks. With a fathometer, it's often possible to locate attractive bottom, or even fish, and to make your drops with unusual confidence. However, don't expect a guarantee, because sometimes a school of fish marked by a fathometer turns out to be spadefish or some other kind of nonpredator.

Without a fathometer (and a great many anglers do enjoy consistent deep-jigging action without one) the approach is to drift over deep bottom that is known to contain at least scattered patches of reef or rock. The practice anywhere off the Florida Keys is to go outside the visible reefline and into deep blue water, then drift back toward shallow water with the usually prevailing east and southeast winds. You should aim to start in perhaps 200 feet of water, drifting inshore until bottom barely becomes visible. Then motor back out for another drift. During Florida's lobster season, which lasts from fall through spring, the outermost floats on lobster traps can serve as a handy reference, since these are usually in about 150 feet.

Keep a marking buoy close at hand while you drift and jig. Instructions for making the buoy are given in Chapter 6. As soon as you connect with a fish, toss the marker overboard immediately—don't wait to land the fish. If your catch turns out to be a grouper, snapper, amberjack, or other reef dweller, you can then keep cranking up and running beyond the marker for new drifts. Chances are more than good that you'll get additional action—maybe a day's worth. And be sure to drift all around the marker, starting well up-current from it.

Should your first catch turn out to be a bonito, barracuda, or other free-roaming species, you may have tossed the marker in vain. But drift by it a few times anyway.

If results don't warrant staying in the area, or if activity wanes, retrieve the marker and start drifting once more. Quite often you will spend long periods of fruitless jigging—or perhaps pick up an occasional surface-type fish—and then finally hit a spot that makes up for all past boredom. But it's possible, too, that you can start getting action very soon, and score in a number of different areas.

FIGHTING GROUPER WITH JIGGING TACKLE

Many of the fish you tie into on jigging grounds are just tough. They'll show you power, or speed, or both. They often test your tackle to its limits—and your boat-handling skills as well. Still, you wage the battle as valiantly as you can, under procedures covered in Chapter 7.

But the grouper is a different proposition. It is both tough and surprisingly speedy at times. And it also has the frustrating habit of diving under a ledge, leaving you to tug against the whole floor of the ocean.

In fact, heavy-tackle grouper fishermen can't even conceive of catching a big grouper on jigging tackle. A grouper, they say, must be dragged to the boat through sheer muscle power, with stout line and a strong back.

It's true enough that spinning line is a poor match for a grouper in shallower water. But a deep-jigger has several factors working on his behalf. For one thing, the depth and the speed of drift often combine to ease a grouper away from the danger zone before it can do too much about it. Groupers are sometimes slow to realize their peril, and can be led away from their shelter. By the time they get their dander up, it may be too far to go back, and there may not be another convenient hole or ledge handy.

Sometimes, too, they travel pretty far off bottom to nail a jig, and if the angler uses plenty of pressure he may be able to keep the fish from getting back.

Many different kinds of fish are caught by deep-jiggers. However, in most waters grouper make up the bulk of the catch. Dan Schooler shows a 12-pounder.

In any event, grouper of average size are caught by deep-jiggers with great regularity, and some very big ones are nabbed often enough.

Many do reach bottom, but a high percentage of them can be coaxed out again, by a combination of thoughtful pressure and a couple of tricks.

Your first decision must come shortly after the strike, when you have to guess how easy your unseen foe might be to handle. If it's a smallish grouper, or perhaps a different species altogether, your best bet is to pump hard, with unyielding pressure and rhythm, to get the fish coming and keep it coming.

Experienced jiggers do this routinely—applying strong pressure at the start and maintaining it until thoroughly convinced that the fish is husky enough to do pretty much as it pleases, despite full drag.

As often as not, the first indication an angler gets that his opponent is a nice grouper comes when the fish makes a power dive and locks up on bottom. If this happens to you, open the bail of your reel at once to provide completely slack line. When a grouper holes up, frantic yanking will only make it more determined to stay put.

But with relaxation of pressure, the fish may well think its troubles have departed. Chances are, it isn't really in a deep hole anyway, but only under a small ledge—or maybe has only its nose tucked under a rock.

Keep the line slack for about 30 seconds. Then tighten up until the line comes tight, and raise your rod into bend-position firmly but gently. If you feel any movement to indicate the grouper has come clear, work on it slowly at first, in an effort to guide it farther from the obstruction. Should this tactic seem to be gaining ground, gradually increase the strength and tempo of the pumping until you're fighting full steam.

If the slack-line caper fails after a couple of tries, crank up the motor and circle over the top of the grouper's position, applying pressure from different directions. Many a grouper has been pulled out of its retreat this way—and paradoxically, the big specimens are usually easier to pry loose than smaller ones. Again, that's because the lunkers may have trouble finding a hole big enough to contain their whole bulk.

Even out of the rocks, a big grouper on spinning or plug tackle is a rugged opponent and the fight is apt to be pretty long.

When you feel the fish definitely rising with your pumps, grit your teeth and pump all the harder. The farther off the bottom you drag it, the harder it will be for it to get back. And if you're in reasonably deep water, it will reach a point where the change in pressure will do it in. Then, for practical purposes, the fight is over, although you still must work a little merely to haul its unresisting weight the rest of the way.

19
KITE FISHING

A lot of weekend small-boat skippers in southern Florida have become proficient sailfishermen without ever learning to rig a trolling bait or estimate a drop-back. The key to their success has been the fishing kite, one of the most

Capt. Bob Lewis, a veteran Miami charter-boat skipper, popularized kite fishing on small boats for sails and other species. He designed a complete portable kite-fishing outfit which is now marketed by Pompanette Products, a company specializing in gamefishing accessories.

useful tools an offshore angler has at his disposal—and one used by some of the best charterboat captains long before any small-boater ever tried it out.

Charterboats still use the kite extensively, and some of them use it almost exclusively. But, thanks mainly to a simple, portable kite-fishing outfit manufactured in Miami, many more kites are seen nowadays on private craft than professional ones.

The kite is such a successful sailfishing device that many folks have the erroneous impression it is used *only* for sailfish. Actually, kite-fishing methods are deadly for every sort of predatory fish, and if more people were aware of this, interest in kites would undoubtedly be a great deal higher.

Also, I have found that a lot of fishermen are still in the dark as to exactly what a kite is supposed to do, and how it is used.

Portable kite reel fits into rod holder. Anglers who build their own kites generally use a large saltwater fishing rod and reel for the same purpose.

The fishing kite is a tool; a piece of equipment. It works no voodoo to produce fish when none are around, but merely serves a particular purpose of great value to the fisherman. And, like all other items of angling equipment, it must be used correctly and in the right places for best effectiveness.

The primary purpose of a kite is to carry one or more live baits away from the boat to any distance you wish. It also enables you to present the live baits at just about any depth—right smack on the surface, just under the surface, or well below the surface—and even to change the depth of the bait at any time you wish.

A complete kite outfit consists of the kite itself, and a kite reel containing the line from which the kite is flown. Attached to the kite line are a pair of clothespins—the first about 50 feet from the kite, and the second about 40 feet below the first. With the manufactured outfit, the pins slide freely on the line while the kite is being let out or taken in, but stop automatically at the distances mentioned above.

The first step is to mount the kite reel in a rod holder on your boat. It goes into the holder exactly like the butt of a fishing rod, and is secured by means of a sliding tapered block and a safety cord.

The kite, which is made of light fabric on a framework of tubular, X-shaped glass sticks, is then snapped to a snap-swivel on the end of the kite line.

In an open boat, and with a steady breeze of at least 10 miles per hour, you have only to hold the kite overhead to let it catch the air. It will start to fly easily. Let out line by cranking the kite reel in reverse. If you've ever flown toy kites, you know that slight pressure on the line or cord is necessary at all times to keep the kite up. That's why you must "feed" line by cranking the reel in reverse, rather than by simply putting the kite reel in free-spool.

ATTACHING THE FISHING LINE

When the kite is about 50 feet from the boat, the first clothespin clicks into position. Now you must lock the kite reel and let the kite hold position while you attach your first fishing line. The line cannot be clipped directly to the pin, because you must be able to give and take line at will for proper positioning of the bait. Therefore, your fishing line must run freely through some sort of ring, and the *ring* must be attached to the pin. Perhaps the handiest and easiest such ring device is an ordinary paper clip.

Fix your paper clip into the clothespin. Now start letting out the kite line once more and, at the same time, let out line from your fishing reel. The fishing line should go out under just barely enough thumb pressure to keep your reel from backlashing (no pressure at all is needed when using a spinning reel).

When the first clothespin is 40 feet away, the second one comes into position. Attach your second fishing line in the same manner as the first, then continue to let out kite line until the baits are as far away from the boat as you wish. Lock the kite reel, and you're fishing.

An ordinary paper clip around the fishing line is clipped to the pin of the kite line. This arrangement allows fishing line to be payed out or taken up at will in adjusting final bait position.

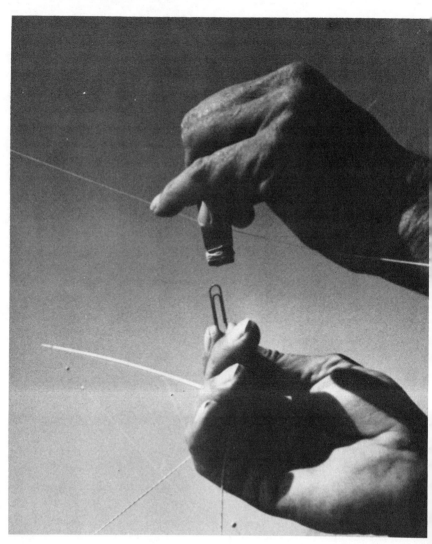

Another detail drawing shows the kite, kite reel, rods, and fishing lines in fishing position.

When first learning the above routine, you should have one person handling the kite reel, and separate anglers for each of the two rods. It will take a little experience before one person can efficiently handle both the kite reel and a rod at the same time.

This shot illustrates how the fishing line runs freely through the paper clip. When a fish strikes, the clip is pulled from the pin, but does not interfere with any mechanics of fighting the fish.

PRESENTING THE BAITS

Once the baits are out, position them as you like by either taking in some of your fishing line, or letting some out as necessary. I feel that one bait should be held just at the surface of the water, so that it is flipping the top at all times. This ruckus attracts fish from great distances. Also, when the bait is at the top, your entire leader is out of water and there is nothing to spook the fish.

A leading reason for the effectiveness of kite fishing is the fact that a live bait can be held exactly at the surface, where its constant splashing attracts fish from long distances.

If using two baits, you can allow one to swim underwater—or you can keep both of them at the top.

You must keep almost constant watch on the surface baits, however, and be ready to adjust your fishing line at any time. Vagaries in the breeze may cause your kite to rise and lift the bait clear of the water—meaning that you must let out more fishing line. If the kite dips and lets your bait swim deep, you must crank it back to the surface. But when cranking your fishing line to position the bait, always do it very slowly. Avoid fast winding or jerking, which could snap the line from the pin.

When a fish hits the bait, the line snaps from the pin. As soon as this happens, begin cranking fast on your fishing reel to take up slack line. Even with a sailfish you *never* drop back or give additional line after the strike. With a kite, you always have more than enough excess line out to provide all you need in the way of a drop-back.

When your line comes tight, strike hard and you should be in business.

There is no need to bother with the kite at all while you're fighting a fish. Just let it stay up there. You can maneuver the boat while fishing, if you wish, so long as you don't head downwind. If you *must* head downwind, or if you *must* run the boat at fast speed, then quickly crank in the kite before doing it. However, it is seldom necessary to chase a fish in a great hurry unless you're using some sort of extra-light tackle. And if that's the case, you should have someone start cranking in the kite as soon as the strike occurs.

COMMON KITE-FISHING PRACTICES

Up to now, kites have been used mainly on the outside reefs and in blue water. If your primary target is sailfish, it's probably best to drift as you kite fish, because you cover more territory, and because it's usually difficult if not impossible for the average small-boater to anchor in sailfish-producing depths.

Drifting provides another advantage, too. Since your kite flies downwind, ahead of the drifting boat, you are free to deep fish on the upwind side if you wish. In this way you can "surround" the fish from top to bottom—but you shouldn't try to take on too much fishing at once unless there is at least one angler free to tend the kite baits in case of a strike.

Anchoring at the edge of a deep reef is a productive kite-fishing method, especially if you dote on variety. Drop the hook in, say, 60 to 80 feet of water, then fly the kite with one surface bait and one underwater bait. You might take grouper, kingfish, barracuda, snapper, amberjack, or other species. Sailfish frequently inhabit the reefs, too, although the majority of them seem to be found in 100 to 200 feet of water. Regardless, a lot of sails have been caught from anchored boats in less than 100-foot depths.

By a wide margin, the most popular kite-fishing baits are blue runners and pinfish. Runners are the most active, but pinfish are active enough and they stay alive better than most species in a bait well. In most areas, pinfish are easier to catch in quantity than are blue runners.

In a pinch, almost any small fish can be used successfully for live bait— jack, snapper, yellowtail, grunt, and many others.

The systems outlined are standard in the areas of Florida where kite fishing has become well established. But it is obvious that the system can be adapted for just about any kind of predatory fish in any waters. After all, kite fishing is nothing more than a sophisticated system for presenting live bait—and what better way is there to entice any gamester than by showing him a frisky live bait in the least suspicious manner?

Scattered use of the kite along Florida's west coast has proved its effectiveness on kingfish, cobia, tarpon, and other varieties.

The complete kite-fishing outfit costs in the neighborhood of $80, which is a hefty bite in the pocketbook but no more costly than some other items of fishing tackle and accessories.

If you wish to economize, you can buy a kite alone or build one out of tubular rod sticks and light synthetic fabric. In that case, of course, you have to rig your own clothespin arrangement, and fly the kite from some sort of homemade reel, or from a heavy-duty saltwater fishing rod and reel.

The two main ingredients for successful kite fishing are a supply of live bait and a good breeze. But in a pinch you can get by without either one. On calm days you can run the boat slowly to keep the kite aloft, and troll either a live bait or a rigged bait such as balao.

20

FLY-FISHING FOR BILLFISH

Any avid fly-caster will instantly recognize and applaud the distinction between the terms "fly-fishing" and "fly-casting." Numerous offshore fish, including an occasional sailfish, have been taken over the years by anglers *trolling* with fly tackle. But not until 1962, when the late Dr. Webster (Doc) Robinson of Key West landed a 74½-pound Pacific sailfish in Panama was the first billfish officially registered to fly-*casting*.

More than any other sportfishing specialty, fly-casting is a game in which the end result is not fully savored unless obtained through adherence to rather rigid rules concerning tackle and technique—foremost being that the fish must accept an artificial fly, presented and given whatever action is necessary to coax a strike only through manual efforts of the caster, and not through boat movement.

To a trout fisherman, the challenge of proper presentation lies in such things as depositing his tiny fly gently to a selected target area, and then employing further skill to drift the fly over a predetermined course, while avoiding line drag or other unnatural motion.

The task of seducing a billfish to a fly is considerably less delicate, of course, but certainly no less difficult. On rare occasions—before and since Robinson's efforts—an offshore fly-fisherman has lucked into the opportunity to toss his fly at a surfacing billfish, only to find that while the fish may exhibit passing interest in the artificial, it is extremely unlikely that it will strike.

Obviously, you could spend a lifetime cruising the ocean, looking for a sail or marlin that would make an inviting target for a fly. And if you did find such a target, and got your fly to it, your odds of being rewarded with a spontaneous strike would be somewhat less than your chance of hitting the Irish Sweepstakes.

Doc Robinson realized this, and when he captured his landmark sailfish in 1962, it was no fluke, but the payoff of an elaborate and carefully planned system. But one winner doesn't prove a system, and so in the next few years

Doc Robinson and Capt. Lefty Reagan with the first marlin ever caught by fly-casting—a 145-pound striper.

he went on to catch more than a dozen Pacific sailfish, plus five striped marlin.

More important, other anglers went on to use the techniques successfully, thereby demonstrating that a reliable system of fly-fishing for billfish had indeed been established. The first to follow was J. Lee Cuddy of Miami, a close friend of Robinson's as well as an angling counselor who had made suggestions which Doc incorporated into the system.

Numerous other fly-casters also began scoring—chief among them being Billy Pate of Islamorada, who was first to show that the Robinson principles are effective worldwide. The first angler to score with *five different species* of billfish on the cast fly, Pate caught Pacific sailfish off Baja California, striped marlin off Ecuador, black marlin off Cairns, Australia, white marlin off Venezuela, and Atlantic sailfish off Cozumel Island, Mexico.

Although the broad techniques of the Robinson system are fairly well known by now among veteran saltwater fly-rodders, a completely detailed description of the entire procedure has never before been given in any book. It is offered here through the help and cooperation of Mrs. Helen Robinson, and is based on lengthy notes left by her husband.

WHERE TO FISH

"This whole thing is a waste of time," Doc wrote, "unless you can fish where there are plenty of billfish and plenty of chances."

Several prominent grounds already have been mentioned—Panama, Ecuador, Mexico, and even Australia. But close to home there are fine opportunities, in season.

From fall through spring, sailfish are usually available in attractive abundance *somewhere* along the southeast Florida coast between Key West and Vero Beach.

And the best bet of all for an Atlantic sail is at Cozumel in the spring.

White-marlin prospects are excellent in the Tongue of the Ocean, out of Chub Cay or North Andros, Bahamas, in March and April. And the determined fly-caster would be almost certain to hook up in Venezuelan waters in October. And, of course, there are the famous white-marlin grounds of Ocean City, Maryland.

TACKLE

The gutsiest fly rod available is called for, naturally, and this means one of the power models used for giant tarpon in the Florida Keys. Length of the rod is not awfully important, but the usual size is around 9 feet. A No. 11 and No. 12 floating fly line is needed to match the rod and to carry the large flies used. Reel should be a heavy-duty, single-action type with positive adjustable drag, and large enough to hold a minimum of 200 yards of 20-pound-test braided Dacron backing. If you can use 30-pound backing and still pack 200 yards or more onto the reel, so much the better.

Since this is a regulation endeavor, the leader must conform to rules. Doc used 12-pound-test tippet because that was the maximum allowed by his club, the Rod and Reel Club of Miami Beach. Under Salt Water Fly Rodders of America regulations, which came later, a 15-pound leader class was established, along with several classes lighter than 12-pound. Presumably, a first-timer would choose either 15- or 12-pound leader.

Rules state that the light-tippet portion of the leader must measure at least 12 inches long. An additional shock tippet is allowed, and this must be *no more* than 12 inches, including the knot or connection to the light tippet.

Doc became convinced that the light tippet should be 2 feet long, or slightly more, to provide additional stretch-cushion and to lessen punishment to the joining knots. This opinion is widely shared by fly-rodders who chase any kind of large ocean fish.

As to the 12-inch heavy tippet, Doc chose Steelon, which he joined to his fly and to a small swivel with crimped sleeves. He tied his light tippet to the swivel, taking care that overall heavy tippet length, including the swivel, did not exceed 12 inches.

Current fly-fishermen would be more likely to tie the heavy tippet directly to the light, using the Albright Special knot. Instructions for making up heavy-tippet fly leaders are given in Chapter 10.

As to the lure, if things turn out right and you tease a billfish into a striking mood near your boat, it just might hit most any large saltwater fly or popping bug you throw at it. But Doc eventually worked out a lure which not only increased his number of strikes, but afforded a much higher percentage of positive hookups.

This was an oversized popper he built with the head of a foam popping cork, a dozen long white hackles, and a 7/0 hook with the point carefully triangulated and sharpened to a knife edge. He flattened the underside of the foam head so the hook would ride point-upright and thus tend to take hold in an exceptionally vulnerable spot in the upper jaw, right at the base of the bill.

THE FISHING SYSTEM

Basically, the system revolves around the use of a hookless teaser bait by a second party. The bait is trolled in normal fashion until a billfish is raised, then manipulated with the teaser rod until the fish is brought within casting distance.

Since it is helpful for the billfish to be allowed to grab and taste the teaser, a strong and durable teaser bait should be used. The answer is a venerable rig which many bluewater anglers know as the "Panama belly bait." It is a rather wide, teardrop-shaped strip cut from the belly of a baitfish—preferably a bonito, although others may be used—then folded over a wire or cable leader with a loop at its end, and sewn to shape. Some of the stitches go through the loop to prevent the bait from being pulled off the cable by the fish. The finished bait roughly resembles a slender fish, and has great swimming action when trolled.

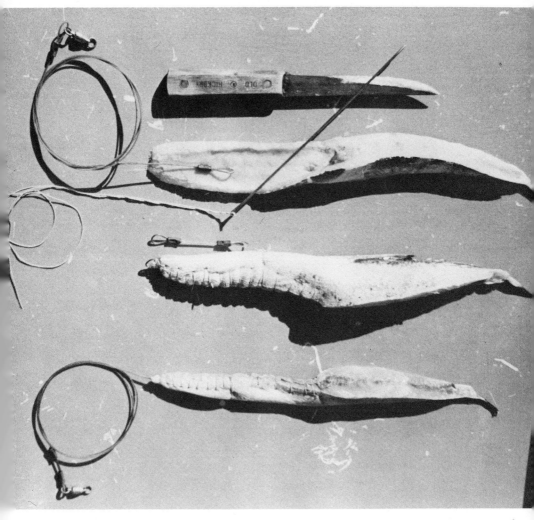

A durable "teaser bait" is made from the belly strip of a bonito, dolphin, or barracuda. The strip is sewn to loops crimped in wire cable.

Rules require that at the time the fly is cast, the boat must be still in the water so that boat action cannot contribute to the action of the fly. Boats differ in the speed with which they lose headway, a factor which the handler must take into consideration in determining when to call "Out of gear."

One more tricky and critical phase still awaits the operator of the teaser: that is, getting the teaser bait out of the water. Helen Robinson, who handled the teaser during all of Doc's billfishing, explains:

"With sailfish it is usually all right to crank the teaser to the transom and lift it out of the water. The sailfish, being dumb and greedy, tends to swim about the area where the teaser disappeared, apparently not disturbed by the still boat. A sailfish rarely rushes a fly, but comes to it slowly with sail erect.

Webster said to me at the time he started this type of fishing that the harde thing he had to learn was *not to cast his fly directly at the fish*. On such cast, the sail would close its mouth over the fly, and the hook would be too f forward to penetrate any soft spot. The fly had to be presented so that the sai fish hit it almost at a right angle to the leader. He would make his cast som what off to the side where the sail would have to turn toward it at an angl This might be classified chiefly as a visual presentation of the fly.

"As to retrieve, slow stripping of the fly seemed to hypnotize a sailfisl Moreover, if it missed on one cast, it would come back for another.

Doc Robinson tenses for the strike as a striped marlin roars toward his po ping fly off Baja California.

"But fly-fishing for marlin was much more difficult and much more excit-ing, because a marlin is wary and suspicious. Webster had to replace many of his sailfish techniques when he went after striped marlin.

"For one thing, he had to 'unlearn' some of the habits which are so in-grained in an angler who fly-fishes by sight for other species, such as bonefish or tarpon. There you attempt to make (1) a long cast so as not to spook the fish; (2) a cast in front of the fish; and (3) a retrieve that catches its eye and interests it in striking.

"With marlin, Webster had to do the opposite of those three things. He made a short cast, behind the fish, and worked the popper as fast and as nois-ily as possible to attract the marlin's attention and cause it to strike suddenly without taking any time to look the lure over.

"The teaser bait must be handled in a way which so infuriates and frus-trates the fish that it loses its sense of caution. No two marlin react the same way. A particularly wary one will have to be given several tastes of the teaser. The first pull-away is done as gently as possible. This is psychological warfare in which the marlin must be deluded into believing the teaser bait is a real fish which somehow managed to get away. As the marlin gets madder, suc-ceeding pull-aways can be harder. In fact, they must be harder because the marlin is grabbing and holding on in its determination to keep its prey from escaping again.

"If, at the other extreme, a marlin from the start rushes the bait with deter-mination, it is better to keep it coming just ahead of him. It should be suf-ficient to give him just one taste.

"There are two conditions which determine when the teaser-handler should call 'Out of gear.' First, the marlin must have become so mad that it will not give up the chase when the bait is pulled away for the last time and cranked rapidly toward the boat. Second, it must be close enough so that when the boat has lost headway, but before the marlin has become aware there is a boat ahead, the caster can make a short cast across the marlin's back trail. By cast-ing at such an angle, the fisherman can set the stage for a right-angle hit from the fish.

"Now the burden of producing shifts from the shoulders of the teaser-handler to those of the angler.

"The marlin, following the teaser bait, continues to rush fast toward the boat. As soon as possible, the teaser-handler flips the bait out of sight by sail-ing it up and forward into the cockpit with a long sweep of the teaser rod. When the bait suddenly disappears, the marlin usually stops dead—com-pletely confused. I've even seen a marlin raise head and shoulders out of the water, searching for the prey it had chased and lost. It's alert for any sign which could explain what's happened. To make it turn and approach the fly at a right angle, you must attract its attention. The angler does this by the way he retrieves the short cast he's made behind the marlin. Since the fish cannot see the fly at this point, it must home in on it by noise. Simply popping the fly isn't enough. Fast hauls of the line, blended with rapid lateral sweeps of the rod, are used to create additional vibration, and send the infuriated marlin wheeling for a spontaneous attack. In its maddened state the marlin has lost all caution, and pounces on the darting fly, determined to recapture the lost tidbit.

"According to Webster, it is important for the angler to synchronize the length of his cast and the timing of his retrieve so that when the fish hits, the

A marlin with what's left of the king-size popping bug that was its downfall.

A Pacific sailfish attempts to shake loose the popping bug in his upper jaw.

line is short enough for the fisherman to put plenty of direct force into setting the hook. With a long line out, much of the upward rod stroke would be wasted simply in straightening the line."

FIGHTING A BILLFISH

It would take a dedicated engineer many long days at the drawing board to design a set of tackle less well suited to battling billfish than a fly outfit. The reel, small-diameter to begin with, is stuck way down at the end of the rod where it's most difficult to reach and crank. Besides that, the crank must be turned four or five times for every yard of line regained. It makes your wrist and elbow tired just to think about it. But that's part of the game.

Billy Pate of Islamorada, Fla., with an Atlantic sailfish he took at Cozumel, Mexico, on a fly. Pate has taken Atlantic and Pacific sailfish, black marlin, striped marlin, and white marlin with the same teaser-bait and fly-casting techniques.

Essentially, of course, you would follow the fighting procedures described in Chapter 7. But since this work is so specialized, it's best to go over the game plan right here—even at the risk of being somewhat repititious.

When the fish hits, you strike hard two or three times to set the hook. Then, as in all fly-fishing, you keep *slight* tension on the excess line with your left hand until the running fish takes out all loose line and your reel drag can take over. The drag should be preset at no more than 3 pounds.

On the first run there's not much you can do except keep a bend in the rod and hang on. But there's a lot the boat operator must do. It doesn't take long for a racing, greyhounding sail or marlin to cover 200 yards, and so threaten your entire line capacity very quickly. The boat must start in chase at once—not by backing down, but forward and at a pretty fast clip.

Throughout the fight, the skipper must stand ever ready to pursue, and it's during these chases that the angler is forced to undergo that abominable chore of cranking the reel as fast as he possibly can for several hundred turns to retrieve his precious line.

On the other hand, the boat should not give chase more than is absolutely necessary to keep a working supply of line on the reel. Whenever possible the angler should fight his fish directly—and fight hard—pumping and pressuring just as much as he would do with light trolling tackle.

Doc concluded that the best chance of victory is to apply as much pressure as possible, as early as possible, while the light tippet has little wear on it.

Sometimes—perhaps several times—during the fight, the fish is bound to go deep. There is little percentage in staying directly over a sounding fish and attempting to pump it up with the fly rod. Instead, have the boat move away. You yield some line in the process, but the distance and angle almost always coaxes the fish back to the surface.

Another important point in boat maneuvering is to keep the fish off to the side of the boat as much as you can. And when pursuing, travel on a parallel course with that of the fish, but off to the side of it. One purpose of these efforts is to keep the leader and line from falling back over the fish's body. In other words, you try to keep the leader at right angles to the fish. It's a challenge which never can be achieved to perfection throughout the fight, but you keep trying. There are other advantages of off-to-the-side fighting position which are explained in Chapter 7.

Everything about fly-fishing for billfish is more difficult than with other tackle, and the final step—landing the fish—is no exception.

You don't have a long and sturdy wire leader that can be grabbed and handled. So you must eventually fight your prize all the way to the boat. Then by holding your rod high and stepping back across the deck, you can bring the fish within reach of the gaffer. A flying gaff is the most efficient landing device, but a regular gaff with 8-foot handle (the longest permitted under angling rules) can be successfully used.

So there's the system, fully detailed. Easy it isn't. But any able fly-caster, in the right waters and with a cooperative teaser-handler, can hook sailfish or marlin by practicing the system with dedication.

And with a lot of chances and a little luck, he can add his name to one of the most exclusive clubs in all sportfishing.

21

THE ROBINSON SYSTEM FOR FIGHTING MARLIN

When big-game fishermen gather at the end of a day on blue water to hoist toasts and gaze wistfully at the glassy stare of a mounted marlin behind the marina bar, they sometimes tell this story.

A once-avid marlin fisherman who had long since given up the pursuit of monsters in favor of light-tackle angling was asked if he ever felt the nostalgic urge to climb back into harness and do battle with giant billfish.

"Oh, every now and then," he replied. "But when I get to missing marlin fishing too much, I just have a friend beat me across the back with a baseball bat while I throw money down the drain."

There may never be a way to reduce significantly the expense of getting a big-game fish on your hook, but there definitely *is* a way to increase your chances of landing a big billfish once you do hook up with him—and at the same time to reduce the physical punishment involved.

It's a system developed by the late Dr. Webster Robinson, and though he worked it out specifically for battling large black marlin in Pacific waters, its principles can be implemented to great advantage by any angler, with any kind of billfish, using any class of tackle from either large or small boats.

Robinson's methods are so different from accepted procedures followed for decades by virtually every big-game angler and captain that his system is bound to create considerable controversy wherever men challenge marlin. But if we start with the premise that big-game fishing does not have to be a sport enjoyed only by those with exceptional stamina and physical strength, the subject takes on another dimension.

The Robinson system was born and polished in the Pacific waters of Panama, where Robinson and his wife Helen made ten multiple-day trips aboard the *Caiman II*, skippered by Theodore and Louis Schmidt. The first three trips, which produced seven black marlin for Doc and three for Helen, during

Using the Robinson fighting system, Mrs. Helen Robinson set two world rec-
ords for women on black marlin after she passed the age of sixty. One was the
796-pounder on 80-pound line, shown here, which has since been bettered.
Her 584½-pounder on 50-pound line still stands. Offering congratulations is
Capt. Louis Schmidt of the Caiman II, *famed Panama sportfishing guide.*

twenty-six days of trolling, provided thrills aplenty. But part of the price paid
included severe physical punishment for every catch—plus more lost fish and
broken tackle than seemed necessary to the anglers.

"After that third trip," Doc told me during one of the many long interviews we held before his death, "I kept thinking there just *had* to be a more
effective way to fight big marlin."

The standard procedure, in Panama as elsewhere, was to keep the marlin in back of the boat, whether the fish was at the surface or down deep, and then try to pump it up by sheer physical exertion. It is not unusual for a really big marlin to be fought for six to eleven hours by muscular men in their prime. The only two exceptionally large marlin Doc hooked during those first trips were lost because of rod failure while he tried to pump them up from the depths.

The rigid pectoral fin of a black marlin stands out in this leaping shot taken at Pinas Bay, Panama. These powerful pectorals influenced Doc Robinson to develop a new fighting system in order to combat their deep-diving effectiveness.

"Fighting a marlin over the stern of the boat didn't make much sense to me," he said, "because the anatomy of a black marlin is against it. Its huge pectoral fins are rigid. They can't be folded back against the body, but they can be angled like the planes of a submarine. When you're working straight down from the stern, all you can do is heave while your marlin planes downward on the strength of those great pectorals. The problem is similar, if not so acute, with other kinds of marlin, even though their pectorals aren't rigid.

"We knew that a deep-fighting black of less than 400 pounds could be handled in the traditional fashion—if you exerted enough strength. But a big fish might take hours, and might even end up dying in the depths and be eaten by sharks while being pulled up.

"I began to think about a whole new approach, and I had some ideas worked out when we went to Panama for the fourth time."

Doc's suggestions were not minor ones. He sought to discard the fighting systems that had been used for twenty years and longer by one of the world's most successful black-marlin crews—and other crews in other black-marlin waters, for that matter. He did not want the stern of the boat pointed toward the fish at any time, nor the engine ever to go into reverse, except perhaps during gaffing.

"Selling the Schmidts on this system was harder than landing any fish I ever caught," Doc said. "They had always backed down on their marlin, and they insisted the procedures I wanted to follow would break the line. But as we worked on developing the new strategy and they saw how handsomely it paid off, they adjusted to it fast."

As a result of the system, the Robinsons' score on the fourth trip zoomed to *forty* black marlin in twenty-four days. Doc landed four in one day, and Helen set a one-day record of five.

From that time on, the Robinson system became standard procedure aboard the *Caiman* and has since been thoroughly tested by many different anglers on hundreds of blue and black marlin. When Helen's one-day catch record was later broken, it was the same system that broke it.

Here's how the system works:

After the fish is solidly hooked, the angler lets up on the drag setting until he has just enough tension to keep the reel spool from overrunning. The boat engine is left in idle while the marlin is allowed to run and jump as far as it's able—the farther the better, since the first burst requires a lot of energy. During this initial period of fireworks, the captain does no maneuvering at all, unless a slight change of boat position is necessary in order to keep the angler facing the fish.

Traditionally, it has been common practice for the skipper to begin chasing the fish as soon as the first run gets underway. This should not be done, since it only takes pressure off the fish. Modern big-game reels have plenty of line capacity, and it should be taken advantage of at this time.

Even though the drag pressure is very light, to guard against line breakage, there is still a lot of pressure on the fish, because of the length of line being pulled through the water.

Obviously, though, if you're using light tackle with restricted line capacity, you may have to give chase sooner. This is a matter for on-the-spot judgment, but if you do have to follow in order to regain line, you should do so as sparingly as is practicable.

When the marlin settles down, the boat is put in gear and begins heading toward the fish, but not directly toward it. Instead the captain sets a curving course, deliberately creating "belly" in the line. Friction against the curved line maintains force on the fish, preventing slack from forming while the boat moves closer. The angler should take up line as the boat makes its circling approach. The drag setting on the reel should remain very light and the boat should proceed slowly.

Under more traditional methods, the captain ordinarily heads directly toward the marlin—either backing down fast or quartering forward at greater speed. Such a direct approach, according to Doc's view, was bound to release pressure on the fish, allowing it a rest period while the line was being recovered. Only by circling slightly can the captain form the arc which assures that some amount of pressure is maintained.

Many anglers and skippers have long believed that a bellied line will break under these conditions, but battles with hundreds of marlin on the *Caiman II* have disproved this. Virtually all modern ocean fishing lines are of synthetic material—monofilament or braided Dacron—which is much thinner for its test than the linen lines of long ago, and of more consistent strength throughout its length.

Once the angler has retrieved most of this line and feels the full weight of the fish, he then tightens his drag to normal fighting stress, which usually is at or slightly below striking drag (see Chapter 7 for drag-setting guidelines, and procedures with star-drag reels).

The angler now goes to work in the traditional manner—applying full rod pressure, pumping, moving the fish as he can.

But if the angler's work is traditional here, the boat tactics are not. This is the crux of the Robinson system. The captain must see to it that the marlin is at all times kept off to the side of the boat and parallel to the keel. If the marlin swings behind the stern, the boat should be turned quickly to put the fish parallel to the other side. If the fish tries to head straight away from the angler, the boat should make a quick semicircle to bring it parallel to the keel once again.

The object is to avoid a straight tug-of-war between the angler and a marlin which is powering away and downward, using its massive pectorals to ideal advantage. This way the fish is constantly being pulled off balance, and cannot really set its "diving planes" well. During this stage the boat should be in forward gear and moving to stay in good position.

When the fish is deep, wide and slow circles should be run around it until it begins to come up. In adapting the Robinson system to billfishes other than black marlin, and especially with lighter classes of line, this is one of the most important points of all. If the fish is down deep, and you're making little if any progress in moving it from a near-overhead station, *move away* and circle slowly as you let line slip from the reel under a light drag. The combination of longer line, better angle, and, again, pressure from the bellying line will almost always bring the fish up.

If, at any time during the fight, the fish should take off on another fast run or series of jumps, the angler again backs his drag to very light setting, and the captain lets the boat idle until the run is over. Then the circling approach, with bellying line, is repeated until fighting position can be reached again.

Often a big marlin will climax its resistance by power-diving toward bottom. Even though it may have been pretty deep earlier in the fight—or perhaps up and down several times—this last dive is all-out, and may reach 100 fathoms or more. And at that depth it is likely to remain, fighting feebly yet doggedly—or maybe dying.

This can be the point of heartbreak for the angler, who is faced with the tremendous task of pumping a great hulk up from hundreds of feet. Even if the fish is dead and offering no resistance at all, the job might well take hours. In most marlin waters, the chances of accomplishing the feat before sharks attack the fish are none too good. And under such prolonged stress, even the best of rods have been known to break, and the finest of reels to freeze.

Instead of lying stern-to and laboriously trying to pump the fish up, Doc again would use boat tactics. He would have the boat proceed at slow forward speed away from the fish, with his drag position light enough to protect against line breakage. Although such a maneuver can cost a lot of line—sometimes almost to the bare spool—the marlin invariably rises as the distance increases and the angle of line changes.

Before the line-capacity danger point is reached, the captain can swing into a circle and quarter toward the fish, thereby allowing fast line recovery.

This technique is called planing up the fish. A similar planing system has been used by big-game anglers for many years, and should be described here for comparison.

In the traditional planing tactics, the boat moves away from the fish, but for only short distances at a time, and the angler keeps heavy pressure, allowing line to slip as little as he possibly can. Then, after a short forward movement, the boat backs down fast while the angler pumps with all the strength and speed he can muster. The forward-and-back routine is repeated over and over.

In the Robinson variation, a long length of bellying line again does most of the work, more efficiently and in less time.

So there's the Robinson system. Given fair trials it should result in an increase in the number of billfish brought to boat, and a welcome decrease in fighting time, angler fatigue, and tackle failure.

While countless marlin, and many very big ones, have been caught by traditional methods based on fighting over the stern and backing down, much depends on the fisherman's strength and endurance. Much also depends on the individual fish. Huge billfish have been boated within minutes, yet relatively small marlin have fought for many hours.

Doc Robinson never maintained that traditional methods were wrong, only that his system was more efficient, especially with large fish.

Black marlin and blue marlin are the undisputed heavyweight champs of the big-game fishing world. Both species can exceed 1,000 pounds, and the Pacific Ocean undoubtedly harbors marlin that top 2,000 pounds.

Considering the punishment that even a 400- or 500-pounder can administer to a healthy and muscular fisherman, the quest for an Atlantic half-ton and a Pacific full-ton marlin going on today would indeed seem to be flagellistic. It might be all the more reason for sensible anglers to give careful consideration and serious testing to Doc Robinson's system.

In recent years, big-game fishermen have benefitted greatly from improvements in rods, reels, lines, and boats. Records change and tackle changes. Techniques can change for the better as well.

22

FISHING WRECKS AND OTHER MAN-MADE STRUCTURES

Navigation markers, artificial reefs, and sunken wrecks can be among the fishiest places you'll ever find. From a single unimposing nun buoy to a mammoth Gulf Coast oil rig, any sort of structure in the water has at least the potential of being a great fishing spot and merits close investigation. Of course, the buoy is not likely to produce with anywhere near the consistency or variety of the oil rig, but it may well have something to offer at given times.

NAVIGATION MARKERS

Consider navigation markers. The "simplest" ones are floating buoys—cans, nuns, spars, bells. Not much fish-cover here, you might think. But there is more than meets the eye. Down below is a hefty anchoring device, and this is connected to the buoy with a large chain. Algae and other small life forms collect there—enough, certainly, to begin a limited food chain. The floating buoy itself adds to this, and provides some shade and cover for baitfish.

More substantial navigation aids—structure types built on pilings and ranging in size all the way up to lighthouse dimensions in some areas—increase this effect. Baitfish and panfish hang around to nibble on algae and crustaceans. Some types of larger fish also feed on crabs and barnacles. More sedentary types of predators may hang close, and the roving species cruise in and out to check the menu.

Also consider that a lot of navigation aids are placed—for obvious reasons—at or close to attractive fishing conditions, such as the edge of channels, entrances to harbors and inlets, or shoal areas rising from deeper water.

Such things must be taken into account when checking out the marker prospects in your own area. Obviously, there are a skillion markers which don't even merit attention, being located in polluted harbors, busy waterways,

Al Pflueger, Jr., connected with his 30-pound barracuda at the buoy in back-
ground—which the fish now seems to be wearing atop its head as a crown.

silted areas, and other places where fishing isn't apt to be good anyway.

Often, the productivity of certain markers is well known, which means that local sources of information can be tapped to advantage. Or you may have to explore on your own. If you have a regular fishing ground, it certainly pays to work the markers in the neighborhood from time to time—not just once, but at various seasons and tides. Maybe you'll find a marker that frequently harbors cobia or tripletail or barracuda or some other major gamefish, and so

merits selective fishing effort. Or you may find that where a string of navigation aids marks a boating route across bay or sound, none seems to be *particularly* preferred by those fish, even though they can often be found at one
marker or another.

Chances are, thorough familiarity with the markers in your own territory
will open up a variety of useful possibilities. This marker may be a consistent
producer of blue runner or other live bait; that one a dependable spot for
sheepshead, snapper, croaker, sea bass, or other bottom feeders; the other one
an especially attractive structure for bunches of forage fish that, in season,
draw schools of mackerel, jacks, bluefish, bonito, or kings.

*A cobia, one of the species most commonly taken around buoys and oil rigs
and over wrecks.*

Procedures for fishing navigation aids must vary, of course, according to your own angling methods and the type of fish being selectively sought, if any. A troller, for instance, would simply troll around it several times—starting in a wide circle, then working in gradually until, finally, his baits swing right by the structure itself. Following is an example of how you might give one marker a thorough going-over:

Start by approaching the buoy at near-idle speed, with one or more anglers at the ready and armed, according to personal preference, with lure, fly, or live bait. Search carefully for fish that might be in sight near the surface, and throw directly to them. Polaroid glasses are a big help here, as fish might be so far under that they are identifiable only as dark blobs. The boat operator should attempt to hang back as long as possible, within reasonable casting distance but not overly close. Your search should last a few minutes, at the very least, since fish might be cruising around the marker and come into sight momentarily. If nothing shows up, make a few casts with a jig or sinking plug—working it from top to bottom if possible, and close to the structure. A good method is to cast upcurrent so the lure will sink by the time it reaches the downcurrent side, which generally is the most productive. If no strong current exists, cast all around.

Lighthouse structures, almost always located on shoals near deeper water, are home to many kinds of fish.

Next, ease away from the marker at low speed. A fast motor or sudden acceleration will spook fish; slow motors usually do not. Circle well upwind or upcurrent and judge a drift that will take you within casting distance of the marker. Cut the motor. Start casting, or drifting a bait immediately, because fast-swimming fish, such as mackerel, are often well out from the buoy, even though they remain oriented to it. Also, bottom conditions around the marker might be very good, especially if the structure marks an area of shoal or sunken reef. Continue drifting and toss baits or lures close to the marker or its pilings as you pass. Drift well to the downstream side for further testing of surroundings.

By now you may have had some action, or some indication of the best way to continue. You might decide to continue making drifts, or to anchor along some portion of the drift path that produced fish or strikes. Or, you might wish to go ahead and take up a station at the marker itself.

It is unlawful to tie your boat to a navigation aid. Believe it or not, some boaters break this law, and I have been told that many villains who do it recommend the following tieup procedure. They pass a long rope around a piling, or over a crossmember, and fasten the end of the rope to a forward cleat in the boat. When fast release becomes necessary—in order to chase a large fish or flee the Coast Guard—they simply cast loose at the cleat; no need to pull up and untie from the marker.

Naturally, the law-abiding citizen would not be secured to the marker, but anchored in close juxtaposition—as difficult, and sometimes hazardous, as this might be. In either case, there are several angling options. Try them all, or select one.

A live bait can be fished straight down, with a sinker, and near bottom. This for such as cobia or grouper or jewfish. Another live bait can be freelined back of the boat in hopes of blues, mackerel, or other ranging types. Cobia would hit that bait too. Bottom baits can be sent down near the piling for potluck. Casting and jigging are also practical.

If you should hook a good fish on light tackle, you should clear away from the marker instantly (see Chapter 6 for rigging an anchor-line float). Cobia, especially, like to weave patterns around the pilings. Many anglers like to set the hook firmly, then relax fighting pressure to almost nothing until the boat reaches a reasonably safe distance from the obstruction, whereupon they tighten up and go to work. At any time, the skipper may be called upon to follow the fish around the marker, and so the motor should be started as soon as the boat is free, though it can be kept in neutral until a chase is required.

Take the fishiest navigation marker in the world, multiply it by a few hundred, and you get an idea of what a good offshore oil rig can produce. Unfortunately (from an angling point of view), Louisiana has a virtual monopoly on this fertile fishing, with hundreds of offshore rigs, some of which date back a quarter of a century.

The foregoing advice on marker fishing applies equally to rig fishing, with adjustment for physical size of the structures involved.

Delighted Karl Osborne with an amberjack he caught on a fly over a wreck off Hatteras, N.C.

ARTIFICIAL REEFS AND WRECKS

The difference between a wreck and an artificial reef is that one was put down accidentally, the other deliberately. Another difference is that many wrecks are harder to reach, harder to find, and so receive much less fishing pressure.

Regardless of origin, any underwater structure that survives long enough for its own little ecosystem to become established is bound to be a productive

One way or another, king mackerel can usually be caught over wrecks or around offshore buoys and rigs. Surface trolling got this one, but if that system fails, try drifting a rigged or live bait, or deep jigging.

fishing spot, and often is a fantastic one. Food supplies build, bottom fish establish residence in and around the wreck, resident predatory fish hang close by, and pelagic or migratory fish are attracted by the presence of baitfish, possibly combined with currents and eddies created by the artificial structure.

Be aware, however, that all artificial reefs do not pay off, despite high hopes. Some are poorly built, or of poorly chosen materials, and they come apart and scatter. Locations have been badly picked, with the result that materials sink away in mud, or are quickly silted over. So don't get too excited over the mere mention of "artificial reef," or by reading the magic words "fish haven"—which is what artificial reefs are called on navigational charts. Check locally to make sure the reef is intact and doing well.

Again, there are several methods for fishing a sunken structure, depending to good measure on water depth, anchorability, or how well you can keep the rather small spot located.

Small bluefish are used as "decoys" to tease amberjack up from wrecks off the North Carolina Coast so that anglers can cast to them with light tackle.

Actually, all the fishing systems employed have been detailed in other chapters. You can anchor and chum, drift over the wreck, troll in its vicinity, deep-jig, cast, or whatever. The only additional advice needed here concerns application of those techniques in a very limited area.

Anchoring generally is the best method, if water depth permits. Try anchoring upcurrent from the wreck, with boat position close to, but not on top of it. Then set up a chum line to pull fish away from the wreck and to your

The angler who caught this amberjack over a Key West wreck couldn't wait to tease the fish up—he used a deep jig to connect near the bottom.

baits. When small and medium-size fish respond to the chum, larger predators in the area usually show an interest in the proceedings and come around as well.

If you can't get your anchor to hold on surrounding bottom, then anchor directly over the wreck and chum to the downstream side. At times this may work equally well, since fish that forage away from the wreck normally work downcurrent.

As always, you have several possible systems, from heavy-tackle bottom fishing to surface casting. Chumming over a wreck is one of the best ways to drum up action on trophy-size fish with spinning, plug, or fly tackle. You may spot customers in your chum line, or right around the boat. And always be alert when small fish are being cranked up, as big boys often follow along.

Of course, there's the danger that a light-tackle prize will find the wreck and cut you off. Sometimes there's nothing you can do about it, but it still pays to have your anchor line rigged with a float, so that you can give chase and then return later to the same spot.

Drifting isn't really an appealing system for fishing a wreck, because you have to keep making short drifts and a number of them—and it may not be easy to keep going over the wreck. Drift directions can fool you. Still, drifting may be necessary in very deep water.

Now chances are you'd never find such a wreck anyway without a depth sounder, but occasionally it happens—by lucky accident, by tedious trial-fishing in the general area, by having another boat with a fathometer put you on the spot to start with, or by an unusual condition of the water's surface.

If you have a depth sounder, of course, you use it to keep relocating the wreck and drifting across. Even with a depth sounder—and most certainly without one—it pays to drop a marker on the spot (see Chapter 6). Since the marker may very well end up off the wreck before it catches, you will have to make several drifts in relation to it, then keep repeating the drift that pays off.

Using a live bait with a heavy sinker, start well updrift of the wreck so your bait can be at the right depth when you pass.

If deep jigging, be sure to use a jig heavy enough to get down quickly. You won't have time to wait around for the jig to sink.

INDEX

Photo Credits